Martini Wonderland

Seth Schechter

Cover Art by Bryant Arnold

for

Sydney

and

Lucas

The following is the true story of my experiences working for Sidney Frank, the creator of Grey Goose Vodka. Most of the names of the people involved in this story have been changed.

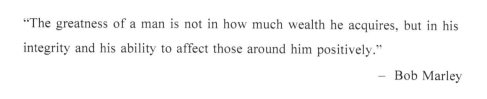

"The greatness of a man is not in how much wealth he acquires, but in his integrity and his ability to affect those around him positively."

– Bob Marley

Contents

Chapter 1

Jungle Juice

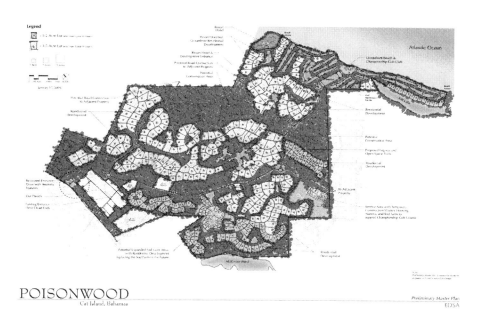

POISONWOOD
Cat Island, Bahamas

Preliminary Master Plan
EDSA

It was a hot fucking day, but it wasn't a familiar heat. It wasn't a Vegas sizzler that melted your credit cards, or a Cajun broiler that blackened your snapper and singed your beans. I was experiencing the slow burn of an authentic Caribbean jerk roast. And worse, I wasn't floating in the Bahamian bathwater with a banana daiquiri and caramel mermaids massaging my feet.

I was deep in the jungle following two machete-wielding Haitians. The Haitians broke trail through dense vines and vegetation as we hiked the property my employer was acquiring. Sidney Frank, the billionaire booze tycoon, was closing on 3,000 acres on Cat Island. Cat was in the Bahamas, next to Eleuthera and about 130 miles south of Nassau. Our parcel spanned from the high cliffs of Mt. Alvernia to the Atlantic Ocean below, and at $14 million for the whole shebang, she wasn't exactly a bargain.

I knew we were near the coast because I could hear waves breaking, but we could've been going in circles for all I knew. I was just following the Haitians and trying to remain optimistic. My body was embalmed in a smeary mixture of zinc oxide, sweat and nuclear-strength insect repellent. Repellent was almost redundant since my personal rum vapors would probably deter Godzilla.

We maintained a grueling pace, and while I focused on avoiding ground hazards, I occasionally looked up through the bamboo canopy and caught glimpses of intense sunlight and humongous spiders. Big sons of bitches perched in golden, hammock-sized webs, some with leg spans bigger than my head. They were playing it cool, but I knew those suckers were monitoring me with their beady eyes and twitchy mandibles, waiting for an opportune moment to lunge for my jugular. The Haitians sliced the spiders like Benihana stir-fry whenever they were within machete range, which was frequently. I hated spiders and shrieked whenever I got hit by flying spider parts. This delighted the Haitians. Every time I screamed the Haitians grinned, and I noticed they had about three good teeth between them.

Cat Island spider

2

The lead Haitian guide, a part-time fisherman named Jean-Baptist Agwe, stopped in his tracks and held up an arm. He pointed at a tree ahead of us and gave me the universal danger signal - his long, boney index finger swept across his throat. I took a deep breath and remained calm. The tree itself was deceptively beautiful. Its elliptical leaves were almost heart-shaped and translucent, with berry clusters hanging like nectar sirens, tempting poachers to reach for its succulent fruit.

"Poisonwood," was one of the three English words Agwe knew, quickly followed by the remaining two, "No touch." I knew poisonwoods were there, but I'd never been *mano-a-mano* with one until that very moment. I was actually relieved to finally see one on our property.

I walked over and examined the tree closely, but not too closely. From a safe distance I could distinguish faint amber stains around its torso. The poisonwood oozed a sap that burned like liquid fire, leaving blisters that lingered longer than most conventional STDs. I took a few steps back to get a better view of the toxic tree in its full glory and splendor. The poisonwood was a giant green paradox. It was the epitome of natural danger, enchantingly savage and exquisitely cruel, beauty with a nasty bite. Poisonwood was going to be the perfect name for our project.

I backed up a little more and looked around. The natural beauty of Cat Island was abundant and obvious. The danger was much more subtle, more camouflaged, but it was there and it was very real. I glanced over at my guides, and they pointed at the tree and shook their machetes. Then it hit me like a sack of coconuts. I was a sick, sunburned attorney representing an eccentric multi-billionaire, and I was following poor, sword-wielding black men through man-eating spider and poisonous tree infested jungles. It hadn't occurred to me, until that very moment, that I should have brought a machete for myself, just to even up the playing field. Even armed, the field was heavily slanted in favor of the opposition. I had $5,000 in my wallet, I was wearing a $10,000 Rolex on my clammy wrist, and I was closer to Dumbo than Rambo in survival skills. My Haitian hatchet men made roughly $20 per day on days when they had work, which were sporadic at best on Cat Island. Cat was a relatively undeveloped outer island, and it had a slippery reputation as a haven for drug smugglers and desperadoes. There was no one around us for miles. I could have easily vanished, sans watch and wallet, and no one would have found me except the spiders.

Small waves of fear started swelling in my periphery, and that familiar cloud of irrational tension began to dull my perception. My pulse quickened and my breath got strained. I reached for my back pocket and felt the lump. My self-defense security blanket was a pack of playing cards that Sidney gave me before the trip, and he said it was the most valuable thing he owned, which was an unusual thing to say, even for him. I supposed if worst came to worst, I could have flipped cards at the Haitians' eyes. I'd seen Chris Ferguson, a world champion poker player, split whole carrots with a single, high-velocity card flip. I lacked proper training and technique, but I was willing to take the eyeshot if necessary. It wasn't much, but it was something. I also had a backpack filled with water and energy bars. I smiled at my tour guides. "Who wants a snack?"

....

We finally arrived at a small clearing after what seemed like hours of soggy bushwhacking. We were up almost 150 feet above sea level, which was rarified air in the Bahamas. Most of the outer islands were flat and swampy, but Cat had the highest elevations of the entire chain, and the parcel of land we were acquiring from the Morton family had the second highest elevation at 201 feet. The Mortons were likely the descendants of missionaries or pirates, or both. Their family had acquired large swaths of oceanfront land from the natives, probably trading shiny trinkets for title or just outright stealing it.

The highest spot in the Bahamas, the peak of Mt. Alvernia, was 206 feet and located on an adjacent Morton parcel. Near the peak of Mt. Alvernia was the Hermitage, a scaled replica 12th century monastery built in 1940 by the infamous architect and hermit priest, Father Jerome. According to local legend, Father Jerome had a penchant for conducting services wearing only his boots. He spent a great deal of time wandering alone and naked in the Cat Island hills, speaking in tongues and flogging himself. The spiders probably gave him a wide berth. I could see the mini-monastery from the clearing.

I walked up to one of the highest points in the clearing to see what else I could see. A light mist was falling, but there was very little cloud cover. It drizzled every day on the island. The locals called it liquid sunshine, and it was refreshing despite the sweltering conditions. From my vantage point I could distinguish most of our parcel, from the mountains all the way down to the coast. The satellite enhanced 3D topographic maps, which had cost a small fortune to render, showed the complete picture, and it was awesome.

All of my searching had finally paid off. I'd now been on Cat Island three different times, and I'd circled the parcel several times in the air, but that paled to standing on the soil and feeling Poisonwood come to life. I could envision the contours and layout, the footprint and structures, and I knew what Donald Trump must feel when standing on the roof of an old building on Central Park South that he was about to steal from some dumb schmuck. A warm, tingly sensation started in my testicles and worked its way up my spine, across my neck, and my ears started buzzing. I suppressed an almost uncontrollable urge to scream and hug the Haitians, but I didn't want to alarm them as they had sharp knives and limited empathy. I was elated and nothing else really mattered. This was it. This was the one. I'd seen hundreds of properties, but the old Union Estate tract on Cat Island had the potential for golfing perfection.

The topography was a course designer's wet dream. Wide, rolling hills and mature foliage reminiscent of Augusta, rocky coastline channeling Pebble Beach, and windy links carved into high bluffs above the breaking waves, equal or surpassing the splendor of Bandon Dunes. Plenty of room for spec homes and a boutique hotel and spa. Building the necessary infrastructure from scratch would be a monumental challenge, but challenge built character. Access was easy from New York - a mere stroll in the park for a Citation X. We would need to lengthen the old runway at New Blight Airport to accommodate Sidney's Boeing Business Jet (BBJ), but extending runways was much easier than building an airport from scratch.

Cat Island was vastly underdeveloped and in need of new schools, good hospitals and improved utilities. We agreed to provide all of these improvements and facilities, at our expense, in our master development plan. Our grand vision would turn this island ghost town into a bustling Caribbean oasis. And we were unfazed by widely substantiated reports that Cat was a hotbed of drug smugglers, pirates and gangs of cold-blooded Bahamian murderers. In fact, we welcomed that challenge also.

And we were also highly aware of the many Union Estate squatters - locals who built humble dwellings on small parcels without any formal ownership or title. Most had resided there and worked the land for generations, and they were more entitled to ownership than the settlers who possessed the deeds. While we would retain the legal right to evict the squatters after the sale closed, there was really no point and we didn't want to stir up any trouble. In fact, we'd agreed to improve most of their land and dwellings, and provide many of them with consistent full-time employment for the first time in their lives.

....

Our future head groundskeeper would probably benefit most of all. His name was Mickey Ingraham, and I knew he was right for the job from the moment I met him. He was tending to the postage stamp yard of his newly painted cottage located just outside of New Blight. Mickey and his cottage were squatting on the

Union Estate tract, and had been for many years. His cottage was beautiful and his yard was immaculate. The grass was trimmed neatly. The bushes were contoured in tasteful, symmetric lines. The palm trees and spiny hibiscus flowers were pruned to tropical perfection. Even the amateur layout and design took into account the natural, flowing beauty surrounding the property.

But it was Myles, the toddler hiding behind Mickey's massive leg, an impish boy with wide hazel eyes, a full head bursting with black and blonde curls, and braces on his legs, that sealed the deal. Myles had muscular dystrophy, and his legs were almost useless to him. Mickey had to take him to Nassau for medical care and physical therapy, but the costs and distance made his treatment almost impossible.

Mickey realized that Sidney's master plan would bring the hospital, doctors and equipment that Myles desperately needed, and he was so grateful he offered to work for Sidney for free. Mickey had almost nothing. He lived in a tiny cottage on land he didn't own, and he wanted to work for a billionaire gratis. When I refused his offer, Mickey didn't understand. After further negotiations, he reluctantly accepted a salary but insisted it be reduced.

When I returned to the states and showed pictures of Myles to Sidney, and explained his situation, Sidney went to the Vault and returned with an envelope. No words or fanfare. Just an envelope, and it was a thick one. Sidney called it an advance. He knew it would take time before the hospital was up and running, and he wanted to sponsor Myles's treatment. When Mickey opened the envelope during my next trip to Cat, I could sense his confusion. He didn't understand, and he was suspicious. Drug runners routinely greased locals and he was obviously concerned that we were aligned with the bad guys and trying to buy him. Mickey had never seen that kind of wealth come out of an envelope, and he initially refused to accept it. It took a little convincing, but I persevered.

....

The mist stopped momentarily, and I noticed an incredibly vivid rainbow extending from the rocky shoreline up to the cotton candy clouds. There were brilliant swarms of birds and butterflies floating up in all directions. I pulled out my camera and snapped some quick shots of paradise. Sidney's dream brought me here, and this is where his inspiration would take flight. It was around 10am on January 10, 2006. We were within days of closing on the most perfect land to build Poisonwood, the world's most beautiful and challenging oceanfront golf course. My balls were still tingling. Sidney was en route to Vancouver for a heart valve replacement, and when he saw these photos he would be in heaven.

I returned to my room at the Greenwood Inn after dropping the Haitians at their shanty campsite. The Greenwood was a shitty little scuba diving hotel, but the rooms had semi-reliable A/C, and they had a staff cook named Annie who made delicious conch fritters, coconut grouper and pineapple upside down cake. Annie was a big, beautiful Bahamian goddess who clearly enjoyed her own culinary delights. She had a loud, infectious belly laugh and wry sense of humor. One night she chased me around the bar with a meat cleaver for helping myself to her last piece of cake. I kept proposing to marry her and take her back to California. She kept rejecting my offers, which was good because my real wife back in California wouldn't have been pleased.

I had paid each Haitian $50 dollars, and I let them keep the machetes. They looked at me like I was crazy. I was warned by developers not to give them a penny more than $20 dollars a day for fear the Haitians would get spoiled if daily laborer pay exceeded the customary wage. The Haitians sailed between the islands on little junk rigs that barely looked watertight. Many of them drown if a hurricane blew through. They lived in tiny shanties scattered around the shores of the outer islands, and waited months at a time for menial work. They worked hard and sent the money back to relatives living in squalor. I had a nagging pang of regret that I didn't give them more.

My satellite phone started to ring and I saw that it was Chad calling from Nassau. Chad decided to skip the Cat Island excursion, opting to stay at the Ocean Club and play a few rounds of golf. Now he was probably sitting on the deck of his $3,000 dollar per night suite perched above the baby blue waves and relaxing after a hard week of doing nothing, thumbing through the latest copy of Robb Report, selecting Sidney's next Maybach or Gulfstream or golf trip boondoggle.

The One and Only Ocean Club was the finest resort in the Bahamas. It was elegant, understated and luxurious. The suites were enormous and beautifully appointed with exotic woods and rich, warm furnishings. They had Egyptian linens, Turkish towels, and bowls of fresh tropical fruits and flowers tastefully strewn about. Chad usually selected a suite with a private infinity pool and spa, although he refused to swim or otherwise blemish his perfectly blown and sprayed hairdo. His Nassau accommodations were always the best Sidney's money could buy, and he insisted that anyone else traveling with him, including yours truly, lodge at the Atlantis or, even worse, the Paradise Island Beach Club.

The Atlantis was like a hostile merger of SeaWorld and Circus Circus, filled with chronic gamblers from Florida and Jersey who wouldn't know the difference between a Chihuly and a Chalupa. It was a glorified ocean front trailer park with sloppy buffets and loose slots, but tolerable for a day or two. The Paradise Club was a different matter entirely.

The Paradise Island Beach Club, affectionately known as the Parasite Club, still gives me night terrors. I stayed there once when the Atlantis was full, but I didn't sleep for more than a few minutes at a stretch. My room was teeming with short curly hairs and big surly bedbugs, and the bedspread was well ventilated by cigarette holes. I couldn't bring myself to get between sheets that were breeding more viral and bacterial specimens than Courtney Love's G-string, so I sat on a chair covered with towels and braced for the nightly jumbo roach rumpus.

After a couple of long rings and deliberation, I answered the phone.

"So, how was it?" The sarcasm was so thick it stuck to the roof of his mouth. Chad knew damn well it was a scorcher, which was why he opted out.

"Hot."

"Anything else?"

"Lots of big spiders."

"Sounds lovely, but how's the land?" Chad was irritated waiting for me to spoon feed some prime intelligence so he could call Sidney and regurgitate. I was not going to give him the satisfaction without a little struggle.

"Relatively hot and buggy." Chad was Sidney's favorite attorney, and I was second favorite of two, although lately my stock had been on the uptick and I was a legitimate contender for pole position. Chad was good-looking, cocky and amazingly arrogant for a 30-year-old punk with no real business or legal experience. But you had to hand it to him for hooking in and clamping down. The guy was a pro. He could be smooth and cool when performing for Sidney and his cronies, and a son-of-a-bitch redneck asshole in private. Chad spouted audacious fibs and outlandish whoppers straight to your face while looking you dead square in the eyes, and you'd almost believe his bullshit even if you'd seen the truth with your very own eyes only moments earlier, and even so you'd still second guess yourself. Chad also told hilarious true stories about Sidney and his nutty wife Marian that cramped your stomach from laughing. He was incredibly charming at times, and he could be rude, crude and astonishingly inappropriate a moment later. Not to mention Chad was a scratch golfer and sociopath.

....

Working for Sidney was Chad's first job out of law school. It was like winning the lottery the first time he bought a ticket, but he was in way over his head as consigliere for a connected hooch hustler. Chad claimed to have a small amount of Native American blood, although he looked and acted whiter than Mr.

Rodgers. His tales of growing up on an Oklahoma Indian reservation had dubious provenance, but you never really knew with Chad. He had a bulletproof poker face, and he told loads of stories that didn't add up or check out. Chad was also, hands down, one of the biggest racists I had ever met. Every other word out of his mouth was "nigger" this or "Jew" that. He despised most races and cultures equally, including his own, but particularly the Jews, which was ironic since a Jew was essentially paying him seven figures to play golf every day.

Chad also didn't discover until close to the end of my term with Sidney that I was a card carrying Member of the Tribe. My name wasn't Shmuly Jewstein, but the name Seth Schechter might cause a mildly savvy person some pause. Chad, the arrogant ignoramus, naturally assumed that I wasn't. I recalled a day we were playing golf at Sunningdale Country Club in Scarsdale. Chad pointed at a guy in a cart, casually leaned over to me, and said, "Hey Seth, look, there's a Jew".

"Really?" I pretended to be shocked and incensed. This was Sunningdale. It was a Jewish country club in Scarsdale, a primarily Jewish suburb of Westchester, a primarily Jewish region of New York, a heavily Jewish occupied state. You could barely drop a golf ball at Sunningdale without hitting a Jew in the foot. "Are you quite certain?"

"Absolutely."

"How can you be sure?"

"I just know." Chad leaned back in the cart and smiled, proud of his laser-like Jewdar. "I can always spot the Jew."

Chad was a natural born salesman, and as long as you didn't listen closely to the bullshit spewing from his mouth, it all sounded pretty good. But Sidney loved Chad, and Chad was his favorite. He was the prodigal child, the kind of son Sidney would have wanted. I think Sidney saw a lot of himself in Chad. Both were slick salesmen and extreme opportunists with raw talent and rough edges. But Sidney and Chad were fundamentally different creatures.

I still enjoyed some rare moments working with Chad, in spite of myself

11

and everything else. He was offensive, depraved and I didn't trust him an inch, but I laughed more during my time working with him and Sidney than during any other job in my life. My favorite memory to this day is flying with Chad from New York to California in a Citation X to meet some golf course architects. Chad convinced the flight crew to perform aerobatic stunts while I was in the lavatory trying to relieve myself after slamming about three beers. I tried to brace myself and aim true, but the plane was doing Kamikaze dives, Blue Angel barrel rolls, turbo tail-slides, supersonic whip-spins and Magic Mountain loopty loops. I alternated between sticking to the floor and hitting my head on the ceiling. The massive G forces actually bent my urine flow's trajectory, and my body was literally airborne in midstream on several attempts before my prostate involuntarily cut the flow to avoid peeing in my own face. At some point, I tried to sit down and white knuckle it, all to no avail. I ended up urinating all over my shoes and pants, and I laughed so hard whilst pissing myself that I almost started crying.

....

"Cut the bull, and tell me about the land."

"Geez, you're Mr. Cranky Pants. Must be all that Ocean Club stress. What's wrong? Did your masseuse have a goatee? Did they forget to put an umbrella in your piña colada?" I was *mushrooming*[1] Chad and enjoying it immensely.

"That's me hanging up." Chad was getting close to his breaking point.

"Ok, relax." I took a deep breath, "The location and topography are perfect. Completely and utterly perfect. It's pristine. The land has never been touched by a hurricane. It's in a naturally protected zone where hurricanes can't build any power

---

[1] *Mushrooming* - keeping someone in the dark and feeding them with shit.

due to the cold and deep currents directly offshore. It's raw jungle now, but the potential is unreal. It has everything we are looking for. It could be better than Pebble Beach. Every hole on the ocean. It could be the greatest ocean course ever, with plenty of room for other development. It's unbelievable," I paused, building up to the zinger, "You should have been here."

Eerie silence. I almost detected some disappointment on the other end, like an exciting journey was coming to an anticlimactic conclusion. Chad enjoyed the hunt more than the capture, and why not? We were paid an exorbitant salary to travel to exotic locations, stay in world class accommodations, eat in the finest restaurants and research golf courses by playing them. I didn't mind being Chad's Sherpa, even if it meant dodging spiders and bunking with flesh eating bacteria. Besides, Chad was traveling less frequently due to family issues, and I was often on my own and much happier.

"Email me the photos." Sidney loved photos and movies. They made him feel like he was a vicarious adventurer.

"On the way. Some mpegs also. Tell Sidney that you did a fabulous job today when you talk to him."

"Whatever." Click, and Chad was back to his fancy magazines and fruity drinks. He would forward my photos and movies to Sidney, and then call him to describe his dangerous safari to the superlative golf course destination. Sidney would probably see right through Chad's shtick, but even if not it didn't matter because we had perfection. And for the mere price of $14 million, with a $1.4 million nonrefundable earnest money deposit, we would own this jungle jewel. The Bahamian government's blessing was a formality at this point.

Bahamians loved wealthy Americans, and Forbes ranked liquor magnates were near the top of the heap. The government used injections of foreign capital to create jobs and commerce, particularly in underdeveloped and underutilized outer islands like Cat and Eleuthera. Nassau and Paradise Island were overbuilt, over-commercialized disasters, but most of the other islands were poor and relatively desolate. Any islander who wanted consistent work had to relocate to Nassau. The government needed to change this trend, and creating infrastructure and industry on the outer islands would help alleviate the problem.

Our attorneys scheduled meetings with government representatives in what seemed like a never-ending parade of private meet and greets, one official cued up behind another. The Minister of Palm Trees. The Ambassador of Bananas. Undersecretary to the Coconut Sub-Committee. All smiles and warm welcomes and so very pleased to make my acquaintance. Thrilled we selected Cat Island. Looking forward to many years of success and good fortune. But there was something lurking behind the forced grins, sweaty handshakes and oversold island hospitality. They could smell big money, and big money owned the Bahamas. Sidney's purchase was a double up in their eyes.

The first pot was free commerce. They needed outer island infrastructure, and if they could get Sidney to help bankroll it, all the better.

The second score was old school Caribbean swindling. Colombian drug cartels and American organized crime families had controlled the Bahamas for generations, and corruption was so customary it was almost expected.[2] The government assumed we were coming to Cat Island to launder currency or bury some hidden treasure, and they all wanted a piece of the action. The officials were sizing up our stack and waiting for the flop. Waiting for the optimal moment to strike, just like the spiders. They were greedy bastards, but this wasn't their first rodeo and they wouldn't spook us too early in the game. They would easily endorse our project and promise subsidies and incentives, mainly to set the hook. They knew they could squeeze more than schools and roads out of a Tommy Bahama piñata[3] like Sidney. The government officials saw a great white whale

---

[2] An important history lesson for anyone considering developing land in the Bahamas, is that the islands were founded by pirates and shipwreckers, and that still seems to standard operating procedure.

[3] A piñata is a wealthy and reckless speculator who spills money when smacked around.

with a big red bulls-eye branded on his backside. Suggested contributions, solicitations, shakedowns and fleecing would all follow in due course, predictably when we were in urgent need of government assistance.

I lay back on my bed and closed my eyes, desperately needing rest but still feeling restless. My body had crashed but my brain was still bouncing. There were divers out on the beach cleaning their equipment and telling fish stories, and I could hear the clinking of Kalik beer bottles and loud belly laughter. On top of exhaustion, I started feeling lonely. I needed to go home and recharge. It seemed like I hadn't been home in years. In fact, it had been almost two months. I closed my eyes and tried to remember Laurel's face. Her warm breath was like the waves crashing in and rolling up the sand. I could picture her strawberry blonde hair and her translucent eyes, which were almost the same color as the sapphire water just outside my door. I could see her eyes looking at me with that same distant and detached expression. I expected her to be happier that we had more money coming in, and the potential to make a lot more and live the dream in a tropical oasis.

It seemed like the higher I climbed and the more money I made, the unhappier Laurel became. She was tired of living alone for extended periods, and sick of living in the shadow of Sidney's flying circus. I could see her flinch whenever anyone asked me what I did, and she'd roll her eyes as I told the incredible stories that she'd heard way too many times. Didn't she realize I was doing this for us? For our family and our future? Granted, the job had some major perks, like traveling the world, playing golf almost every day and all the free liquor I could drink. But this wasn't all about me, at least not entirely. Didn't she realize it was a sacrifice to be far away from home and my loved ones for months at a time, all in the quest to fulfill the visions of a batty billionaire? It was a daily struggle, albeit more tolerable as said struggle was staged on luxurious tropical locales with five star resorts sporting Michelin rated restaurants and championship golf courses.

I still missed Laurel and Cooper, our big red Hungarian pointer. Sometimes

I missed Cooper more than Laurel. He would sit in the corner of our bedroom and turn his back as I packed my suitcase. He hated the suitcase. The suitcase meant I was leaving. I remember backing out of the driveway and turning back to see his wrinkly cheeks smashed up against the window, hot breath creating a cloud of misty slobber, his woeful green eyes watching me go. I knew he'd be there when I returned, in that exact spot, sad eyes and smudged face, whether it was days or weeks or months. It broke my heart every time.

I didn't want to think about home any more, so instead I tried to think about everything we had to do to close the deal. I needed to call the agents, attorneys and accountants, and set up meetings with the brokers and the bankers, maybe add some bakers and candlestick makers for good measure.

My phone rang, rousing me from a fairytale acquisition daydream. I saw it was Chad again, and I almost let it go, but I picked up just before it rolled to voicemail.

"Keep your pants on, I just emailed some photos and a few..."

"Don't worry about it. He's dead."

"What?"

"Sidney's dead." Chad was subdued for a change, and I knew immediately that he was serious. I felt the blood drain from my head, and my knees got wavy. Everything was suddenly upside down and pear shaped. It was like I'd gotten shot but couldn't figure out who pulled the trigger or where the hole was. I experienced bizarre waves of panic and *déjà-vu*, probably because I'd played this scenario over and over in my head. I knew it was coming, I just never thought it would actually happen.

"What happened?"

"Massive heart attack on the flight to Canada. I'm flying to New York in an hour. Get your ass there pronto."

The line clicked and went dead. I was reeling. In mere seconds the day went from elation to bewilderment. I felt powerful waves of grief and loss swelling up around me. The world lost an extraordinary soul with a limitless heart connected to a limited heart valve. Sidney had been my patron and mentor, and I owed him for giving me the greatest opportunities of my life, and for teaching me that wealth wasn't everything I thought it would be. If nothing else, his pain was finally gone.

I walked out of my cabin and looked around the beach. It was starting to cool down a little, and most of the divers had retired to their air-conditioned quarters for the evening. The sunlit reflections on the water were still bright and hypnotic. I was in paradise, but I didn't know which end was up. My lungs were stiff and I couldn't catch my breath. The Fear was building and closing in, and I was on the verge of a massive anxiety attack. I needed a drink.

I walked to the bar and grabbed a bottle of rum. No glass needed. The bottle and I reclined together in a hole in the sand in front of my bungalow. I started taking long slugs while struggling to breathe, but it felt like my lungs had collapsed. I kept drinking, but the rum wasn't relaxing me. I needed a distraction.

I reached in my pocket for the pack of cards Sidney had forbidden me to open. This qualified as an emergency. I opened the pack and slid the cards out. They were extremely crisp and stiff, although they were not as sticky as I expected. The pack was definitely new, but someone had opened it and shuffled a few times. I spread the cards around the sand in front of me and tried to play a game of solitaire, but the cards started reminding me of people. Sidney was the undisputed king of congestive hearts, Chad the one eyed crackerjack of racist spades, my wife the queen of ideal cut diamonds, and Marian the wildest joker of them all. The cards weren't helping.

As I was sliding the cards back into their box, I noticed a small glimmer in the corner of my eye. There was a tiny square of glossy paper stuck in the sand, almost imperceptible except for a bright reflective edge. It must have fallen out of the pack when I opened it. The sun caught it just at the perfect angle, and it was practically radiating red and yellow rays, like it was on fire. I picked it up and examined it. It was a small photograph and it was old. In an instant, I understood what Sidney was trying to tell me when he gave me the deck. He knew what was coming, and that I wouldn't make it back in time to say goodbye.

I could see the dark waves building in the distance, but I was safe for now. My breath was returning and I felt calmer. I returned the photo to the pack of cards, and the pack to my pocket. The rum was also starting to kick in, and it was making me warm. I took another long drink and examined the bottle. Rum always reminded me of the Coyopa bottle Sidney invented that lit up and played reggae music when it was tipped. Way ahead of it's time. I silently toasted Sidney, and closed my eyes. I listened to the waves crashing and rushing up and down the sand. I could hear the steady and reassuring rhythm of the sand and water, the trillions of tiny crushed shells and coral chips, grinding and chiming in infinite repetition.

My mind started to wonder with waves pounding my chest and rum warming me like hot blood. Something fluttered near my cheek, and I opened my eyes to see a Monarch butterfly touch down on the rim of the rum bottle inches from my face. Its wings were brilliant shades of yellow and orange, and its body and wingtips were covered with tiny white polka dots. It was one of the most phenomenal creatures I'd ever seen, and for a few moments I wasn't sure if it was real or the rum talking. It froze momentarily, and then its wings started to flap in perfect synchronicity with the waves.

I leaned back in the hole and took a few more deep breaths. Everything was going to be alright. I watched the butterfly for several minutes, closed my eyes and passed out cold.

Chapter 2
Tequila Sunrise

I was born during the 1968 winter of foreplay, immediately preceding the 1969 summer of love. My parents were both originally from Ohio, but they had the good sense to move to southern California in 1970. It was the promised land of fruits and nuts, bursting with the sea, sunshine, and opportunity. My father became a successful surgeon, and I grew up with the indulged children of other wealthy La Jolla families. We were the privileged progeny of doctors, lawyers, businessmen and gangsters. Many of my classmates were affluent Mexicans and South Africans whose families had, until recently, owned slaves.

My peers were shuttled to private schools in large German sedans by neurotic mothers wearing cashmere and suffocating French perfume. We spent weekends at country clubs and holidays in Hawaii. I learned early on that I needed everything. Horse estates, beach bungalows, private jets, exotic cars and yachts. Everything would bring happiness. Everything was the great expectation, and I was expected to chase it.

One of my father's close friends owned several casinos in Las Vegas, and he had a son who was my age. When I was a toddler we had play dates at their palatial estate, and only later did I realize the huge, armed men playing with us were not cowboys. I attended the son's birthday party and returned home with a life sized teddy bear and drivable electric car as party favors. Their compound was equipped with an intricate maze of tunnels and panic rooms, and we had endless fun exploring and playing hide and go seek. Sadly, my adventures at the enchanted fortress were suspended indefinitely after another friend of the casino owner got five bullets in the head, three under the chin, from a small caliber handgun equipped with a silencer.

I experienced my first full-blown panic attack in kindergarten. The school nurse diagnosed it as a seizure, but I knew better. I knew from an early age that I

19

had the Fear. I was sitting in a tiny plastic chair at a tiny plastic table, struggling to paint a piggy bank, when suddenly everything around me started to expand while my body simultaneously shrank. My teacher, Mrs. Dusenberry, looked titanic. My classmates morphed into huge moronic monsters. Crayons became sharp pastel logs and safety scissors gigantic plastic guillotines. The entire classroom reeked of Sharpies and burnt Styrofoam. My heart was racing and my vision blurred, and I could not focus or think coherently. The distorted piggy bank in front of me had grown to the size of a razorback, and it was staring at me. It looked hungry. I needed to feed it, but there was no food around other than my classmates. I dared not move lest the half painted hog devour me, and I felt a serious twitch creeping up. I could see my future unfurling before my eyes like a papier-mâché boar melting under the searing glue gun sun. I was a nuclear powered pressure cooker, and I needed to get away before the damage was irreversible.

I ran from the pig and locked myself in the bathroom for two hours. The janitor finally picked the lock and I was sent home. I took a short scholastic leave of absence and was sent to a renowned therapist who played with puppets and sent my parents ghastly bills. I was cured expeditiously. My parents enrolled me in public school to toughen me up, plus the savings were immediate and substantial. My father made his boat payments, and I locked myself in bathrooms and held my breath until I turned blue.

My parents took me to Mammoth Mountain to celebrate my fifth birthday. I got severe altitude sickness and threw up for two days straight. But on day three I skied for the first time, and it changed my life. I would point straight down hill and close my eyes, and it felt like I was flying. I ended up with a broken arm and concussion after I crashed full speed into a tree.

When I turned six, I tried to walk to Disneyland because I'd seen the commercials, and I knew that Disneyland was the place where all my dreams would come true. All I needed was to get myself to the enchanted kingdom, and I'd live happily ever after amongst talking mice and nymphet princesses. I knew that at Disneyland I would have everything I could ever wish for, so I packed my worldly possessions into my Evel Knievel suitcase and set sail for the happiest place on earth. I made it a few blocks before a neighbor caught and returned me.

Shortly after my eighth birthday I drank half a bottle of Canadian whisky. My parents were hosting a dinner party and I treated myself to six or seven generous pours while no one was the wiser. Crown Royal came in a cool purple sack, and it was surprisingly smooth on my tender palate. It went down real easy, but it didn't stay and I heaved spiked macaroni and cheese all over the coffee table before passing out. My mother informed the guests that I had aggressive food poisoning. I'm sure they all poked suspiciously at their salmon.

During my eleventh year I tried to hitchhike to Las Vegas because I'd seen the commercials, and now Vegas looked much happier than Disneyland. Everything in Vegas was brilliant neon and ripe for the picking, and the showgirls looked like fun babysitters. I ran all the way to Interstate 5 before the cops picked me up.

The following year I won the San Diego Marathon for the 12-and-under age bracket, primarily because I was the only person in that age bracket to finish all 26.2 miles. I had achieved Kenyan-like endurance from outrunning invisible predators and hours of hyperventilating. When fleeing imaginary elephant stampedes, there are the quick, the dead, and the insane.

I almost became a man at the tender age of 13 with a girl who was several years my senior. We were in the process of dry humping on a loading dock behind a popular skating rink, and my biscuit was bumping her basket when two drunk hockey players resembling the Hanson brothers heckled me into the boards. Four years later that same girl got gonorrhea from a marine in Tijuana.

About a week after I turned 16 and got my drivers license, I decided to drive my parent's station wagon to Tierra del Fuego. I loaded up my surfboard, passport, a five-pound jar of Price Club peanut butter, and my Bar Mitzvah winnings, and I rolled. I made it to La Paz, but my car died in a mud field and I was forced to abort the mission. I discovered the Fear leases a 2 bed/1 bath timeshare in Cabo. My parents were displeased.

After high school I enrolled at Cornell University. It was the only Ivy League school that would take me, and it sounded good on paper. I would descend upon Ithaca like a conquering California god and guzzle the milkshake of Cayuga paradise. Cornell was about as far as you could possibly get from La Jolla, but I figured with an Ivy League degree everything would be mine in no time.

My freshman year went well. I excelled academically and made the varsity ski team as a freshman. But winters were abysmal – frigid arctic winds choked the Finger Lakes and caused months of the coldest, greyest and most depressing weather west of Siberia. I missed the Pacific coast desperately, but I knew there would be suffering along the road to everything. Most of the suffering I endured involved frostbite and failed attempts to fornicate. I noticed the artistic guys seemed to be getting laid, so I decided to become a suffering artist even though it would take much longer to get my mitts on everything.

I grew my hair out, bought a bong and guitar, and changed my major to English because the attendance policy was flexible and the suffering level was bearable. At some point during my senior year, I made another misguided decision and registered for an intensive Japanese program called Falcon. I failed all 7 Falcon units due to the inflexible attendance policy and lack of empathy for pseudo suffering artists. Plus, the Fear would manifest during my rare classroom appearances, and the Fear was surprisingly fluent in Japanese. My suffering was unconditional at that point.

Another classmate who excelled in Falcon was invited to teach English in Japan following graduation. He was later invited to leave Japan after he went skipping down Shibuya Crossing in his birthday suit, flinging his feces at terrified motorists and screaming obscenities at flocks of hostile vampire bats.

After college I relocated to Utah and tried to qualify for the U.S. Ski Team. I tore my ACL during a training run, and that dream was done. I threw it on the growing pyre of dead dreams and hobbled back to California.

I got my knee fixed and moved to Sacramento to study winemaking at U.C. Davis. I quickly determined that winemaking was either a cruel mistress for poor fools, or a fun hobby for the uber-rich. There was very little middle ground during the early days of the California wine boom, and most developing wineries were money pits with limited upside. That situation would change, dramatically, but I needed immediate gratification. Nonetheless, I enjoyed the time I spent studying at Davis and staggering through Napa. Little did I realize that this brief enological interlude, and the minimal amount of fermentation science (and massive amount of fermented grape juice) I ingested would become pivotal to my destiny.

I returned to San Diego still limping like Achilles. I was close to broke with slim prospects and dismal options. Everything seemed more elusive than ever. I hadn't surfed for years, but I needed to rehab my knee so I bought a board and started paddling out whenever I had free time. I hit the waves almost every morning before sunrise and most evenings at sunset. It was amazingly calm on the water just as dawn broke. The coastal fog layer evaporated and warm light drenched cottages and palm trees dotting the bluffs. The frigid Pacific would slowly come alive, and playful dolphin pods, rogue seals and tight packs of wave skimming pelicans would join me for breakfast.

But evening surf sessions were even better. There was something magical about watching the sun slip leisurely into the Pacific, followed by the greenish afterglow and ghostly clouds streaking across the horizon. Sometimes there were vivid blue pockets peeking through the dense cloud layer like small portals to heaven. Occasionally there were sunsets where the sky exploded in red and violet auroras so beautiful and intense that it looked like God spilled fluorescent finger paints. I knew these brief moments, sitting in brilliant stillness and watching the surreal fade into shadows, were the closest I would ever get to anything resembling divinity.

After surf sessions I would recline in a sand hole and listen to the waves for hours. The sand would course between my fingers and toes, and the musky air would fill my lungs. If I closed my eyes I could almost feel the ocean breathing as waves rushed up the beach. I just sat, not a care in the world, peaceful and lost in the seaside rhythm. But moments never last, and the stresses of life would return like the building swell.

I became aware that if I wanted to attain happiness and everything that came with it, I needed to spend more time surfing. And although beach time was ostensibly free, everything else in California was absurdly expensive. I had to make some fast cash, and I needed a big score. Naturally, I decided to go to law school. After all, I was still a Jew and law was one of the Tribe's chosen professions. My other option would have required me to attend medical school, touch blood and save lives. Law was much cleaner. Your mother could still tell the ladies at the club about her son the lawyer, and they would all nod their heads and flash a lipsticky smirk while picking arugula out of their teeth. Lawyers made big shekels and drove Bentleys and lived in beach houses with Nordic blonde trophy wives. They capitalized on the misfortune and misery of others while sucking the life from anything with a hole and a heartbeat. It sounded ideal.

In 1994, I enrolled in a third tier San Diego law school that didn't scrutinize academic records.[4] After graduating and passing the California bar in 1997, I met a beautiful woman named Laurel, got married and prepared for everything to fall in my lap.

I attempted to practice law and loathed it. I then tried my hand at day trading, and I was a genius from 1999 to 2001. Every stock I bought turned to gold, as did every stock I didn't buy. Everything was going my way, and everything was in sight. In 2001, the bubble burst, the clock struck midnight, and all my shekels turned back into shit. I lost just about everything, tucked my tail

---

[4] Free advice to anyone considering attending a low tier law school = spend your money on something more practical, like a Taco Bell franchise or a hundred thousand lottery tickets.

and limped back into legal misery.

I ended up working as an associate in the dead-end law firm of Butterbean Schnitzel LLP. Schnitzel was a chubby palooka who sported cheap suits, wide ties, and game-show-host-hair. Unfortunately for me, I worked for the other white meat, Barney Butterbean.

Butterbean was the host of a local AM radio program that dispensed free legal advice to unsuspecting callers, but in his mind he was Perry Mason of the tax bar. Butterbean was the walking epitome of everything wrong with the legal profession. He cared little about adding anything meaningful to the world. Everything to him was billable hours and maximizing profits.

Butterbean had a bulky, sweaty head with sticky hair and small eyes that were set close together, giving him the appearance of a large, oily rodent. He rarely made eye contact when speaking, persistently focusing on some indeterminate point in space, his squinty eyes blinking behind smudged, wire rimmed spectacles that seemed disproportionately small to his pumpkin head. Butterbean never stopped moving, even while seated he constantly fidgeted and jerked, his body in perpetual, unbalanced motion, like a huge drinking bird toy.

Butterbean's personality did not compensate for his appearance. He treated his employees like garbage, only communicating with associates via email or post-it notes because he was too busy billing. His inaccessibility was a blessing due his grossly inadequate hygiene. I don't think Butterbean owned deodorant, a toothbrush or shampoo. He'd wear the same suit every day for weeks at a time to save money on dry cleaning, and he was shrouded in an acidic cloud of foot odor and halitosis.

It was rumored that Butterbean once fired an associate using a post-it note. His notes were rife with constructive criticism and liberal application of endearing terms such as 'stupid', 'awful', 'idiotic' and, the ever popular, 'this sucks'. He left daily uplifting and affirming voicemails advising me to monitor the classifieds for job opportunities.

But the most distressing aspect of Butterbean was his uncanny ability to charm his clients. They thought the Bean walked on water. He was a completely different person when a client walked through the doors. He was smooth and cool. He was informative, helpful and almost humanlike. He was Butterbean Esq., legal superstar. Butterbean was a textbook Dr. Jekyll, and his oozing hypocrisy was an unsettling yet invaluable introduction to the underworld of humanoid zombies. Until then, I'd never met anyone as phony and soulless as Butterbean. He made me aware that chameleonic rats scurry amongst us, and he inadvertently helped to prepare me for greater challenges lying ahead.

....

I was sitting in my office, dreading another day with Butterbean on the island of legal misfits. It was the end of summer 2003, and the days were getting shorter and cooler. Beach time was limited, and now I had very little to look forward to besides an occasional Santa Ana swell or weekend camping in Mexico.

As I sat moping, Todd Bradley ran into my office. "Dude, you have to check this out. Has to be a joke."

Todd worked for Schnitzle and was equally disgusted with himself and the firm. Todd and I had very similar backgrounds. We were both second tier Ivy Leaguers. Todd had attended U Penn for undergrad, and we both attended law school in San Diego solely as a means to an end. We shared a deep disdain for our employers and office mates, and we knew there was no future at this firm. We frequently sent each other interesting job postings and compared notes after interviews.

One crucial difference between us was that Todd loved soccer and I loved golf. Todd played semi-pro basketball in Europe before law school, but his passion was soccer. He freely admitted that he never actually played soccer, but he loved watching it. Todd often woke up at 3am to watch live streaming World

Cup matches in Europe. Fortunately for me, he didn't watch or play golf, because my golden opportunity may never have happened if he had been any good.

Todd handed me the printout of an ad on Monster.com. I read the printout. I looked up at Todd and smiled. I tried to read his face. I was looking for a twitch, a suppressed grin or at least poor eye contact at a minimum. He was looking at me with a straight face. I read the printout again, slowly and deliberately. I still have a copy of it in my files. Below is the exact wording.

Highly successful liquor importing company is seeking an experienced attorney with a golf handicap of five or better to join a private traveling staff. This exciting opportunity requires extensive executive travel with company chairman and staff. Candidate must be licensed to practice law in either New York or California. Experience in real estate law, business law, trusts and estates or the wine and spirits industry preferred. Candidate will assist both the chief legal counsel and general counsel on various projects. The candidate will frequently accompany the chairman on golf outings and will be expected to post highly competitive scores at par or better. Demonstrated golfing excellence is required. This is a six-day-per-week position that will rotate between New Rochelle, NY, Rancho Santa Fe, CA and various domestic and international locations. The ideal candidate will be team oriented, highly motivated and well organized.

A big booze company was hiring an in-house attorney to play golf, travel and drink extensively with the chairman? Either Todd had found the Holy Grail of legal jobs, or I was getting punked. I studied his face. We'd played pranks on each other in the past, but he didn't hide the bluff well. I'd taken a chunk of his paycheck home a few times after our monthly poker nights. Plus, this would have been an elaborate and expensive charade. I was skeptical, but he looked completely innocent. My eyes were wide and my hands were trembling.

"What the hell is this?" I stared at Todd and narrowed my eyes. "Is this for real?"

"Swear to God, it's on Monster. Go look for yourself."

"Holy shit." I felt lightheaded and a little wobbly. I wanted to believe it, but my bullshit meter was squealing that this was way too good to be true. There had to be a catch or an elaborate scam lurking somewhere behind this. Some conman was probably compiling a mailing list of sucker attorneys who bit on preposterous advertisements. Someone would instruct me to wire a $5,000 deposit to the home office in exchange for a multi-million dollar bequest from my recently departed long lost uncle, the crown prince of Nigeria. But maybe, just maybe… it was just too damn strange not to be true.

"Holy shit is right, and you're welcome dickhead. If you get the job, send me some free samples." Todd shook his head and walked away.

I immediately fired up my resume and started editing feverishly. Serious golf skills were apparently integral to landing this job, and I was going to need to channel the poor judgment of my resume muse to get this job done. I was a good golfer, but not nearly a five or under. Golf was not cool when I was growing up, and I hadn't taken it up until after college. All the cool kids were dropping in the chutes at Mammoth Mountain or charging the point breaks at Windansea, and the nerds were cleaning their balls and polishing their putters at La Jolla Country Club. The hot girls wore stretch pants and bikinis and loved skiers and surfers. Big gals with braces and bad skin loved golfers. Tiger Woods didn't make golf cool until decades after my glory days.

Nonetheless, I was able to put a game together, and I played a lot during law school. Work and marriage limited my free time, but I still managed to squeeze in a few rounds a month. I never maintained a serious handicap, but it probably would have been around seven or eight at my peak, and it was definitely closer to a 15 as I prepared to conjure up some curriculum vitae voodoo. Honesty wasn't going to make this cut, so I rounded down and estimated my handicap at a three. With a little range time, I could get close enough to fake it. Besides, they would never actually test my golf skills as part of the interview process. That would be crazy. I also made sure to point out that I had been captain of the Cornell University varsity golf team, which was a complete fabrication.

In closing, I added a few sentences describing my inspired and inebriated post-graduate fermentation research at U.C. Davis, which had one of the top ranked enological programs in the country. I then emailed my resume and cover letter as the posting instructed, and figured I had a snowflake's chance of getting a legitimate response.

It couldn't have been more than 10 minutes later that my phone rang. It was a New York area code. "Is this Seth?" The voice was very professional and cordial.

"Who is this?"

"My name is Gary, and I work for Sidney Frank. Sidney owns Grey Goose Vodka. You emailed your resume for a position with him and he wants to meet you. How soon can you catch a flight to New York?"

"Right." My suspicions were confirmed. I looked around my office for hidden mics and cameras. The owner of Grey Goose wanted to interview me? Well, he better bring a big net to catch the monkeys flying out of my butt. Gary would probably first ask me to wire the retainer payment to Uzbekistan to secure my interview slot. Even so, Gary did sound genuine and convincing, and his English was surprisingly authentic. "Dude, are you serious?"

"Serious as a heart attack. Mr. Frank wants to consider you for the staff attorney position. He likes your resume. He has offered to fly you to New York, first class, all expenses paid. Are you available to catch the red eye here tonight?"

"Sure." I only had six estate plans to draft and four client meetings scheduled for tomorrow. Other than that, I was wide open.

"Great. I'm emailing you your ticket and agenda as we speak." My eyes nearly popped out as a first class, round trip e-ticket to JFK hit my inbox, and those didn't come cheap. Almost instantly, I knew this was the real deal.

"Wait a minute." I tried to catch my breath and get my bearings, but things were happening fast. "Who is Sidney Frank?"

Gary laughed. "Hang on. I'll shoot you an article." I didn't have to hang on long, because a link to a Wall Street Journal article popped up in my inbox. "Call me if you have any more questions or need anything in the meantime. See you tomorrow, and don't forget your golf clubs."

Ironically, two of my most indulgent and expensive vices, golf and wine, were the two crucial factors that landed me the interview with Sidney. I opened up the link to the Wall Street article and read it. It detailed the history and extraordinary financial success of Mr. Sidney Edward Frank. According to the article, Sidney revolutionized the spirits industry and spawned the superpremium vodka category by creating the Grey Goose brand in 1996. Grey Goose quickly became the best selling superpremium vodka, and Sidney owned most of it personally. He had also taken Jägermeister from obscurity to the number one selling liqueur in the country. Further, the writer credited Sidney with introducing sex into advertising by hiring curvaceous women to shake their goodies while hocking his products. Naturally, this vice visionary had also been prosecuted by the EEOC for sexual harassment. Several Jagerette models claimed they were subjected to unwanted groping from Sidney and his executive team. Sidney settled the case in 1999 for $2.6 million, the largest EEOC settlement ever recorded at the time. The New York Attorney General who crusaded against Sidney and made a name for himself was a brash, straight-shooting newcomer named Eliot Spitzer.[5]

I sat in my office in stunned silence. How was I going to explain this to my wife? "Honey, I am flying to New York tomorrow to interview with a

---

[5] Eliot Spitzer served as the 54th Governor of New York from January 2007 until his resignation in March 2008 after exposure of his involvement with a high-priced prostitution ring.

superpremium vodka maverick for a golfing attorney position. Oops, almost forgot to mention, he also employs thousands of strippers. I'll see you in a few days." Laurel wasn't a woman who appreciated spontaneity, and this probably wouldn't qualify as a pleasant surprise. She had recently been downsized from a large Internet company, and she wouldn't be in the mood to hear about my exciting new adventure to the enchanted kingdom of superpremium spirits and molested models. Sometimes I suspected Laurel secretly enjoyed watching me struggle at Butterbean's, like a subconscious case of Schadenfreude. Maybe not overtly, but it seemed like my misery made her feel a little better about her situation. I knew I was going to be in for a battle going to New York, but I knew that if I don't go, I'd regret it more than the multitude of other squandered opportunities bobbing in my wake. This was probably my last shot at getting everything, and I wasn't going to let it get away.

Chapter 3
Cosmopolitan

My flight landed at JFK around 6am on September 21, 2003, and I was still half asleep. I popped two Ambien and a double Don Julio chaser when the plane took off around 10pm, and the effects of the medical grade margarita were lingering. The first class seat was quiet and roomy, and I was able to get a little restless sleep, but not much. I was still in a semi-stupor when I saw a Taliban-trained driver holding my misspelled name on a cardboard sign at the baggage claim. He collected my golf bag and shuttled me to the Frank compound in New Rochelle.

I don't remember much about the ride, other than feeling detached from my body and that swarming aroma of Arabian town cars. It's like a symphony of cigarette butts and Windex, with a pinch of moldy curry, a splash of Brut, a smidge of oniony sweat and just a whisper of hummus breath. I rolled the window down and was tempted to stick my head out. We eventually arrived at 11 Hillandale Road, and my wild expectations reverted into niggling suspicions. I expected opulence and splendor. I expected a sick MTV crib with all the whistles and bells. I got bells. Cowbells.

Sidney had occupied an old white farmhouse in a modest, sleepy New Rochelle neighborhood for almost 40 years. It was nothing special, and certainly not where you would expect a liquor mogul to reside. There was a New Rochelle city police car parked in the driveway with an off-duty cop serving as security. I looked into the car's window and observed the policeman. He was in full uniform with several weapons visible, and he was sleeping.

As I walked up the decomposing stone driveway, I disturbed a huge rabbit hunkered down in the shrubs. It jumped straight up in the air and scared the living shit out of me. I must have jumped also due to my fragile nerves. This bunny was a fucking monster, and I swear it looked at me dead square with its squinty pink eyes, like it wanted to tell me something important, or possibly warn me about dangers lurking ahead. Or maybe it was an ingeniously disguised and covert member of the security team. It was certainly more alert and intimidating than the cop. The huge startled hare ran up the driveway and disappeared in an overgrown bush.

I collected myself and followed a weedy cobblestone path to the front door. The door looked original, and I noticed it was completely separated from its hinges. There was a note on the door directing deliveries around the side of the house to the service entrance. I would learn that the front door was warped and sealed shut from decades of floods and neglect. I'm sure it was a major fire hazard, but Sidney was simpatico with the New Rochelle fire chief, and everything was kosher.

As I walked around the house toward the service door, I started to smell the fragrant aroma of fresh flowers. It was an intoxicating bouquet, and it kept getting stronger as I walked but I couldn't actually see any flowers. At first I thought it was my imagination or a reaction triggered by the lingering stench of the town car, but it was so pungent and pervasive that it had to be real.

I finally arrived at the equally unimpressive service door, and next to it was a large brick wall blocking off the back yard. I rang the doorbell and waited. Nothing. I rang the bell and knocked loudly. Still nothing. The floral scent was so powerful that I felt like I'd stepped into a hothouse. I sauntered over to the wall and peeked over. The view was dazzling. Thousands of flower bushes stretched for acres, along with perfectly pruned trees, mazes of hedges, fountains, waterfalls and ponds. Sidney's backyard had one of the most beautiful gardens I'd ever seen, and everything was exquisitely arranged. I could also see several sitting areas, picnic tables, a croquet court, and scattered arbors and pergolas. It seemed surreal and completely out of place, like some kind of botanical oasis in the middle of Death Valley.

I walked back to the door and knocked again, this time more forcefully. I waited for a few more minutes and still no answer. I didn't know what to do, but I wasn't about to wait at the servant's entrance all day, so I hitched my skirt, girded my loins and turned the doorknob. It was unlocked, and the old wood door creaked open. I took a deep breath and entered. It seemed bold and presumptuous, but I was insulted that the welcoming committee was unprepared for my arrival, especially after all my trouble to get there.

I proceeded down an unusually long, narrow hallway, and even though it was dimly lit I noticed unusual paintings and posters on the walls. Some of them were beautifully framed and others had been slapped up with scotch tape and pushpins. One painting in an ornate frame caught my eye, and I stopped momentarily to examine it. I was no art expert, but I could have sworn the painting was an original signed Picasso. It had to be a fake since it was stained and hanging between two neon Jägermeister posters, but it was an excellent forgery.

There was an old bookshelf in the hallway that contained hundreds of dusty VHS tapes and DVDs. I glanced at some of the titles. Mostly classics and old westerns. I did notice several WWII movies, some JFK conspiracy-theory documentaries, an entire section devoted to Winston Churchill, and one or two classic porn titles. It looked like a collection you might find at the local swap meet or flea market, or possibly in a hoarder's basement.

As I continued down the curious tunnel I experienced a brief and vivid wave of *déjà vu*. I knew I'd been here before, in this hallway looking at these curious artifacts. It was all totally foreign and intensely familiar at the same time. I was groggy and dazed, and I seriously questioned whether I might still be asleep on the plane. Maybe this was all a very queer Ambien fueled delusion and I was about to wake up sprawled out on my tray table with a long string of drool under my chin and a bag of peanuts stuck to my forehead.

Remembering the armed guard out front, I shouted out a few warning

35

"hellos" to make sure I wasn't mistaken for an intruder and gunned down before my interview. No one answered back even though I could plainly hear pots and pans banging and clanging from somewhere down the hallway.

I finally emerged in a dumpy little kitchen. Two cooks were intermittently making breakfast and mopping up a major flood on the floors. An antique pipe under the sink had cracked about 20 minutes prior to my arrival, and puddles were everywhere. Old towels and newspapers were strewn about the floor, forming tiny dry islands that enabled staffers to walk through the kitchen without soaking their shoes.

The kitchen looked like nothing had been updated or cleaned for the past 40 years. The appliances were rusty and hazardous-looking. The flooring was cracked and stained from previous floods, golf spikes, spilled coffee and massive amounts of dog urine. The wallpaper was dingy and peeling, and I spotted what appeared to be a large chunk of petrified burrito stuck to the ceiling. The kitchen counters were covered with dirty dishes, empty boxes of cereal, old magazines, playing cards, coffee grinds, utensils, bowls of rotting fruit and dog biscuits. Small swarms of fruit flies hovered and flew in synchronized formations every few feet. As I marveled at the micro air show, I noticed many sets of young, curious eyes and amused faces observing me.

All around the kitchen were small card tables, and the young people sitting at these tables were delighted by my perplexed reaction. None of them looked much older than recent college graduates. Most of them were wearing golf hats and rain gear. I would later become friends with many of them, but at this point they were just smirking strangers. They had all been in my wet shoes at one point. They had all entered this strange world through the nasty kitchen, and they'd all walked the grimy linoleum line. They could empathize with my fear and uncertainty. And they'd seen the same response from everyone who came through. Every suitor who came calling on Sidney made their grand entrance through the grungy tunnel and squalid kitchen. World leaders, sports heroes, movie stars, porn stars, hedge fund hedgehogs, vulture capitalists, investment bangsters, gamblers, politicians and professional alcoholics. All of them had walked the same crooked path looking baffled.

I noticed an old Jamaican woman sleeping at the kitchen table with her head resting on one of her hands. I would later discover that her name was Donna, and that she was the housekeeper. She had been the housekeeper for over 30 years, although she was strictly forbidden from cleaning anything. So in between long naps she watched soap operas on a tiny old TV in the kitchen.

I also couldn't help noticing a very peculiar looking older woman glaring at me from behind one of the refrigerators. She had a bushy nest of grey hair and dark, sunken eyes. She was wearing crusty rubber boots, muddy gloves, grubby overalls and a maroon Members Only jacket. One of her mud gloves had a death grip on a big wine glass that was nearly filled to the rim with something resembling chilled white wine. I suspected it was apple juice at that hour of the morning, although it definitely looked like wine. I thought it was nice that Sidney allowed the mentally challenged groundskeeper to come in and have some juice in the morning, and I was impressed with her handiwork in the backyard. I smiled at her. She shot back daggers.

"Who the hell are you, and what the fuck do you want?" she snarled. It took me a moment or two to process her response. At first, I assumed she was kidding, or that I had misunderstood her. I smiled at her again, and she just stared at me with glazed, hollow eyes.

"Excuse me?" The welcome wagon was not as I expected, and furthermore I wasn't about to suffer insults from a gardener. I took a menacing step towards her. She didn't flinch.

"You're not excused. Are you deaf *and* retarded?" She took a menacing step towards me, and I stepped back. "Actually, I know exactly what you want, you little shit. You want to eat my food, drink my wine and steal my money, like all the rest of these assholes here." She nodded at the kids who were now beaming in our direction. "If it were up to me, I'd fire the lot of you. Good day sir!" I glanced around and noticed the observers' expressions had morphed from curious amusement to unbridled glee. They loved what they were watching, like Romans baiting a rabid hyena.

"Mrs. Frank, why don't you relax and let the nice man go bout his business. He not here to hurt you. Nobody want to hurt you." Donna had emerged from hibernation and put her hand on the old woman's shoulder. The woman shrieked and ran upstairs into a bedroom, slamming her door so hard that I felt the floor shake. I realized that I had just been verbally assaulted by Marian O. Frank, or MOF as she was known to the staff. She was Sidney's wife, and she appeared to be drunk and deranged.

MOF

. . . .

At some point after I started working for Sidney, and I can't recall the exact date, one of his obese and elderly Labrador retrievers named Jagey lost his will to live, and he lay down in an attempt to die peacefully. He'd had enough, and he was ready to cash-out and retire to the big lazy dog ranch in the sky. After everything he'd been through, I can't say that I blamed him.

He wasn't even the original Jagey. The original Jagey drown in a pool when he was a puppy - he got trapped under a pool cover when staffers were supposed to be watching him. Sidney swapped him out with a similar looking puppy before MOF returned to town. She probably noticed the switch, but she went along with the charade.

Now it was the imposter Jagey's turn to kick it, but instead of taking the suffering animal to the veterinarian for a humane and dignified departure, MOF loaded the gloomy beast onto a makeshift gurney and pulled him around the house, like a schoolgirl pulling a leaky stuffed animal on her radio flyer. Jagey couldn't move, but you could clearly detect an anguished look in his eyes that pleaded for a quick mercy kill.

Jagey was held hostage on that cart for almost six months, with MOF trying to nurse him back to health. She fed him a fishy concoction of gruel and fairy dust, and she chanted mystic spells in his floppy ears. Sometimes she bathed and cleaned up after him, unless she was busy gardening or flying about on her broomstick. Donna begrudgingly assisted, unless she was sleeping or watching soaps. Occasionally, we found Jagey in a spot where he'd been left for several hours, cold, hungry, whimpering, and coated in his own shit.

Several staffers conspired to intervene and deliver Jagey to the vet for his final journey. Then, as luck would have it, Sidney decided to go to Hawaii with MOF and most of the staff. Donna and I were appointed to stay behind with the dogs, which was perfect because euthanizing Jagey would be a much smoother process with MOF out of the picture.

I made all the arrangements, and Jagey was scheduled to depart the morning after MOF's flight. His suffering and misery would soon be over.

On the day of the big trip, the Franks left the house around 2pm. About eight hours after their jet departed, my cell phone rang. The call was coming from the Frank's house phone.

"Seth?"

"Yes?

"This is Donna." Her accent was unmistakable, but she sounded excited and uneasy.

"I know. Are you okay? It's late."

"Yes. Yes. Everything is fine, but you need to need come see something. Hallelujah." I could hear her reciting prayers, possibly voodoo, and crossing herself.

"What's going on? Are you sure you're alright?" I was getting worried. Donna was no spring chicken herself.

"Yes. I'm fine. It's...it's Jagey."

"Is he dead?"

"No, no...."

"What's wrong?"

Silence. I could hear her crying softly and breathing hard.

"Donna, what's happening?"

"Jagey's walking. Praise Jesus, it's a miracle."

Eight hours after MOF departed, on the night before he was scheduled to take an extended dirt nap, that damn dog rose from his deathbed and walked. He'd lost a lot of weight, and he moved a little gingerly for the first couple of days, but he was back to his old unwieldy gait and spastic perambulations by the time everyone returned from Hawaii. It was one of the craziest things I'd ever witnessed. I had irrefutable proof, at that very moment, of something I'd strongly suspected. MOF was a witch.

....

Gary finally greeted me in the kitchen after what seemed like an eternity. He apologized for his earlier absence, but he'd been occupied shutting down the main water valve. Besides serving as resume screener and main point of contact, Gary was also Sidney's lead bodyguard. Gary was enormous and yoked. He'd served in the Marines, and went on to dabble in mixed martial arts and cage fighting. Gary had once knocked an opponent out in the first 30 seconds of a fight, and he never regained consciousness.

"How was the flight?" Gary smiled and slapped me on the back with an arm that was more like a meat hook. I almost fell over.

"Great."

"Outstanding. You must be hungry. Want some breakfast?"

I looked at the flooded mess in the kitchen and shook my head. My stomach was in knots, but I still wouldn't have touched anything cooked in that kitchen with a Kevlar oven mitt. Gary smiled again. "Yeah, I wouldn't eat this shit either. It's for the dogs and the golfers. I'll get Sidney's personal chef to whip up something for us. Let's go see the big man."

Gary escorted me through a maze of decrepit hallways and Havishamian rooms that appeared to have been untouched since the late 60s. The entire house was carpeted wall to wall with brown shag that had supposedly started out pearly white. Sidney's two massive black retrievers, Jagey and Meisty, lumbered down the hall in front of us sniffing and foraging for food remnants buried deep in the pile. There were racks of old clothing and stacks of old shoes everywhere, and large cardboard boxes piled on top of each other. Rows and rows of bookshelves with more tapes and DVDs. There must have been thousands of them.

41

I also noticed a vast number of Agamographs covering most of the walls. Agamographs were colorful, holographic prints created by the artist, Yaacov Agam. Agam was an experimental kinetic and optical fabricator who rose to prominence in the late 1960s by using lenticular printing to present radically different images that morph as you change your angle of viewing. Essentially, he devised a clever method to mass-produce psychedelic artwork at a highly opportune point in American history. I had seen one or two Agams in books and museums, but I was amazed that almost every wall in Sidney's house seemed to display an Agamograph, and some walls had more Agam than wall showing.

We eventually came to an imposing metal door at the end of another long Agamed hallway. The door looked brand new and sparkly clean, in stark contrast to all the other decrepit doors we'd passed by or through. There was a table and chair next to the door, and another hulking man was sitting at the table playing solitaire on a laptop. The only other item on the table was a baby monitor with a small video display, but I couldn't distinguish the blurry image on the screen. The hulk didn't acknowledge us or look up from the laptop. There was a security keypad mounted on the wall next to the big metal door. Gary punched a code into the keypad, and I could hear the sound of heavy bolts unlocking and thick steel bars retracting into the door. It sounded like we were opening the door to Fort Knox. The keypad beeped a few times and the door slowly opened. Gary walked through and motioned for me to follow him.

I looked into the dark abyss beyond the gates of Babylon, and I felt a sudden urge to turn and run as fast as I could. I knew beyond a shred of doubt that if I stepped through this highly fortified portal, everything in my life would change permanently. I would not be the same person on the other side. Something inside me would be lost forever, and something was waiting for me out there in the darkness.

I stood frozen for what seemed like hours, but was probably only a few seconds. The Fear was building, feeding on uncertainty and doubt. The clouds were rolling in and I was getting a cold chill up my spine. I took a deep breath and calmed myself. I was here for a reason. I had come this far and I was not turning around. I was not going to run away. Not this time.

I took another deep breath and entered Sidney's suite. It was immediately apparent that this was not going to be like any other interview. Ever. It was very dark at first, and I was having trouble seeing. I was not sure if it was my fatigue and mild lingering narcosis, or whether this was the darkest, coldest and weirdest room I had ever seen. The air temperature was freezing, and I was doing my best to keep from shivering. I could almost see my breath. As my eyes adjusted to the darkness, I started to focus in on the peculiar surroundings.

The room was massive, probably 4,000 square feet. An enormous bed was situated directly in the middle of the room, and there was a pulley system with cables attached to a beam above bed to help its occupant in and out, like a makeshift forklift. The walls were covered with priceless works by Picasso, van Gogh, Renoir, Matisse, and huge sculptures by Dali, Calder, Giacometti and Henry Moore were strewn about, seemingly organized so the bed occupant could have a clear view of all of them. Agamographs were conspicuously absent from this room.

Hanging from the ceiling in front of the bed was an enormous Sony LCD TV, and it was broadcasting a pre-recorded Yankee game. One side of the suite had been converted into a professional gourmet kitchen, and there were several chefs quietly preparing food and drinks while pretending not to notice me. Another part of the suite was a vast wine cellar with the capacity to store several thousands of bottles. A massive conference table stood near the bed, and it was covered with bottles, pictures, magazines, various knick-knacks and assorted chotchkies. I also couldn't help noticing a freestanding toilet directly next to the bed. A large white porcelain apparatus, prominently and proudly displayed without any pretense of privacy or vanity. The two pudgy dogs and an equally chubby cat were now lounging under the toilet. The carpet in this room was even more revolting than the rest of the house.

Sidney Frank was splayed out butt naked and flat on his back in the center of the king-sized bed. He was puffing away on a cigar, and his eyes were pointed straight up at the ceiling. I was somewhat startled by Sidney's appearance, but what made the sight even more disturbing was the gorgeous blonde masseuse pounding on his legs and feet. I would later learn that Sidney suffered from poor circulation, among a litany of other potentially lethal medical conditions. Almost every single day, Sidney was visited by a strikingly beautiful massage therapist who kneaded his extremities, usually while he reclined in the buff.

I was not sure what to do. I stood for a few long minutes, alternating between watching the game and trying not to gawk at the grotesquely fascinating spectacle in front of me. I felt like a voyeur, but everyone in the room was going about their business as if nothing unusual was happening. Apparently this was just another day at the office. I watched Sidney closely, and I wasn't certain he was awake, although he grunted every time the masseuse hit a hot spot. I cleared my throat a few times, hoping that he'd realize I was there. I got nothing. Gary noticed and walked over to the bed. He grabbed Sidney's huge foot and shook it.

"Mr. Frank, Seth is here."

"Oh yeah? I been waiting here for you. Sidney Frank, Brown Class of 1942. Good to meet you." Sidney grunted and held out the *claw* to shake my hand. His right hand was gnarled and claw-like with fingers that were permanently curled from old football injuries. He never moved his head or looked at me. "Care for a drink? Pierre, bring us two Dirty Geese, big ones. They're made with Grey Goose. That's my vodka, and the world's best tasting vodka. I invented it in 1997. Everyone thought Russian vodka was radioactive after Chernobyl. So I said, fuck Russia, lets make vodka in France. They got the best of everything. Best food, best wine, best women. You name it, them Frenchies got the best. And now they got the best vodka. You drink, right?" His eyes never left the ceiling, which was fortunate since I was transfixed on his genitals. They resembled a dehydrated mushroom dangling from a ragged grey tumbleweed. Franks and beans, twigs and berries.

Sidney was approximately 80 years old and considerably overweight. He was mammoth, probably tipping the scales at close to 300 lbs. He had a full head of grey hair and wrinkly, ruddy skin from years of golf and beach blanket bingo before the advent of sunscreen. He had been an accomplished football player in his prime, and there was trace evidence of ancient muscles in his arms, thick neck and broad chest. Decades of hard work, hard drinking and the good life had turned his once athletic physique into a bloated mess. He looked like a slightly older Brando after an extended Krispy Kreme and Quaalude bender.

Sidney

One of the chefs popped a huge dirty martini into my jittery hands and gave me a wink. He dropped another enormous martini on Sidney's night table. It was 7:15am local time (4:15am in California) on a Tuesday morning, and I had no clue what was going on. I was standing in my wrinkled suit, holding a 32-ounce martini and trying to process everything around me. My brain wasn't cooperating, so I took a few slugs of my breakfast cocktail and immediately felt better. The strong drink was warm, and everything that seemed peculiar started to make more sense, or maybe I stopped analyzing it. I felt more like a guest than an explorer who'd found a lost and forbidden world.

"Gary, up." Gary used a remote control and adjusted Sidney's hospital bed so he could see me. As the bed tilted and his torso was lifted up, the beautiful masseuse never missed a beat. The bed stopped moving and Sidney and I made eye contact for the first time. He was much older than I had expected. I had envisioned a mature person, just not ancient. His eyebrows were so grey and bushy that it was difficult to see his eyes. But once his shaggy gaze was locked on me, I could feel a connection. His eyes had a bright sparkle of energy that seemed magical and mischievous. The naked stare down made me a little uncomfortable, so I broke eye contact and looked around the room. Sidney flashed a toothy grin, like he was thrilled to have just won the impromptu staring contest. He took his martini glass and lifted it.

"Here's to getting honor!" Sidney lifted the glass to his mouth and downed the entire martini. I couldn't believe it. I'd never seen anyone chug a martini, and I'd seen some accomplished chuggers. He spat a big olive back into his glass, and without a flinch or missing a beat, he said, "And staying on her!"

I laughed out loud. Sidney smiled and I could see almost every tooth in his mouth. I looked at my glass and momentarily considered making a toast, but I couldn't think of a good one, and I really didn't want to attempt the gallon martini chug on an empty stomach. I doubt it would have stayed down very long, and me hurling breakfast martini was not the optimal first impression.

"So you went to Cornell? Beautiful city, Ithaca, but a little dreary. I went to Brown. Providence, now that's a city. And Brown is a much better school. What was your SAT score?"

I opened my mouth to answer, and it occurred to me that I hadn't the foggiest idea. I had drawn a complete blank. I couldn't even lie convincingly because I couldn't remember if the top score was 800 or 1600. Fortunately, Sidney continued talking before I said anything incriminating.

"So you were captain of the Cornell golf team. Three handicap?" I nodded, and felt the hair on my neck start to stand up. Damn, this guy was good. I saw him studying me with that wry, toothy grin on his face.

"Well, what the hell are we doing here? Let's golf. Gary, toilet."

Gary gingerly helped Sidney to the toilet next to the bed. He plopped down on the seat and proceeded to move his bowels, shamelessly, for the next five minutes. I tried to excuse myself and wait outside, but he kept asking questions about wine and golf, and I kept answering. I attempted to look away during the crescendos, but eye contact is important and I didn't want to be rude.

....

Sidney didn't care to move very far to take care of business. He could walk, but he preferred to roll. His full-time paramedic and security crew rolled him directly from bed to car when he went to golf courses, restaurants, airplanes or romantic trysts. Almost all business meetings were conducted from his bed, and when nature called, he wasn't shy. Sidney occasionally failed to reach the bedside apparatus in time to answer the call. Some speculated that he didn't even try to hold it, just to prove a point.

Looking back on it, Sidney's immodesty might have been a psychological defect or power play, or combination of the two. I once witnessed Sidney dropping a deuce a few feet away from a high-octane meeting of investment banking hotshots and hedgehogs, several of whom were women. Most of them tried to conceal their shock by averting their eyes and pretending not to notice, but morbid curiosity reigned supreme and we caught a few covert peepers. Sidney grinned and waved. All of the staffers were fairly desensitized to his antics, and almost nothing shocked me. I recalled another time when Sidney dropped his trousers on the third hole at Trump National, bent slightly, and blew out all over the perfectly manicured tee box. MOF, playing a group behind Sidney, was convinced that a rabid bear or sick wildebeest made the mess. She called the club manager on her cell phone to complain about the unseemly conditions, and she urged him to warn all players that a diseased and possibly dangerous animal was lurking somewhere on the course. When the manager politely declined, MOF called the Donald directly to demand the manager's termination. I also recalled holding a cell phone next to Sidney's ear during a conference call while he defecated loudly. He yelled at his executives, most with salaries well into the seven figures, in between grunts and growls. The scene would have repulsed a normal person. I found it oddly endearing.

....

Sidney was whisked from the toilet into a wheelchair, and Craig rolled him out the door. I was shown to a guest bedroom and given two minutes to change into my golf attire. Gary assured me that if I took even a second longer than two minutes, Sidney would be gone and I'd be on the next flight home. The guest bedroom was almost as repulsive as the kitchen, and I tried not to touch anything with my hands or bare feet.

I made it to the car in one minute and 57 seconds. We departed Sidney's house for Sunningdale Country Club three seconds later at exactly 7:30am. I couldn't believe this was actually happening. I assumed there was a remote possibility we'd play golf at some point, just not right out of the gate.

I was seated across from Sidney in the back of one of his customized bombproof Maybachs, and Chad was seated next to him. Chad had introduced himself back at the house, and he jumped in the car as we were departing. He was much colder and distant than the other staffers I'd been introduced to, and during most of the car ride he was immersed in some kind of business report. Chad was dressed impeccably in a brilliant white polo and pressed tan trousers, and he had a pastel green cashmere sweater tied over his shoulders. It looked like he'd undressed a Ralph Lauren manikin to create his look. Sidney was scanning the Wall Street Journal and intermittently watching MSNBC on his TV monitor. Another big cigar was smoldering in his mouth and the windows were closed, creating a campfire-like air quality in the rear of the $500,000 automobile.

Chad was visibly displeased. "I can't breathe, and my sweater is going to stink like a Havana whore house." Chad grimaced and reached for the window button.

"Don't touch that goddamn window," Sidney barked and blew a huge cloud of Davidoff dust in Chad's direction. Sidney had a very gruff and gravelly tone that many staffers mimicked, never in front of him. I became fairly adept at impersonating him. Sidney was also in the habit of calling staffers at all hours to ask ridiculous questions or make bizarre demands.[6] He expected unwavering loyalty, and he enjoyed pushing buttons and boundaries. Sometimes I would call people from Sidney's cell phone and mess with them. Marty, Sidney's personal biographer, was a favored target. One time I called him at midnight and demanded that he deliver chilled lychee nuts and baby loquats. He drove all over Chinatown and finally delivered them to Sidney at 2am. Sidney woke up and looked at Marty like he was crazy. Then he shrugged and ate the fruit.

---

[6] After a few staffers claimed they "missed" his calls due to poor Nextel coverage, Sidney ordered that everyone pack two phones – with both Nextel and Verizon service - just to be on the safe side.

Chad sat quietly and pouted. He looked pensive and furrowed, but it was difficult to take Chad seriously. Even when he was trying to maintain solemnity, there was always a spark of depravity flickering just beneath the surface. Sidney enjoyed tormenting Chad, and everyone else dear to his heart. It was part of his mentoring technique. Tough love. Thick skin. It wasn't puppy dogs and rainbows in the real world. It wasn't breakfast bloodies, golf all day long, and happy endings every night. The world was competitive. It was cutthroat. It was dog eat dog, and Sidney wanted us to maul pitbulls. He wanted to make sure everyone in his liquor neverland got a little reality spank now and again. Sometimes you would worry if Sidney hadn't yelled at you recently. You knew he loved you when he barked in your face. It meant he was thinking about you and that he gave a shit. In fact, if he really adored you he'd fire you, only to hire you back for more money. That was a little trick he'd learned from his mentor Rosenstiel, who'd fired and rehired Sidney a number of times. Of course, Rosenstiel hired Sidney back at a discount. By the time I started working for him, Sidney had already fired Chad three separate times. One time he'd been terminated for sending a box to the wrong Bermuda address. The box was filled with cash

We arrived at the pristine links of Sunningdale Country Club at 7:57am on a glorious late September morning. There was glistening dew on the grass and a slight chill in the air, but the course was breathtaking. Sunningdale was built in 1918 by A.W. Tillinghast, and it was a work of art. The course was not long, but the contours were carved out of the natural topography, and every hole had its own unique character. Similar to Winged Foot and Quaker Ridge, it was a rare privilege to play a course steeped in such distinguished history and tradition.

Waiting for us in the parking lot were two of Sidney's professional golfers, Trevor and Kevin. These guys were actual PGA touring pros, and I recognized them from TV. They crushed the ball and had short game skills that were beyond my conception. They didn't miss shots, and I was worried. I could hold my own against any country club chump with a big mouth and a fat stack of high society, but I was going to get caught with my pants down this time. The rubber was fucking the road, and I was going to get my ass spanked, bow tied and handed to me on a silver platter with a frilly doily. My muscles felt weak, my neck was stiff as a board, and I was nauseated and groggy. And to top it off, I was a little buzzed from the big gulp breakfast martini.

Fortunately, Trevor and Kevin were also professional partiers. Unbeknownst to me, they had just rolled up from an all-night bender with two female exchange students from New Zealand, and they were in no condition to be driving, much less playing golf.

I would come to learn that staffers drank for free. The Sidney Frank Importing Company ("SFIC"), the staff's de facto employer, had a program called "Brand Promotion" and it was the greatest perk ever enacted for a company of professional alcoholics. You could essentially expense all of your drinks no matter where you were, but there were two small catches. The drink was supposed to be made with a company brand, such as Grey Goose, Jägermeister, Corazon Tequila, etc. (although that restriction was rarely enforced), and you were expected to buy drinks for fellow alcoholics boozing at the bar. It was designed to encourage corporate salespeople to buy drinks for the house when they were making sales calls or attending events. It was not intended to allow Sidney's staff to party like rock stars on SFIC's dime, but that was the happy consequence. The company would eventually pull the plug after the staff racked up a hundred thousand dollars in brand promotions during one quarter, but it was a fun quarter.

Trevor and Kevin removed their sunglasses to greet me and shake my hand. Their eyes were puffy and bloodshot, and I could smell vodka fumes radiating from them. Trevor was limping from a minor altercation that occurred sometime during the prior evening involving his foot and a moving car. Their condition made me feel a little better, but not completely.

I walked to the tee box and beheld the splendor of the first hole at

Sunningdale. It was magnificent - long and straight, with a wide-open fairway and very few hazards. A perfect opening hole confidence booster. Kevin pulled Sidney's cart up onto the tee box, and positioned the cart a few feet behind the first tee. Sidney always rode shotgun, and his cart was positioned so he could have the best view of the action, even if it meant parking on tee boxes and greens. If you tried that shit at most other clubs, the manager would revoke your membership. $5,000 tips to club managers afforded unique privileges.

Trevor was first on the tee. He ripped it 320 yards straight up the middle. Kevin then slammed his drive about 300 up the right side. So much for my assumptions that alcohol would even the field. I later learned that many professional golfers actually play better while shitfaced. Golf is 95% mental, and a little nip can help calm the nerves and improve focus in some people. Kevin and Trevor were prime examples of alcohol-enhanced warriors. I was not.

I walked up to the tee box more anxious and jumpy than I'd ever been in my life. I leaned down and tried to tee up my ball, but my hand was quivering so violently that I could barely get the ball to stay propped up. I took a few deep breaths to calm myself. I imagined that I was on a beautiful beach with a stick, and that I was going to hit some shells into the water. I pictured voluptuous bikini girls reclining in sand traps, waiting to lube my body with cocoa butter. I tried to smell the warm seaweed, but it smelled like mown grass. I listened for the sounds of waves and seagulls, but the only sounds I could hear were a droning lawnmower and my heart palpitating inside my chest cavity. My skull and ears were keeping perfect rhythm with my heart. I took a few sad practice swings, but my driver felt like it weighed 100 pounds. My chest was pounding and my ears were hot and intermittently buzzing and ringing. I took my stance and looked at the ball, but I felt like I was floating above my body, watching myself sway to and fro, swallowing hard with a dry tongue, waiting for the inevitable convulsive explosion, like a mosquito diving into the beautiful blue light. I felt like everything was moving in slow motion. Just hang on and breathe. I took a deep breath and held it. I felt like I'd been standing above my ball for an eternity. I worried that if I waited any longer I would faint or vomit, or both. I wondered if anyone noticed how dreadfully long I'd been frozen above my ball. I took another deep breath. My brain activated autopilot, and the fat lady started screaming.

My body instinctively coiled, followed by an infinitely slow wind up. I reached the apex after what seemed like forever, paused, and convulsed imperceptibly. I could feel my blood clotting. I could hear a caterpillar yawning. I could smell a mosquito smoking.

I closed my eyes and fired my driver down the line as hard as I could. I heard the egg crack and sizzle, and I opened my eyes just in time to see, to my amazement, that I actually made decent contact, followed by sheer horror as I watched my skyrocketing slice fly miles out of bounds.

My heart came roaring up through my throat, struck my medulla oblongata squarely and then sank back down into the pit of my stomach like a human high striker. I wasn't sure what to do, but I was certain that I'd just blown the possibility of ever working for Mr. Grey Goose. He would know I wasn't a three handicap, and the world's most overreaching attorney would limp back into obscurity. I looked over at Trevor and Kevin, and they were making no effort to conceal their cocky grins. We all looked over at Sidney. He was sitting in the cart, big cigar smoldering in the corner of his mouth, head slumped to the side, passed out cold.

Trevor fished a ball out of his pocket, dropped it and smashed it 300 yards dead center. It was driver off the deck, and I swear he hit it on the bounce. It was one of the most incredible shots I'd ever witnessed. Trevor then walked straight over to Sidney and tapped his leg. Sidney's head popped up and his eyes opened, but he looked disoriented.

"Did you see that? Seth crushed it." Trevor yelled near Sidney's ear.

"Oh yeah? Good." Sidney nodded and cackled a little. "Looks like we found a player."

Trevor climbed in the driver's seat and winked at me. "Nice drive, Shooter." I would later learn that you never wanted to be called Shooter.

When they told me I'd be playing a round of golf with the Chairman, I naturally assumed the Chairman would be playing golf also. Sidney never left his cart once. He hadn't played a full round of golf in several years, although he'd hit an occasional shot or putt if he felt inspired. But his love of the game was obvious.

As we played, Sidney told me stories about playing Sunningdale through the years, and he pointed out subtle changes that were made to the course. A tree removed here, a tree planted there. He talked about playing with Arnold Palmer, Sean Connery, Michael Jordan, Bill Clinton and Donald Trump. He claimed that he almost got Al Pacino out on the course. He also talked a lot about his closest friend, Gene Borek, a true blue collar golfer and former head pro at Metropolis Country Club. Borek's claim to fame was that he shot a course record shattering 65 in the U.S. Open at Oakmont in 1973, only to be one upped two days later by Johnny Miller's scorching 63.

Sidney was a student of the game, and he considered golf to be the truest test of a person's character. Almost all staffer candidates were interviewed on the golf course, even if they couldn't actually play. They didn't need to be skilled; they just needed balls and a good attitude. As we talked, I started to relax and enjoy myself, and my golf improved immensely. Sidney scolded me when I hit bad shots, grunted on the good ones, and he was so pleased when I beat the pros on one hole that I thought we was going to jump out of the cart and kiss me.

Another undisclosed perk of golfing for Sidney's amusement was his motivational sprinkler system - $500 for birdies, $1,000 for eagles, and $5,000 if a player carded a hole-in-one or beat the course record. We finished the round and stopped for lunch in the clubhouse. I felt pretty good. I made a couple of birdies and had a thousand bucks cash in my pocket. It was definitely the most money I'd ever made during a job interview. Trevor and Kevin each made a few grand that day. Most of it would end up in the chefs' pockets after the afternoon poker game. Most of the chefs' spoils would trickle down to card rooms, bookies, casinos, OTB outlets, lawyers and massage parlors.

"You play okay for an lawyer, but you're no three," Sidney chuckled and coughed a little. He looked a little flushed and sweaty, but he smirked and jabbed me in the ribs. "I used to be a five, and I could've won a couple of bucks off you today." He winked at me. Sidney had never been a five, but he knew I wasn't a three so technically we were even.

Opportunism was not foreign to Sidney. He'd grown up next to Cochegan Rock, the biggest glacial boulder in New England. It's about 50 feet high and 7,000 pounds, and it served as a spiritual meeting place for the Mohegan Indian tribe centuries earlier. Sidney's first business enterprise was charging horny teenagers a nickel to use his ladder to scale the rock so they could smoke cigarettes and make out. When they realized they were stuck, Sidney would charge them a dime to get back down.

Sidney used his entrepreneurial ingenuity to get into Brown University. He was not an academic superstar, but he managed to convince, and by convince I mean bribe, his school's record keeper to change his grades to *A*s. My golf handicap was a similar deception. It was more harmless embellishment than malicious fraud. Sidney wasn't upset. To the contrary, he was impressed that I had the nerve to chase a dream and get my foot in the door of a priceless opportunity. In a sense, I bluffed for the pot, and Sidney appreciated a good bluff.

"Lying about golf is like lying to your wife." He wheezed and smiled again. "If she didn't see it, it never happened." Sidney took a long drag on his Davidoff and leaned in. "Just never lie to me. Understand?"

"Understood."

"Good. So what do you know about taxes?"

I'd just received a Masters degree in taxation, and I knew that Sidney had memorized my resume. "Well, to be perfectly honest, I have a lot of useless tax information stored in my brain, but I realize that none of it matters as long as you play golf with the judge."

Sidney belly laughed. The jester amused the king.

"I like you, kid. You remind me of someone. I can't place it. Someone from my past. Someone I knew from Ohio."

My eyes widened, and I caught myself. Was he serious or pulling my leg? Had he done research on me? Looking back on it, it wouldn't surprise me if he'd compiled an entire FBI dossier.

"My entire family is originally from Ohio."

"Really?" He was inscrutable, and if this was a bluff, he had me sold.

"My mom grew up in Cincinnati, and my dad is from Springfield."

"You don't say." Sidney smiled and slapped me on the knee. "My first wife was from Cincinnati. Good people out there."

"The world's best."

Chapter 4
Screwdriver

After golf, I found myself back in the Maybach riding with Sidney to his corporate offices in New Rochelle for my formal interview. SFIC occupied two dilapidated floors in one of the oldest buildings in downtown New Rochelle. I was beginning to think crappy accommodations were Sidney's hallmark. Chad was riding with Trevor and Kevin, leaving me all alone with Sidney.

Sidney sat in his seat quietly, but he wasn't reading or watching TV. He was wearing mirrored sunglasses and his head was not facing me, but I knew he was watching me. Observing my reactions. Reading my face and body movements, trying to pick up my tell. I would learn that Sidney read people better than most professional poker players, and those guys read people better than FBI profilers. It was an aptitude, like artistic or musical ability. It couldn't be learned, taught or even practiced. Sidney was a people-reading savant, and it was a gift that served him well through life. It made him a deadly effective salesman. He could see right through almost everyone.

Sidney leaned forward, very close to my face. For the second time that day, I had the uncomfortable feeling that he might kiss me. He leaned right up to my ear and whispered, "I know what you're thinking."

"You do?"

"Yes."

I waited. He leaned back in his seat and smiled. He remained silent for a long time. I felt like I should say something to break the tension, but I kept quiet. Finally, he spoke.

"One word."

"Plastics?"

"No, smartass. Innovation. If you take nothing else away from today, take innovation. You must constantly innovate, or you will die. You need to keep things fresh. Keep it new and interesting. Whenever you look at something, don't think about what it is. Instead, think about what it can be. Think about its potential. Everything wants to be better. That's why you're here. That's exactly why you're in my car right now. Am I right? Of course I'm right. And how do you make something better? That's exactly what I'm thinking right now." Sidney smiled and took a drag from his cigar. "Innovation made me a fortune, and trust me when I tell you I'm no genius. I just see things different. I see potential. I skate to where the puck is going, slap the goalie with my stick and go home to fuck the head cheerleader. I can make you better than you thought possible. But you got a lot to learn, and I'm short on time. Time is the most precious resource of all. It's one of the few things I can't buy more of. So the question is, are you worth it?"

Sidney leaned back and was silent for a few minutes. I wasn't sure if he was waiting for me to answer.

"Lesson two. Marry a rich girl. Filthy rich. Let her family do the heavy lifting. You can make more money and connections in a 20 minute ceremony than most men make in a lifetime."

"Too late for me, Mr. Frank."

"Next time then." Sidney smiled and took a long drag on his cigar, exhaling slowly. "Did you know that I married the richest girl in America?"

"Really?"

Sidney grinned and put his hands behind his head. His face lit up and his eyes twinkled. "Skippy Rosenstiel. The love of my life. Most beautiful girl I'd ever laid eyes on." Sidney could sell it, and I might have bought it if I hadn't already seen photos of the bride. Skippy was no picnic. "I brought her fresh flowers every time I saw her." Skippy and flowers seemed at odds, like she would have been more comfortable holding a basketball or a carburetor.

"So, I'm at Brown," Sidney smiled and looked out into the distance, "And I meet Eddie Sarnoff." Sidney puffed away on his stogie like a choo-choo train. "And that's when my luck started to turn." He sat back and put his hands over his eyes, very slowly and dramatically. "Eddie had the car, and I had the cock. He had this beautiful Ford convertible, but he would park far away from everything else in the lot. He would circle it three or four times, inspecting the paint for dings and scratches. He was one meticulous bastard. Drove me crazy.

"One night, me, Eddie, Skippy and one of Skippy's sorority sisters piled into Eddie's car and went to see Casablanca at the drive-in. We got cheeseburgers, milkshakes and handjobs. It was great.

"On weekends, I would go with Eddie to the his family's little place in the city. Eight stories on Park Ave. Their place had a private elevator and a media center. Everyone in the family had their own floor. Eddie's father David was head of RCA. He later started a company called NBC. Made a fortune back in those days. Eddie and I would walk in and their cook would have fried chicken and beer waiting for us. That was gracious living, my first real taste of the good life.

"Sometimes I would go visit Skippy. Her family's apartment took up the 26th floor of the Sherry Netherlands Hotel. The views from up there. All the people and cars moved real slow, and you barely heard cars honking. Everything seemed small and insignificant.

"But it was a lot different than Sarnoff's place. No warmth. No fried chicken. Her family treated me like a janitor. Her mother looked me up and down, and I could see she didn't care for my rough hands and cheap clothes. I couldn't afford fine suits back then. Shit, I could barely afford shoes. Probably looked like a bumpkin to her, not a respectable suitor. And their apartment was full of priceless antiques, masterpieces of art and uncomfortable furniture. She always watched me, like I might break something or steal the silverware. I should have, miserable assholes. They had some of the first security cameras ever made. Skippy's father Lew was always lurking, speaking on the phone in hushed tones, meeting with suspicious characters, or just walking by lost in space. Always wore big thick glasses. Always smoking the biggest cigar made.

"So one day, Lew was walking by us. He looked angry about something.

Skippy tried to introduce me. I said something like 'pleasure to meet you sir' and reached out to shake, and that bastard just stared at my hand. He studied me carefully for a few minutes. I was amazed he could see anything through those glasses, but whatever he saw he didn't like. He frowned, blew a mouthful of smoke at me, and marched past me like I was a ghost."

Sidney was quiet for a few minutes, looking out the window and lost in thought. I thought the history lesson was over for the day.

"Lewis Rosenstiel. Ever hear of him?"

I could have tried to bluff, but I knew Sidney would sniff it out. "Nope."

"One of the most ruthless criminals of all time, and you've never heard of him. Guess what? You ain't alone. Amazes me that the Italians get so much press, and most of the biggest Jew gangsters are relatively unknown, except a few. Rothstein. Lansky. Siegel. That's about all the media knows, but let me assure you there are bones buried out there. I've seen them myself. Lansky was the man behind Lucky Luciano, and the Jews bankrolled a lot of Italian action. Did you know that?" Sidney looked at me closely.

"No."

"No. I didn't think so." He looked out of the window and was quiet for a moment or two. "You probably learned a lot in those fancy Cornell classes, but all that crap won't help you in this business. You got a lot to learn, kid, and the clock is ticking." He was running some kind of crude equation in his head, deciding whether mentoring me was a worthwhile investment.

We pulled up in front of the SFIC corporate building, and one of Sidney's senior executives was parking his candy apple red Ferrari in a handicap space. He sauntered over and gave us a greasy, obsequious welcome. His name was Lenny Sidewinder. Lenny was losing his hair, so he shaved and polished his scalp. It looked like he spent hours detailing it. You could almost see your reflection if you looked closely. Lenny had an unusually small head and several large fat rolls near the base of his neck, and from behind his head and neck region resembled a large, circumcised penis. Lenny suffered from mildly apelike facial features coupled with a pronounced lisp, and he was wearing a tight, silky shirt unbuttoned almost to his navel. He had thick gold-chains around his hairy neck, and his tight polyester pants were tucked into Gucci biker boots. Lenny was the quintessential juice-slinging pimp. He reeked of Drakkar Noir and loud desperation.[7]

I was led to a waiting room and detained for several minutes, and then escorted into Sidney's office through a side door. Sidney was already seated with a cigar in his mouth and an ice-cold shot of Jägermeister in front of him in a small snifter. There was another shot in front of a chair next to him.

"Take a seat." Sidney pointed the claw at the chair. I sat and slowly surveyed the room. His office was a converted boardroom, with his desk chair at the head of a long conference table. It had recently been renovated, and was much nicer than the other offices in the suite. On almost every flat surface sat a bottle of company product. The walls were adorned with priceless paintings, and more priceless sculptures were scattered about. I also noticed many candid photos of Sidney with all sorts of professional athletes and celebrities. I had definitely rolled back into the old school medicine show of snake oil wheeling and dealing.

There was a pile of ancient photos of on the table next to me, and I started thumbing through them. "Those are mostly old photos of Lew." Sidney chuckled and pointed out some of the more interesting ones. "There's a rare photo of Lew, Lansky and Bronfman". It was like something out of *Goodfellas*. None of them was smiling, and they all looked a little nervous. I saw a photo of Rosenstiel shaking hands with J. Edgar Hoover. Both of them had big grins on their faces. There was another photo of Rosenstiel and Roy Cohn locked in an unusually tender looking embrace. There was a shot of Rosenstiel, Al Capone and Frank Costello in a casino that looked like a government surveillance photo. There was a

---

[7] Lenny would later appear on several episodes of the *Real Housewives of New York* as a potential love interest of Bethenny Frankel. It was difficult to watch without a heavy dose of antiemetics.

very stiff and serious looking photo of Lew standing near President Dwight Eisenhower at what looked to be a formal White House function.

I noticed a large print of Lew, Sidney, and a beautiful woman on a huge yacht decked out in fancy bathing suits. "Funny suits, right? Different times back then. Recognize her? That's Lee Rosenstiel, now better known as Lee Annenberg. She was Lew's second wife. I went on their honeymoon with them, on that big floating toilet. Don't ask me why, I'm not even sure myself." Sidney grinned and shook his head. "She eventually dumped Lew for Walter Annenberg. Went from underworld princess to high society duchess, from moll to doll with a divorce and an I do. That broad had king-sized cajones and some crown jewel chutzpah to dip them in."

Sidney pointed the claw at a small black and white photo. "There's me and Abe Schechter." I saw a picture of a much younger and handsomer Sidney standing with a lanky, balding man wearing thick glasses. He had a familiar look to him. "Abe was a good man. Bought a big distributorship back in Cincinnati. Paid a fortune. He soon discovered that the brands had no contracts. No loyalty. He ended up with a big bag of bagels. Abe made some bad decisions, but he was a good man. He was always fair and upright, and I'll never forget that. I never forget a friend." Sidney chuckled gruffly and patted me on the shoulder.

"Uncle Abe was a good man." I didn't know for certain if I had any relatives named Abraham, but it seemed plausible. Had to be an Abe or two back in the Schechter woodpile. Abe or not, I had some distant connection to Sidney's past. Our family trees had been fertilized by related manure.

All of my relatives were from Ohio. My mother's father, Leon Goldman, was a physician and laser researcher, and he spent the bulk of his career in Cincinnati. Leon started building lasers and integrating them into dermatology in the 1960s, long before any surgeons recognized the utility of a scalpel made out of light. He is now considered the father of laser medicine. Leon was old school, and he didn't protect or patent any of his inventions or intellectual property.[8] Although he is celebrated in the medical community, Leon retired and passed away quietly in San Diego.

My father's father, Jack Schechter, was in the scrap metal business in Springfield. I am not entirely sure what the scrap metal business involved, but he played a lot of golf. Jack eventually retired to Florida and expired on the fairway of some swanky club near a deli that served sour cabbage soup and massive pastrami sandwiches.

Sidney married into the most well connected Jewish family in Ohio. We shared a tribal kinship well beyond that of two random Jews walking into a bar, and it afforded Sidney a certain comfort level and security he didn't share with the other staffers.

He raised his Jäger shot glass, "To Ohio!" and slammed it down without flinching. He then trained his steely gaze and toothy grin on me.

I picked up the glass of Jäger and sniffed it. The odor reminded me of bombed nights at Cornell followed by concussive mornings, with me searching for my underwear and praying that whatever was hibernating next to me wouldn't regain consciousness until I'd escaped. I noticed that Sidney was still staring at me, now with a slightly bemused expression. I raised my glass. "Ohio!" and I slammed the shot. My esophagus burned and I feared the shot was going to come right back out. I managed to choke it back and smile.

"No poker face." Sidney chuckled gruffly and coughed a little. "You've tasted it before?"

"Sure. Many times." Jägermeister was fast becoming the number one selling liquor in the United States, and it would eventually sell over a million

---

[8] If he had I probably wouldn't have been looking for a job with Sidney, and you wouldn't be reading this book.

cases per year and overtake Kahlua to gain the top coveted number one spot.[9] But I'd known Jägermeister for a long time. It was a fairly easy shot, especially ice cold. Colleges put Jägermeister on the map, but the popular mainstream combination of Jägermeister and Red Bull (aka "JägerBomb") was skyrocketing and pushing Jägermeister sales past the million case per year mark.

"What does it taste like?"

"Let's see, it tastes a little like Nyquil, licorice, maybe a touch of...."

"No Stupid!" Sidney shouted in my face with such force that it stunned me momentarily. "It tastes like...MONEY!" Sidney grabbed his stomach and burst into convulsive laughter. I had face-planted into one of his favorite proverbs. He laughed so hard that it triggered a coughing spasm. Sidney turned beet red, his nose started running and I could see phlegm dripping from his mouth. He was dry heaving and appeared to be in serious pulmonary distress. I ran over and patted his back, hoping he wouldn't expire during our initial meeting. I worried his ribcage would splinter if I hit him any harder.

Polly, Sidney's executive secretary, burst into the office. "Everything all right, Mr. Sidney?" Polly always called Sidney "Mr. Sidney". It was one of her more annoying behaviors, presumably copied from Sam Bronfman's infamous "Mr. Sam" sobriquet. Polly was at best incompetent, and at worse dangerously reckless. My favorite Polly story was when she mistakenly duplicated a $50,000 wire to a British technology company that was helping SFIC with website design. Fortunately, that company's accountant was exceeding honest and he brought the error to our attention. I thanked him profusely, we reversed the wire, and I made sure Polly was aware of her mistake. She thanked me for catching the error, we shared a few laughs, and she drove home. The very next day, Polly drove to work, fired up her computer, and wired another $50,000 payment to the same company.

---

[9] This was particularly satisfying for Sidney since Schenley Distillery (Lew Rosenstiel's company) had previously owned the Kahlua brand.

The accountant was laughing when he called me. He thought we were wankers.

Polly was the byproduct of multiple generations of inbreeding in desolate regions of the upper northeast. She was gaunt and lanky, with a subtle hunchback and an alarmingly shrill voice. Her squawks could shatter leaded glass, and possibly lead. She had a protruding forehead and eyebrows so plucked they were missing, though she traced them in with colored markers that coordinated with her mood swings and ensembles. Polly's outfits were bright and sparkly with big colorful buttons, and she spent hours shopping online and on TV for snazzy blazers and accoutrements. In between shopping, Polly watched funny cat videos and sang along to Brittany Spears songs. Her chin was completely missing, making it difficult to tell where her face ended and her neck began. Her mouth was a useful landmark because it was always partially open, and her discolored tongue was constantly licking her scaly lips, darting in and out like a hermit crab guarding its crusty den.[10]

Polly's husband, much younger than her and equally repellent, tried to convince me, within 10 minutes of our introduction, that he was a retired male model, professional surfer, and MMA cage fighter. Notwithstanding his uncanny resemblance to Napoleon Dynamite, I was skeptical.

Polly saw me holding Sidney as he was hacking and gagging. "What are you doing to Mr. Sidney? Let go of him you little asshole." Polly's shriek scratched both of my eardrums, and every hair on my body stood on end. "Security. Security. Mr. Sidney is being strangled." Polly pushed a button on a fob she wore around her neck while attempting to brain me with her scaly elbow.

Before I knew what was happening, the doors to the office blew open and three huge black security guards with guns drawn came bearing down on me. The

---

[10] Polly would later receive a reported $12 million bonus when Grey Goose was sold to Bacardi. After Sidney died and Polly was terminated, she received a reported $2 million severance payment. She would later sue Sidney's heirs for allegedly diluting her interest in Sidney's energy drink company. Her case was eventually dismissed.

Homeboys of the Apocalypse. I was confident that it was game over, so I quickly made my peace and waited for quick pops and searing pain followed by extended streaking through Elysian fields and riding perfect cloud breaks into infinity.

"Stop, stop, Seth was trying to help me." Sidney's raspy voice gradually became louder as his airway cleared. The guards holstered their weapons and apologized. Polly looked confused. "For crying out loud, Polly, I was laughing." Sidney looked directly at her. "Get out."

"Yes sir, Mr. Sidney. My mistake." Polly tried to smile, but the skin around her mouth was so tight and puckered it looked like she was scowling. Her teeth were tiny, and all I could see were braces and enflamed gums. She picked up a stack of papers and started sorting through them. "But before I go, I need you to sign this authorization to...."

"No." Sidney growled.

"Mr. Sidney?"

"Get out of my office, now!" Sidney pointed the claw at the door.

"Yes sir, Mr. Sidney, right away sir." Polly and the security squad exited as quickly as they came.

"Sorry," Sidney sat down and took a long drag from his cigar, "Polly ain't too bright, and not much to look at, but she's loyal. Above all things, I value loyalty, and I reward it." Sidney smiled and gave me a little wink. "Did you know my executive VP made seven figures last year?"

"Not bad." I tried not to smile. We were about to negotiate my salary, and he had just pulled his pants down before the flop.

"Yeah, not bad at all." Sidney glared at me, realizing the admission a little too late. Then he reached out and grabbed my hand. If he had been anyone else, I would have run out of the room. But from Sidney, it was another endearing moment that only he could pull off. This was the proverbial offer I couldn't refuse. Money was not the point. We bonded, and we were family now. "I have a special project for you, and I think you're going to like it."

Chapter 5
Manhattan

I was sitting in my New Rochelle hotel room wondering what the hell happened. The entire day seemed like a bizarre fantasy. How was I going to explain all this to my wife? Honey, you aren't going to believe this. The Grey Goose dude wants me to move to Napa to start a wine brand. She wouldn't believe me. I said it to myself, and even I didn't believe me. The phone rang. It was Craig.

"Please hold for Mr. Frank"

The gravelly voice was unmistakable. A rough, low phlegmy clatter produced by 60 years of dirty martinis and smoky cigars. "Dinner tonight at eight. I'll send a car." The line went dead before I could respond.

I wasn't sure if dinner started at 8pm, or if he was picking me up at 8pm, so I played it safe. At 7:45pm I was standing in front of the New Rochelle Marriott in a tie and jacket. My palms were sweaty and I was getting nervous again. I waited for a while but nothing was happening. 8pm came and went, and I was starting to worry that I messed up somehow. Was I supposed to meet him at the house? At around 8:30pm I was dialing Sidney's house when a limousine rolled up. It was a Mercedes Benz, and it was a convertible. In fact, it was the world's only convertible Mercedes limo.

Sidney had it custom built by combining two 1995 S500 sedans at the hip. It slowed down just enough to allow me to jump in.

The top was up, and as expected the limo was filled with smoke, just not the kind of smoke I was expecting. Not cigar smoke. Not cigarette smoke. The limo was filled with the sweet, pungent smoke produced by primo weed. It was like the opening scene from *Fast Times at Ridgemont High* in a much nicer ride.

The next thing I noticed was that Sidney was not in the limo. I would later learn that he rarely left his bed, especially at night, unless it was important. Rendezvous with high society lady friends were important. Dinner with Seth the hack golfing attorney was not high priority. Inside the limo were five other staff members, including the Trevor, Kevin and Gary. Chad opted out of the welcoming festivities. Gary was beefy, and he occupied a generous swath of the limo's seating area.

"Here you go," Gary smiled and handed me a large burning joint, quickly followed by a freezing cold bottle of Jägermeister. "Hit this shit, and then take a shot while the smoke is still in your lungs. It's called a JägerBong." Everyone in the car started laughing.

I held both items in separate hands and paused, trying to remember in which order I was to proceed. I hadn't smoked weed since college, but I wasn't opposed to the occasional puff. Personally, I considered smoking weed much less harmful than drinking, when used in moderation. Stoners didn't usually kill people while driving or beat their wives and children after a hard night of bonging. Potheads played hacky sack and listened to Pink Floyd while munching spicy Cheetos.

I took a look at the joint in my right hand and admired the craftsmanship. It was rolled well, thick and tight. I then turned my attention to my other hand. The Jägermeister bottle was ice cold, and my hand was starting to feel a little numb and tingly. I examined the bottle closely. The label showed a Stag's head with antlers with a crucifix above it. Odd label for a product distributed by a Jew, but then again it was manufactured in Germany. I looked at the back label and noticed the tiny *Sidney Frank Importing Co.* notation on it. I had seen this bottle and label hundreds of times, but SFIC's name had been meaningless.

I looked up and noticed that everyone in the limo was staring at me in anticipation. It occurred to me that this was part of the initiation, like a secret handshake or swallowing goldfish. This was the corporate Kool-Aid, albeit smoky, wretched and illegal in many states unless prescribed by a doctor.

"Eat me!" I took a deep drag on the joint and downed the shot. A little brown spray of smoke and Jägermeister came back up through my nose. "Thank you sir, may I have another?" My lungs were burning and my nose was running, but I managed a sly, *Cool Hand Luke* grin. Everyone in the limo started laughing and chanting "Eat me! Eat me! Eat me!"

"Where's Mr. Frank?"

"Who?" Gary smiled and smacked me on the back so hard that I nearly fell out of my seat. "Sidney? Well, he had some highly important business to take care of in the city." I noticed that the assembled crew exchanged knowing glances, relaying some kind of inside joke. "He told me to take extra good care of you tonight."

The limo took us into Manhattan for dinner. Our first stop was dinner in the private room at Asiate in the Mandarin Oriental. As we walked in I could feel electricity coursing through my body, radiating through all of the tiny hairs on my neck and arms, clogging my ears and making me a little punchy. Gary walked up to the host, a slim and fastidious man with a tight black suit, slick black hair and perfectly trimmed goatee. Gary whispered something into his ear and gave him the signature Sidney Frank handshake. Generally, the reader might assume Gary folded a C-note into his palm and slid it into the host's manicured fingers. Not in this case. Gary handed the thin white man a thick white envelope.

The host opened the envelope, and I could detect an almost imperceptible eyebrow twitch and moment of rapture. But he was a pro and cool as a cucumber.

The host closed the envelope, smiled internally, and went to see if our private room was ready. It had probably been ready for hours, and we still would have been seated there with or without the $5,000 tip. But that was how the big man broke bread, and he wouldn't have expected anything less from his crew entertaining a guest on his behalf.

The restaurant's huge windows, light wood floors, warm brown tones and tree branch chandelier exuded both tranquility and understated excess at the same time. I might have enjoyed the pleasant ambiance but for the fact my insides were exploding. I could feel my stomach churning, intestines twisting and my eyelids were twitching in synchronicity. The host was giving me a funny look. Could he tell something was wrong with me? Was it obvious? The freaky flickering eyelids were a dead giveaway.

I tried avoiding eye contact by looking out the windows. I could see Central Park and it looked inviting. I imagined standing in the park near the big duck pond. If I closed my eyes, I could hear the ducks quacking and the children laughing. I wanted to be one of those children, laughing and playing duck, duck, goose. I tried to find my happy place, but I felt like I'd inhaled a tank of nitrous while sitting on a subwoofer pumping out convulsive techno beats. I took some deep breaths and imagined that Central Park had transformed into an exotic beach, and the pond was now the infinite turquoise sea. The sun was reflected in the tiny brilliant waves, blinding me as I walked along the shoreline. As my eyes slowly adjusted, I noticed the ducks had morphed into super models in feather bikinis floating on duck-shaped rafts, beckoning me to engage them in coconut oil wrestling and topless Marco Polo. I marched towards them like a zombie, unable to resist their mesmerizing magnetic pull. As I got further and further from the beach, I noticed the tide was dropping at a proportional rate and I was not getting wet. The receding tide was keeping pace with my maddening march, and I was not gaining ground on the titillating sirens. The girls were continually just beyond my reach. As I quickened my pace, the tide countered by accelerating its recession. I attacked, it parried. I counter-attacked, it counter-parried. I was still no closer to my objective, and I had walked a good distance into an area that had only minutes before been the ocean floor. There were fish flopping, crabs bobbing and snapping, and lobsters backing under rocks and mounds of seaweed. I reached into my pocket to snap a photo with my phone, and I noticed something moving in my periphery. A monster shadow on the horizon was heading rapidly in my direction, gaining momentum and growing exponentially as it lurched and gurgled. I turned to run back to the beach, but my feet were stuck in the deep wet sand. My hands dropped instinctively to my hip to retrieve my weapon, but I was naked and helpless to resist the titanic black beast bearing down on me.

I snapped back to reality. The dim light appeared even dimmer, and the room was subtly spinning. My knees felt wobbly and the last place I wanted to take a dive was in a restaurant surrounded by Sidney's team. I quickly excused myself and staggered into the men's room. I sat down and took some deeps breaths. I was sitting on a cold toilet in one of the most exclusive restaurants in New York, and waiting just outside the door were people entertaining me on behalf of the martini king. I was anxious and unsure of myself. I didn't feel worthy of this rock star treatment. I felt dangerously exposed, like an impostor waiting for my cover to be blown. I was a simple lawyer from California with an Ivy League degree, a taste for good wine and a decent short game, and I'd stumbled into an alternate reality that seemed way too good to be true. What did they want from me? Why had I been chosen? What purpose could I possibly serve? Was it pure dumb luck, or was there a darker, more sinister reason for my recruitment? Did they want to use my organs as possible replacements for Sidney's? Was I being groomed as a live donor buddy? A transplant sidekick? He looked like he could use a new liver, at a minimum.

I took several more deep breaths and held them until my heartbeat pounded on my eardrums and darkness started setting in. As my brain cleared and reloaded I could feel my body getting calmer. I flushed the toilet several times and listened to gallons of water being sucked out to the sea. Everything was going to be alright. I left my stall and walked to the sink area. My heart was still racing, but my legs felt more secure. I splashed cold water on my face and slapped my cheeks. Tranquil sea air. Calming ocean spray. I took a few final deep breaths and prepared for my ascent.

I exited the men's room just in time to see our group being escorted away. I caught up and blended as the group paraded through the main dining area to the private room. I could feel all of the attention suddenly on us, although none of the other diners overtly stared. They were all dropping significant coin, and they wouldn't tolerate diminishment by a group of intoxicated and over-indulged punks. But they were keenly aware of us. I overheard muffled whispers from several tables saying something like "the Grey Goose guys" or "Sid's kids."

We were seated in the private room and menus were distributed. The host handed the wine list to Gary. The only beverages I'd seen him consume were Jägermeister and Red Bull. Gary didn't even open the list.

"Six bottles of the 2000 Chateau Petrus. Please open and pour all of them."

My eyes widened and my pulse quickened again. Gary ordered each diner a bottle of wine that listed for almost $5,000. Stay cool. I always wondered if anyone actually ordered those astronomical bottles on wine lists, or whether they just remained dormant and dusty in the cellar for years and years. I sometimes wondered whether restaurants really had the bottles on site, or whether they just fluffed up their lists with imaginary magnums of 1961 Chateau Lafite and non-existent jeroboams of 1997 Screaming Eagle. I assumed the Mandarin maintained a fairly accurate wine list, and most of the patrons could afford to pair an extravagant wine with their exorbitant meal. As six pristine bottles of Petrus were delivered to our table, I had confirmation.

The sommelier filled my glass and left the bottle in front of me. I was frozen. My first inclination was to take a photo of the bottle and send it to my friends. I lifted the glass and took a sip. It was delicious. Robert Parker had rated it at 100, and he was much more reliable than Wine Spectator. I read lots of reviews, and I didn't always taste the unctuousness leather or pencil lead that many wine critics claimed to taste, but I knew a good wine when I tasted it. This one went down real easy.

I looked around the table. Everyone had a bottle of this magical potion in front of him, and it was clear that most of them had absolutely no clue what they were drinking. Two of the golfers guzzled their glasses and then chased the wine chug by passing a flask of Jack Daniels. One of Sidney's chefs raised his bottle and chugged about half of it down in one long guzzle, followed by an even longer belch. Another staffer decided he'd rather have a light beer, and he simply pushed his wine bottle aside. Simply pushed a $5,000 bottle of wine away in favor of Bud Light. This was new and unchartered territory. I was accustomed to fighting my tablemates for the dregs of a wine we considered precious at $50 a bottle.

"How's the wine?" Gary smiled and smacked me on the back again. I could feel a hand shaped welt starting to sprout between my shoulder blades.

"Good." I tried not to spill any of the wine in my glass, but I think a few precious drops may have been liberated.

"You think the wine's good...wait for the food."

Gary wasn't kidding. It was, without a doubt, the finest meal of my life. I was served duck with a selection of six different salts. One of the salts was allegedly from the Jurassic era. The pompous *Salt Steward* [the restaurant employed a server dedicated solely to serving salt] claimed the salt was millions of years old. He went into a long harangue about the history and details of the salt, where it was mined, the delicate metallic nuance and subtle spicy undertone. It tasted like salt to me. I ate a tiny cut of Wagyu beef that melted in my mouth. My tablemates were also enjoying their food, immensely. Many of them ordered seconds and thirds of the beef dish. At almost $200 per Wagyu slice, we were quickly racking up an obscene bill, not to mention over $30,000 in beverages. But no one really seemed to notice or care. Everyone was telling stories about their crazy experiences with Sidney and his wacked family.

I heard about Sidney taking the entire staff to a stuffy Saturday buffet night dinner at Sunningdale. Coat and tie required. Sidney dressed in his signature luminous ensemble. Neon pink sports coat with a fluorescent green tie. To add even more injury, Sidney invited four Jagerettes, all gussied up in their floozy finest, to escort him down the chow line. Sidney was so bombed that he barely kept his face out of the potato salad. He grabbed food selections with his hands, sampling and returning partially used portions into the serving dishes if he wasn't completely satisfied.

I heard about Sidney ordering one of the cooks to dump a bottle of $4,000 Louis XIII Cognac down the drain, and refill it with his $40 Jacque Cardin Cognac so he could prank some unsuspecting guests who thought they were sipping one of the finest Cognacs in the world. I heard about Sidney inviting friendly Jagerettes back to the house for private parties while Mrs. Frank was puttering in the garden or out walking the dogs. I heard about Sidney fouling his trousers during a round of golf because he'd had an enema administered just prior to leaving the house, and the golfers having to clean sewage out of his golf shoes.

I laughed so hard that I couldn't breathe. My stomach hurt and I was pretty certain I was going to regurgitate a fortune in food and wine. But even through all of the drinking, and eating, and laughing, I was keenly aware that they were all watching me. They were observing my actions and reactions. This was an integral part of the initiation. It was a test. They wanted to make sure I was a good fit for the family. They would submit a full report to Sidney during the first few holes of the next morning's round.

The bill was finally presented to Gary. He opened it and I saw a slight grin cross his face.

"Guess how much?" He held up the folder and looked around the table.

No one said a word.

"Come on. Worst guess has to pay."

Everyone's eyes widened and they looked nervous. They played this game frequently, but the stakes were a tad bit higher tonight.

"Relax." Gary pulled out Sidney's Black American Express and placed it in the folder. The release of tension was palpable.

"Well?" one of the golf pros finally asked. I was dying to know but never would have mustered the courage to inquire.

"Forty-Seven" Gary said very matter-of-factly, as if the fact that we had just spent almost $50,000 on dinner was not at all unusual.

I tried hard to keep my game face, but inside I was reeling. I looked around, expecting to see amazed or horrified reactions on the faces of my compatriots. No one seemed surprised or even bothered. Just another meal, another $47,000.

The limo shuttled us directly from the Mandarin Oriental to Scores. Gary reserved a private room with four dancers. There were two bottles of Grey Goose on ice, and the golfers started mixing strong drinks and passing them down the line. The dancers were flexible, the lap-dances were nasty, and it didn't take long before the room was spinning again, but in a much more pleasant direction this time. I have extremely vague memories of the remainder of that evening, but I vividly recall waking up in the limo holding a Big Gulp cup filled with my own expensive vomit.

I would learn that, in addition to our dinner, Gary also expensed a $25,000 bill from Scores. I had officially been welcomed into the Sidney Frank staff family.

....

I woke up the next morning fully clothed on my bed. My head was pounding, and every muscle in my body was stiff and aching. I had dried vomit all over my face and shirt. My underwear was missing, which was worrisome, but all my parts seemed to be intact and operational. I could barely move, but I was expected to report to Sidney's house for another early round of golf.

By the time I was dressed and at the house, five minutes after the designated time of departure, the golfing group was long gone. Sidney waited for no one.

I found myself wandering around the house with nothing to do. I had a late afternoon flight home, and almost the entire day to kill. I shot the bull with the cooks for a while, and they served me a delicious hangover cocktail followed by a gracious invitation to play a few friendly hands of poker with the prize money I'd made while golfing the day before. I politely declined.

I walked to the rear of the house, and there were windows looking out to the garden area. The view was breathtaking, and again I was struck by the contrast of the garden and the house. They just didn't seem to belong together. Someone took meticulous care of the garden, but the house was rotting from the inside. I finally found a little door that led to the backyard. It looked like a door made for dwarfs, about half the size of a normal door. It almost looked like a slightly oversized dog door with a doorknob. I bent down and tried to turn the knob but it was locked, and the only way to unlock it from the inside was with a key.

I was about to give up when I heard a loud commotion coming from somewhere behind me. I turned just in time to see MOF coming down the hallway dressed in overalls, galoshes, a big straw hat, and carrying a golf bag on her shoulder.

"Clear the way. Clear the way. Marian Frank reporting to the first tee." She was walking fast and she meant business. I stepped aside just as she came to a stop next to me at the little door.

"Are you new here?" She turned and looked me in the eyes with her glazed, vacant stare.

"Me? Ah, yes. I think we already had the pleasure..."

"Here, take my bag." She pushed her bag towards me, and I grabbed it just before it came crashing into my chest. It nearly knocked me over. The bag felt like it was full of bricks. I took a look in her bag and saw two real golf clubs, a 7 iron and a putter. I also noticed a croquet mallet, a crowbar, a fishing pole, several tree pruning instruments, a fully functional (and sharp) replica Samurai sword, and a plunger.

"When is my tee time?" she looked at her watch, a large Mickey Mouse timepiece that did not appear operational.

"Tee time?"

"Yes, tee time. When?"

"How does 8 o'clock sound?"

"8? Why so late? Am I behind the fucking Lipshitz group again? I'll tell you, those idiots are slower than molasses. There goes my day. Might as well go and warm-up for a few hours." She grabbed the doorknob and tried to turn it. "You have the key?"

"Me?"

"You see any other retards here? Do you or don't you have the key?" Her brow was starting to furrow and she looked a little more skittish than usual.

"Well, I don't think...."

"I know you don't think. Aren't you the starter? Don't you work here? Call someone and get the key you incompetent little shit."

I noticed Donna quickly shuffling around the corner and towards us with a key. "I'm sorry Mrs. Frank. I should have given this to him yesterday." Donna winked and handed the key to me. I opened the door and MOF stooped and exited, banging her golf bag violently against the small doorframe.

"She think the backyard is a golf course, poor woman. We keep the door locked because some of the boys go out there and tee off on her flowers. Little assholes." Donna laughed and walked away. I watched MOF intently. She picked the 7 iron out of her bag and took a few swings at an imaginary ball. She then used it as a walking stick and started marching around the property, fingering the flora, teasing the fauna, and extracting suspect shrubs and weeds. I could see her mouth moving, but I could not make out the words that were coming out. I cracked the door open so I could hear.

"Why Madame Ladybug, don't you look glorious today. Shall we meet Ms. Hydrangea for 9 holes, and then have tea with the Wasps? Splendid. Just splendid." She would garden as she conversed, watering here and there, pruning and repairing anything that was out of place. Whatever she was doing seemed to be working. She was a weed whisperer.

"So, Mr. Oleander, did you know that I recently unearthed the fact that our planet is really a big muddy golf ball? We are flying through space on a big dirty golf ball, and we move the mud ourselves. We build cities, skyscrapers, dams and bridges, and we relocate our manmade mud all over the cover of the earth ball. And then we expect the earth to rotate evenly and fly straight. Have you ever seen a muddy golf ball fly? Didn't think so. Please don't call me crazy. That's just rude."

As I watched her, it dawned on me that this garden was MOF's happy place. This was her bizarre little world, and these plants were her friends. Possibly her only friends. In all my time with her, the garden was the only place I ever saw her smile.

Chapter 6
Moscow Mule

My plane landed in San Diego the early evening and Laurel picked me up at the airport. She barely looked at me during the car ride home. I knew she was irritated and too angry to talk, and that she would eventually want answers and details that I didn't have. I sat in my seat and tried to lighten the mood by humming along to the radio. She turned the music off and stared at the road.

When we arrived home Laurel marched straight into the kitchen. I watched her slim, graceful figure walk casually towards the refrigerator. She looked really good, and she knew it. She opened the refrigerator door and leaned in, pretending to look for something. She was still wearing her work clothes - a short skirt with a blazer - and that outfit was one of my favorites. The skirt and tight silky blouse accentuated her petite curves. She knew she was teasing me, but that was part of her game.

I sat down at the kitchen table and watched her. She lingered for several more minutes before finally grabbing a bottle of Fiji water. She slammed the refrigerator door and turned abruptly, catching me staring at her. She stared right back. Her deep ocean blue eyes always captivated me. I would get lost in them sometimes. She still didn't say anything, but I'd had enough. I couldn't play the game any longer.

"It's the chance of a lifetime." I blurted out.

"What the hell were you thinking?" She was clearly upset. Her voice was wavering and she was working hard to control her emotions.

"He wants me to start a wine brand."

"You already have a job."

"Are you listening to me? He wants me to move to Napa and make wine."

"You're a lawyer, not a wine maker. You don't know the first thing about wine making. You do estate planning."

79

"Well, I studied enology in Davis for a few months, but that's not the point. This guy turns shit into gold, and he wants me to make his wine. It's a one in a million opportunity. I can get out of that fucking law firm where I'm dying a little more every day. And I can make wine. We could make a fortune if the brand is a success." I was getting angry, and my tone was rising. I'd found the golden ticket, and she wasn't about to yank it out of my G.I Joe kung-fu death grip.

"Great. You go make some wine. Whoop dee doo for you. And what about me? What am I supposed to do? Drop everything I have worked for because some old fart thought it would be brilliant to hire an idiot to make wine? Did you stop to think about me once before you accepted the job? Did you think how your decision would affect your family? Did you consider consulting me before you made a life altering decision? You remember you have a wife, right? And your wife has a job here in San Diego. We're a team. It's not just about you and your delusion to become the Jewish Robert Mondavi." She came closer, and I kept a sharp eye on her balled up right fist. She had a temper, and she was creeping slowly into the red zone.

"Sorry. You're absolutely right. I should have called you first. I assumed you would have supported my decision and realized that I was doing this for us, for the team. I was selfish and stupid. Can you find it in your heart to forgive me?"

"Don't patronize me, you asshole." She walked into the bedroom and slammed the door shut.

I sat in my chair and wondered what the hell just happened. It was the most extraordinary opportunity ever. The kind of chance most people never get, and it would never come around again. I had enough experience and sense to know that I was amazingly fortunate, and I was not going to let it get away.

I loved Laurel more than anything, and I knew she'd been having a rough time and deserved better. I never wanted to hurt her, but there are some times in life when you have to follow your gut, even if it means hurting someone you love. I knew it would mean compromise and sacrifice on both our parts. I knew she was going to doubt things, and I also had plenty of doubts. How serious was this little venture? Was this the fanciful whim of an eccentric fool? A flaunty private-label trophy or holiday hostess gift? Or did he really want to create something real? He was over 80, and from the general looks of things he was playing the closing holes of his final round.

How long would this position last? What if he died? What would happen to the wine project? What would happen to his company, and more importantly, what would happen to me? Was this fantasy worth risking a career, notwithstanding the fact that I dreaded and detested every single day of that career?

I had more questions than answers, but the only thing I knew for sure was that I was diving in head first with no idea how deep the pool was, or what was lurking at the bottom. I was hell-bent to see where the rabbit hole would lead, and Laurel could hop in or get out of the way.

Chapter 7

Kamikaze

I was on my way to the San Diego Airport at 10am on October 1, 2003. My cell phone rang. It was Sidney's private number in New York.

"Good morning Mr. Frank."

"You at the airport?"

Now how the hell did he know that? With everything going on around him, he knew when my flight departed.

"On my way."

"Good. Are you prepared?"

"Prepared?"

"This is important, you realize that?"

"I do."

"Are you nervous? You sound nervous."

Damn, this guy was unbelievable. He could read me through the phone. I was nervous as shit. I had not slept more than a few restless minutes, and even that sleep was haunted by visions of floods, draught, phylloxera, frogs and crabs. I was drained, my stomach was in knots, and I had no idea what I was doing.

"Maybe just a little."

"I knew it. Remember, never blow sunshine up my ass. Let me tell you a story. When the old bastard first hired me to work for Schenley, he sent me to Scotland to figure out why Dewar's was such a donkey. Production was limited and inconsistent. I had never been in the cocktail game, but I had a good head on my shoulders and the old man trusted my judgment.

"So I land in Scotland, and the foreman greets me with a toothless grin and hearty handshake. I like him. Seems like a good man. He drives me to the factory. The first thing I notice is that the factory is closed. It's Monday at 11am local time. Prime time. Monday. Why's it closed I ask him. It's Monday he tells me. Yes, I realize that. Closed Monday. I see, well what about Tuesday? Closed. So then you're open Wednesday. You'd think so, wouldn't you? I would. Well, you'd be wrong then. I look at the grinning toothless man, and I can't figure out if he's sincere or mocking me. I'm nearly double the man's size. Would you mind telling me when you're open? Not at all. There is silence. We look at each other, waiting. Well then? I thought you wanted me to tell you when we're open. I do. Well, I'll have to wait until Thursday to do that he tells me with a straight face.

"So I came to find out that there's an interesting Scottish law to keep the country sober. The factory is only opened two days a week, Thursday and Friday. The rest of the week, doors are bolted closed. Workers didn't seem to care. I wouldn't mind that schedule either. It didn't take a genius to figure out that if we kept the factory opened six days a week, and ran two shifts, we could increase production by nearly 1,000 percent in the first year alone. I met with officials and greased the wheels, and in no time we were producing more whisky than we could sell. Three months later, the old man doubled my salary. He still came out way ahead on that one. So my point to you is don't worry. Just follow your head and your heart. You're a smart kid, and I have a good feeling about you." Sidney paused, and I could almost feel his toothy grin through the phone. "I know you won't disappoint me."

My plane landed in San Francisco, but I was still walking on clouds. Sidney's pep talk had taken a load off my mind. All I had to do is follow my head and heart. How hard could that be? Plus, I was out of the office from hell, and about to embark on a brand new life. I was shuttled to the rental car lot, and I selected a compact car. I wanted to make a prudent and responsible decision, regardless of the debauchery that occurred the night I was hired. I reconsidered my thriftiness every time I hit a bump and loosened a filling, but I was still riding high.

I headed north to meet Gary at our highly classified wine headquarters. Gary was assigned to help me set up operations, and he flew out a week early to scout out locations and select a suitable site. He was being very cautious and covert, and he refused to tell me the exact coordinates before I left San Diego. Gary insisted that his primary objective was maintaining confidentiality, and leaking of any sensitive information, including our whereabouts, to competitors could jeopardize the integrity of the entire operation. I thought he was taking himself a little too seriously, but I appreciated his help and was happy to have some company.

October in Napa was the start of the crush, and the vines were just hitting their peak perfection. This was the best time to drive through the valleys and up the Silverado Trail. The wavy, rolling hillsides were quilted in brilliant shades of green, red, orange and yellow, and thousands of heavy, gnarled vines were hiding small clusters of purple treasure. I was so excited about living and working in the wine country that I was singing at the top of my lungs to any dumb song on the radio. I honked my horn and screamed unintelligible lyrics at passing motorists. I felt young and alive and ready to take Napa by the balls. I was following my heart, and my head was enjoying the ride. I called Gary from the road to get the secret code, as I'd been instructed. My heart sank a little when he gave me detailed directions to a highly secret and remote location outside Healdsburg.

"But that's in Sonoma." I had my cell phone cradled between my shoulder and ear as I looked at the map and tried to drive through Santa Rosa using my knees to steer the car. I had considered upgrading for a GPS device, but the additional $10 per day seemed decadent.

"You're exactly right, Stud. The house is in Sonoma, and it's sick. Right on the Russian River. Super secluded. You're going to fucking love it here."

"But I thought we were doing this project in Napa." I couldn't hide my disappointment. I'd been fantasizing about driving the Silverado trail on my daily commute, private tastings at boutique wineries, sampling the finest wine country cuisine, and hiking the breathtaking hills above Calistoga and St. Helena. Napa was the promised land.

"Dude, listen to me, Sonoma is way better."

Sonoma was like that stoned neighbor who never mows his grass or returns the lawnmower he borrowed. Sonoma winemakers made decent whites and Pinots due to their cool coastal microclimate, but the Cabs couldn't compete with Napa. Big red wine grapes needed heat, and the Napa microclimate was ideal. All of the California cult labels - Screaming Eagle, Harlan, Bryant, etc. - were made from Napa sourced fruit.

I finally found the rental house after driving through a maze of windy dirt roads and hairpin turns that led down to a large wooden structure on the edge of the Russian River. Gary's rental Escalade was parked in front, and I immediately felt silly for renting a glorified go-cart. And another big surprise was in store. The house was secluded and directly on the river, as advertised, but it was not actually a house. It was a *barn*. A big fugly brown barn. Gary the genius rented a converted barn to serve as our secret winemaking base and my living quarters.

The Barn was owned by Jack Warnecke, a famous San Francisco architect who also owned the 80 glorious acres surrounding it. It served as part of a working river ranch at some point in the long distant past. Warnecke had been a close friend and confidant of John F. Kennedy and one of the inner Camelot circle. He'd allegedly become even closer with Jackie after JFK was killed. Legend had it that Warnecke mounted Jackie more than a few times in the Barn's stable area. I hoped it was a little more charming back then.

The outside scenery was idyllic, totally isolated from civilization. It sat directly on the bank of the Russian River, and it was one of the most beautiful locations I had ever seen. But the inside of the Barn was a different story. The Barn had been 'converted' to residential purposes, but not by much. You could still detect the faint lingering stink of cow patties and horse piss. Warnecke left many of his personal mementos and artwork in the Barn, creating a shrine to himself for the world to behold. The walls were covered with wacky 60s and 70s posters from San Francisco art exhibitions, as well as a number of old newspaper clippings of

Warneke's glory days as a linebacker on Stanford's football team. He was part of the 1941 squad that went undefeated and beat Nebraska in the Rose Bowl. There were also many framed photographs of Warneke hanging out with the Kennedy cronies. The floors were dilapidated and creaky, the beams housed armies of spiders and colonies of assorted vermin and varmints, and the water that ran through the plumbing system came directly from the Russian River. Unfiltered. Untreated. It was a putrid fusion of sulfur, river muck, dead fish and duck shit.

"Dude, are you serious?" I looked at Gary as foul brown syrup came slithering out of the kitchen faucet. "How am I supposed to live here?"

"Jesus, what a princess. Hey, your majesty, come look at the deck." Gary opened the balcony door and walked out.

I had to admit the deck was spectacular. It literally floated above the river, and the views were phenomenal. Green rolling hills and valleys sprinkled with farms and vineyards spread far and wide, split by the sky blue rushing Russian. It was dreamy, and it was to be my temporary backyard. I knew I could camp out here for a while, but it wasn't going to be easy.

I spent the next week outfitting the office and preparing for our launch. Gary spent most of that week sleeping on the couch. In rare moments of consciousness, he occupied himself by drinking Redbull, smoking weed, playing online poker and downloading disturbing porn movies. Things had changed drastically since my hiring, and Gary had transformed from ultra high efficiency to mega-slacker mode. The two useful things he managed to accomplish that week were purchasing a high velocity hunting rifle (for security and entertainment needs) and arranging my meeting with Karl Brissel, the winemaker.

....

"Welcome to Chateau Red Nose." Karl gave me moist, jittery handshake as he greeted me at his door. Red Nose was Karl's private label brand that produced on his own time. Karl also lived in a quaint house above the Russian River, but it was a real house as opposed to a utility building. He had clean, fresh water in his pipes and the house was only a few miles from Healdsburg, the hipster town in North Sonoma.

Sidney read an article about Karl wining a gold medal for his Roshambo Imago Chardonnay in the Sonoma county fair, and since he just so happened to be looking for a winemaker, he called Karl.

"And, as it turned out, I was available." Karl emitted a knowing smile and nervous throat-clearing cough, as if about to explain, but thought better of it and kept quiet.

Sidney liked Karl and immediately hired him, over the phone, at double his previous salary - a classic Sidney procurement despite the fact that Karl never had to play golf. Sidney's recruitment methods were strikingly similar to Howard Hughes who was notorious for hiring high-level executives on a whim. Sidney was also a firm believer in trusting the gut. Karl was in fact unemployed at the time, having been dismissed as head wine maker of Roshambo Winery. Karl had experienced artistic differences with Roshambo's founder and conceptual artist, Naomi Brilliant. Ms. Brilliant started Roshambo with a huge sum of her grandfather's money and a limited supply of business experience and common sense. Her brilliant concept was to market moderately expensive wine to the hipster, pierced, inked, and funky fuck you hairdo crowd, who incidentally don't generally drink moderately expensive wine unless someone else is footing the bill or sticking it to the man.

Brilliant decided that Roshambo would produce and bottle 23 separate and distinct varietals. Most wineries produce three to four different varietals at most. Some of the most successful wineries only produce one.

Roshambo's outrageously expensive, ultra-modern winery was billed as low-key and unpretentious. Brilliant thumbed her nose at boring convention and decorated the interior with video games, plastic gnomes and monkey piñatas. She bucked the wine establishment and imported buses of performance artists, Elvis impersonators and drag queens. She held huge rock, paper, scissors tournaments, and hired a DJ to play deafening speed metal and acid rock in the tasting room. When older patrons requested the volume lowered, the DJ was instructed to turn it up and teach them some respect for her art. This wasn't a winery for old farts sipping Chablis while a string quartet played moonlight sonatas. Roshambo was designed for San Francisco's new elite breed of wine daredevils, and old Karl wasn't edgy enough.

Karl was a journeyman winemaker who'd been employed by just about every valley winery at one point or another. His father had moved the family from the frozen tundra of Nova Scotia to the lush Sonoma hills when Karl was young, and he had grown up in the wine business. He was a shy, reticent and slightly nervous man. He always seemed anxious, and he spent an inordinate amount of time wandering around his house looking for misplaced objects and second guessing inconsequential decisions. He was slender and soft-spoken with a large unruly beard that looked out of place on his finely boned face. Karl and his wife had several large cats and no children, but the air at his house was full of life.

"Let's sit out on the deck and enjoy the view." Karl poured two glasses of his house rosé, one of his specialties, and handed me a glass. I'm not a huge fan of rosé, but it was rather delightful. Crisp, cool and refreshing, with a subtle, fruity kick. Perfect for a hot summer day on the river. As we moved towards the patio door, Karl slowed down and gave me a serious look. "Don't make any sudden movements out there, and don't be afraid. They can smell fear."

Karl's deck also overlooked the Russian River, but we were higher up on the mountainside so there was a nice panoramic perspective of the River and valley and the beautiful hillside vineyards and meadows surrounding it. As we walked towards the deck chairs, I sensed that we weren't alone.

Karl's wife had surrounded their property with hummingbird feeders. There seemed to be hundreds, connected by a complex network of storage tanks, pipes, and hoses. The space above and around the feeders was a spastic frenzy of buzzing bird missiles, and the air was alive and beating. It was a living cloud of adrenaline and frenetic energy. Sitting in a deck chair verged on a psychedelic experience. It was almost impossible to stay focused on anything as thousands of tiny, razor-sharp beaks streaked through my periphery and strafed my ears. It made me dizzy and a little jumpy, and I suspected that I'd isolated a major source of Karl's anxiety.

"Keep this over your glass," Karl handed me a thick piece of cardboard. I noticed he kept several spare chunks of cardboard on the table. "Sometimes they dive-bomb the glasses, and they are especially attracted to the rosé for some reason." Probably because it looked exactly like the pink solution in their feeders.

I spent the entire day with Karl sampling many of his past vintages and avoiding feathered kamikazes. His whites were quite crisp and zesty, but I was a red guy. I'd never been a fan of white or sparkling wines. Fine to have a sip before a meal or to cleanse the palate, but most whites tasted interchangeable.

Bring on the big reds. Karl's Syrah and Zinfandel were very good. They were bold and spicy, with lots of fruit and nice balance. His Cabernet was also good, but not great. His style was very similar to most Sonoma Cabs. It was balanced and drinkable, but nothing special. Plus, it had a vague green bean flavor that was common in Sonoma grapes. I preferred hefty Napa Cabs with sweet tannins and flavors of chocolate and caramel cherries, not lightweight reds with essence of steamed broccoli or nuance of boiled Brussels sprouts.

All California winemakers had their signature red wine style. Some produced big beefy blockbusters with lots of tannin that needed years of aging. Others produced more elegant, Bordeaux-style reds that drank well right out of a barrel's bunghole. A few winemakers had a Midas touch when it came to their craft. They all started with grapes and barrels, just as all painters start with paint and empty canvas. But the cult winemakers created priceless masterpieces. California cult Cabernets consistently received 100 point scores from critics like

Robert Parker and James Laube. I wasn't sure how they did it, but I was certain that Karl's wines were not close to cult status, and likely never would be.

"How do you like the Cab?" Karl hovered around me like a hummingbird sommelier, refilling the glass that I was politely sipping. "It took a silver medal at the Healdsburg fair."

"It's delicious." I smiled and kept sipping, hoping a myopic bird would bomb my glass.

I made the dreaded call a few days later.

"How you doing out there in winoland? Looks like you got a nice place. Gary showed me the photos." I detected some laughter in the background, and I knew Gary was probably telling the cooks and nurses about the plumbing.

"I'm good Sidney, but I think we may have a little problem here."

"Oh yeah? What's that?" Suddenly, it got a little quiet on the other end of the line. I knew whoever was in the room or monitoring the call was now listening closely.

I took a deep breath and steadied myself. I hated playing the buzz killer, and I definitely didn't want to blow my greatest professional opportunity, but I had to tell him. "We need to move the operation to Napa."

"Napa? Why Napa, for crying out loud. I just spent a small fortune putting you in a lovely lake house in Sonoma, and now you say Napa?"

Lovely lake house? That was like calling Alcatraz a quaint island spa. "Listen Sidney, Sonoma wasn't my idea, and we aren't going to get the best results if we stay in Sonoma. The grapes are better in Napa. Also...we should probably consider hiring a different winemaker." I paused. It was quiet, but I knew there were about five or six sets of ears listening to me on the other end, so I kept talking. "I like Karl. He makes good wines, but they aren't great, and I think we need someone who can do better. We need to hire a top-notch wine consultant like Heidi Barrett or Manfred Krankl. Someone who knows how to make cult level wine. You hired me to be innovative and find a way to make the best possible product, but I can't do that with Karl, and I can't make it in Sonoma."

Crickets. I began to sweat and my heart was pumping. Fear bubbles lurking just beneath the surface started floating up. I worried that I'd just blown it. My platinum club membership was getting revoked because I couldn't keep my mouth shut and follow the blissful lemming parade. Now he would probably dismantle the entire operation and fire my dumb ass.

"Seth, I appreciate the information. You're a smart kid and you might be right, but I hired Karl to make wine in Sonoma. So do what you need to do, but a deal's a deal." He paused, puffed his cigar, and slowly exhaled. "You'll do fine."

The following few months flew by like a hummingbird on meth. We were so busy I barely noticed I was living my dream. Karl and I produced six different varietals, all without vineyards or a winery. We toured vineyards and purchased grapes, ordered barrels, bottles and materials, and staged our production at high-end custom crush facilities. Wineries were expensive depreciating assets (just ask Ms. Brilliant), and there were many crush facilities that catered to small productions like ours. Most were former wineries that couldn't make it producing only a single label.

We managed to keep our costs low, but our operations were becoming a logistical nightmare. We had wine fermenting in different facilities all over the valley, and after barreling we would have to transfer the barrels to storage facilities for racking and aging. We would later transfer the barrels to a bottling facility when the wine was done aging, and then back to storage after bottling and before shipping. Another big problem was technology. The crush facilities we were using were not exactly state-of-the-art, and we were relying on antiquated equipment, unpredictable utilities, and undependable staff. We were forced to relinquish some measure of control over the wines and the winemaking process. We still showed up almost every day to check on things, but it wasn't the same as turning off the lights and locking the door on your way out.

Laurel stayed back in San Diego for her job, and I saw her on weekends if I could get away. She took a job as a pharmaceutical sale rep, and our running joke was that we were popular party guests because I had the booze and she had the pills. Cooper came to live with me, and he loved the Barn. I took him for long walks when I needed to get away, and he went crazy splashing around in the river or bounding through vineyards chasing rabbits and birds. I plucked five or more ticks from his neck and ears almost every night - they were fairly easy to spot on his short red coat. Occasionally I would miss one, and inevitably discover it a few days later, all swollen with blood and burrowed deep in one of his crannies. I worried about Lyme disease, but he was having so much fun I couldn't deprive him.

Every evening I would grill two steaks - one for me and one for the dog. I also sampled many of the local wines, strictly for professional purposes. Getting completely shitfaced made cold nights in the stinky Barn slightly less odious. I lit fires in the old wood-burning stove, which was the sole source of heat in the house. Cooper and I snuggled under a heavy down comforter trying to keep warm since the Barn was not insulated. Cooper was a squirmy bed hog and I didn't get much sleep, but at least I had company and he didn't mind that I didn't bathe. He also boycotted in his own way by refusing to drink out of the toilets.

Karl showed up at the Barn one cold morning carrying six little glass bottles. "What the hell is that smell?"

"Ah, that's the smell of Barn in the morning. Smells like victory, right?"

"Not really. Smells more like shit." The sad truth was that I almost didn't notice the stench anymore. I was getting desensitized from continuously inhaling it. "I have some barrel samples, and they are really showing well"

We tasted them, and they were all fairly good for such young wines. Karl's rosé was fruity and crisp, the Chardonnay nice and not too buttery, the Syrah was powerful yet elegant, the Zinfandel ripe and beefy, and the Pinot complex and balanced. The only wine that again disappointed me was the Cabernet. It was a little funky and pretty average, but there wasn't much we could do about it now. To be honest, my senses were so blunted from huffing river sludge that every wine had a subtle sulfuric aftertaste, so I really couldn't be too sure myself. Plus, I was overdue for a change of scenery.

"Let's go see the big man."

Chapter 8
Mud Slide

"Do you smell something?" I took a deep breath and looked over at Karl. He nodded and smiled. Even with my dulled nostrils, I caught a deep whiff of good dope.

We were at the top of the driveway leading into Rancho Limon, Sidney's winter retreat in Rancho Santa Fe, California. Rancho Limon took its name from the acres of lemon groves surrounding the house. Located just north of San Diego, Rancho Santa Fe was one of the most affluent cities in the country. In 2011, Forbes listed the Ranch as having the third most costly ZIP code in the United States, and the most expensive in California, with a median home sale price of $2.6 million. Most properties sold for well north of $10 million. Bill Gates, T. Boone Pickens, and Jenny Craig all owned sizable properties in the Ranch. Many properties were vast, sprawling horse estates on multiple acres of land – a rarity in coastal Southern California where stamp sized lots were a luxury.

Sidney's estate was gated and secured, and it had a long, steep driveway leading from the road down to the main house. As Karl and I were walking down we saw a group of young black men with dreadlocks and baggy clothing coming up the hill towards us. Lil Jon and his posse were returning to their limo after a successful business meeting with Sidney, and they'd decided to spark a spleef to seal the deal. And it was a sweet deal for Jon. He was offered the opportunity to be the face of Crunk!, Sidney's new energy drink. Sidney would pay him one dollar for every case sold. That was the deal, and it didn't get much better. Jon didn't have to contribute a penny to the venture, just his distinctive name and face. Sidney assumed all the costs and risks. At the time, Jon was a relative newcomer to hip-hop, but he was a savvy marketer. He'd coined the term Crunk! (a blend of 'crazy' and 'drunk') to describe his music and lifestyle, and his personal brand was busting out virally and exponentially.[11]

Big Sid the Pimp

As we passed next to them, Lil Jon looked at us and smiled dazzlingly. He was wearing a diamond crusted gold grill and his teeth were almost blinding. One of his posse members reached out, handed Karl the burning blunt, and kept walking. Karl looked at the huge, smoldering joint in his hand, and then he looked at me.

The noise coming from Sidney's suite was deafening. He was blasting Lil Jon's song *Get Low* on his Bose system with the subwoofer turned up to maximum, and the walls were vibrating. There were empty cans of Crunk! and Jägermeister strewn about, and a large red plastic gas can with the words Crunk!

---

[11] In 2011, Jon was a contestant on Trump's *Celebrity Apprentice*. Although he didn't win, his appearance probably boosted Crunk! sales. He also guest hosted the TV show *TMZ*, posing with a Crunk! can in his hand.

Juice stamped on it was prominently displayed on Sidney's bedside table. I noticed that one of Sidney's nurses, Danny, was also loitering around the bedroom. Danny was Sidney's self-appointed Chief of Staff, even though his official duties were nursing and running errands. Danny was a squatty, cherubic Filipino who desperately wanted to be all gangsta. His balding head was clean-shaven and he sported a small tattoo of a $100 bill at the base of his neck. He was wearing a tight black t-shirt, tight black trousers, expensive black Nike kicks, and tiny square mirrored sunglasses. Danny was constantly sweating and wiping his face and brow, but his head still had a perpetual glistening sheen.

Danny turned and looked at Karl and myself. "What up, niggaz?" Danny constantly dropped the "N" word in keeping with his thug image, but it seemed awkward and contrived, especially since he was a Pacific Islander. Danny quickly sat down in a chair next to Sidney's bed, leaving Karl and I standing.

Sidney saw us from his bed, "Yo guys. How you doing? Welcome to Crunkland." Sidney turned to Danny, "Dan, turn it down and give us a minute."

Danny stood stiffly, walked to the sound system and turned it off. He walked back to the bed and hovered over Sidney, "You alright, champ? You need anything before I go?"

"Bring some sample glasses." Danny stiffened again. Serving up tasting glasses was miles beneath him, but he wasn't going to make a stink. He'd simply delegate the task to Craig. "Sure champ." He walked past me with a big smile on his round face and punched me in the arm. I had a momentary urge to knock his crooked little teeth in, but I resisted.

"Hey homeboys, did you meet my new buddy, Little Johnny? Nice guy. Brought me some presents." Sidney smiled and displayed a gold and diamond grill similar to Jon's. He looked ridiculous. But even better, Sidney was holding a large golden goblet that was studded with dazzling faux diamond clusters. The diamonds spelled out *Big Sidz Pimp Chalice*.

Sidney removed the grill. "I don't know how the schvartzas wear these damn things. How the hell do they eat?" Sidney looked at me closely, "Seth, you look tired, and what's that crap on your face? You look like a damn hippie. Clean it up, you're scaring the dogs." I didn't have the energy to defend my aversion to shaving with foamy frog feces.

"Hi Karl, how are those fucking humming birds?" Sidney was in a good spirits. He was always happier at the California compound, probably due to the temperate weather and more golf days. The Rancho Limon house was better than the New Rochelle house, but not by much. Sidney's master suite had been renovated and outfitted with many of his signature features. High security, gourmet kitchen, sparkling bar, priceless artwork, wine cellar, commercial air conditioning, black out curtains, and shameless white toilet next to the bed.

A big LCD TV on the wall was showing a WWII documentary he'd probably seen 50 times, and the room was extremely cold and dark. Sidney loved keeping his room unreasonably cold and dark. The room was so cold it felt like a meat locker, and it wasn't uncommon to see visitors wearing parkas and gloves. The technician who installed the A/C unit swore that if it was turned on high and the humidity level in the room rose above 70%, it would snow.

The room had all the necessities to accommodate Sidney for extended stays, but Sidney was very careful not to spend a day over 6 months in California during any given year for fear of the dreaded California community property laws. He and MOF had been married in New York, and separate property law still applied to their unholy union. If he spent a day over six months in California, MOF could conceivably make a claim to half of Sidney's estate upon divorce or after his death. [12]

---

[12] Sidney would eventually buy MOF out of the marriage with a post-nuptial agreement estimated at $100M, although he still couldn't get her to leave.

....

Why Sidney married MOF is one of life's sweet mysteries. At the time of their courtship in the early 1970s, Sidney's first wife, Skippy, was losing a prolonged fight with cancer and other demons, and MOF provided him with an escape. MOF came from a good family, she was supposedly well educated, and she was, above all else, exceedingly quirky. MOF and Sidney both loved drinking, dancing and playing golf, plus MOF had a mouth like a sailor and she didn't take shit from anyone. Her erratic behavior was enchanting to Sidney, and he was so smitten with his peculiar playmate that he almost completely forgot about his train wreck of a wife. In fact, on the cloudy day in 1972 when Skippy officially succumbed to a heart attack after unofficially choking down several bottles of painkillers, there was one conspicuous absentee from the house they shared. Sidney claimed to be on a business trip, but his true whereabouts were never confirmed.

Rancho Limon was in desperate need of cleaning and renovation that it would never receive under MOF's demented reign. She roamed Rancho Limon's long tiled hallways with her perpetually full goblet of chilled white wine in one hand and a potential weapon in the other. She wore ratty Coogi sweaters, stained parachute pants and moldy duck hunting boots, and she screamed at anyone who tried to clean or fix anything. MOF employed a Mexican housekeeper named Maria who, like Donna in New York, was forbidden to work. Maria sat at the kitchen table and watched Spanish soap operas until it was time to go home. She would then return the next day for another extended soap viewing session.

MOF had stockpiled several hundred cases of SFIC's finest products in the center of Rancho Limon's living room, and she surrounded her treasure trove with fences and security cameras lest anyone try to snatch a bottle. One Christmas, Sidney decided to give each staffer a case of every alcohol brand in the company's portfolio. The cases were delivered to Rancho Limon's driveway for distribution, but before the staffers received a single bottle, MOF loaded the entire shipment on a flatbed cart and transferred the load to her living room hoard without allowing anyone a single bottle.

....

"Did you guys know that college kids are drinking Red Bull and Jägermeister by the truckload? Sales are going through the roof. So, I think to myself, why are we helping Red Bull sell their shit drink? They got an 80% market share and they're making billions using my product. So I say to my executives, let's make something better. So we did. Try this." Sidney handed me two cans of Crunk! I gave one to Karl and took a big swig of mine. It was cherry flavored and sickly sweet. I didn't care for the taste, but I wasn't fond of Red Bull either. It's synthetic flavor reminded me of eating Baskin Robbins bubblegum ice cream as a child, mining for petrified gum balls entombed in the icy substrate, oblivious to the beastly taste of the actual ice cream. But for some reason I didn't mind Red Bull mixed with Jägermeister. It was like the two bad tastes canceled each other out, and two negatives made a positive. "What do you think?" Sidney was studying my face.

I considered telling him Crunk! was delicious. I saw him scrutinizing me and I quickly reconsidered. "To be honest, it's a little too sweet. Tastes like bubbly Kool-Aid."

Sidney smiled broadly. I could see every remaining tooth in his mouth. "Perfect."

"Excuse me?"

"That's exactly what I want. We're trying to sell this shit to the inner cities, and what do they love more than Kool-Aid? I'll tell you what. Fizzy Kool-Aid with a motherfucking kick." Sidney was trying to market Crunk! to the urban demographic, which explained his enlisting the services of Lil Jon. They were going to sell it in the southern states first, and then expand virally and hope to go mainstream.

"Enough Crunk! I was reading about *Yellowtail* from Australia. Bastards are moving a million cases a year. A million cases of shitty shiraz in ugly bottles for fuck's sake. I'm making the best wine in California, much better than cheap kangaroo piss. We can do better than that, right?" Sidney's huge Jägermeister ashtray was sitting on his chest with a burning cigar in it. The ashtray sat on top of a large blanket made out of asbestos or Kevlar or something fire resistant. Sidney frequently dozed off while smoking, and he more than once burned holes through his shirt. This would sometimes wake him up. He insisted upon wearing his burned shirts as a badge of honor. Winston Churchill had also favored grubby, burned-up shirts. Sidney wore them everywhere, including Trump National Golf Club. Donald Trump was horrified when Sidney showed up wearing a shirt that had more holes than his golf course. Trump disappeared momentarily, only to reappear with a flashy selection of brand new *Donald Trump* brand golf shirts. These babies were so sharp you could slice bread with them, and the Donald displayed them with more panache than the ShamWow guy. Sidney flatly refused to wear any of them. Only Sidney could reject the Donald's thinly veiled dress code enforcement and still retain his Trump membership.

"Let's taste those samples. Hey Dan, where are the fucking glasses?" As expected, Danny punted his tasting glass delivery duty. Craig entered and deposited a tray of small glasses on the table next to Sidney's bed. Karl poured a round of the Chardonnay into three glasses. Sidney put his cigar in the ashtray, spit a half sucked Halls cough drop out and drank. His face was expressionless. "Good, real good. Tastes just like the Imago." Sidney picked his cigar back up and took a long drag. I seriously doubted that anything he put in his mouth could be distinguished from smoke or Mentho-Lyptus. The chefs were confident Sidney had completely lost his ability to taste. He dumped several packets of artificial sweetener on almost every dish they served him, including steak and ice cream.

As we concluded the tasting, Craig loaded the glasses on a tray and left them near the sink in Sidney's kitchen area. There was still plenty of wine left in the glasses. Out of the corner of my eye, I noticed some movement. I turned in time to see MOF nonchalantly breeze into the kitchen, look around, lift the tray, and swiftly exit stage right.

Sidney leaned back on his pillow and put his arms behind his head. "So, how much do we have?"

"How much?" I was confused and looked over at Karl. His face was blank.

"Yeah, how much wine? How many cases of wine do we have? What are the numbers?" Sidney was getting annoyed, and he started coughing. "Craig, Hall's." Craig appeared with a roll of cough drops, and he deftly popped one in Sidney's open mouth like he was feeding a mackerel to Shamu.

"500." A small production kept our costs low, allowed us more quality control, and the limited supply would drive demand and prices up if we got good reviews. I hadn't discussed my limited production strategy with Sidney, but it was a no-brainer and I assumed he'd be on board. After all, Sidney was in the business, and he had one of the most extensive wine collections in the United States. I was assigned the duty of inventorying his cellar. It was both euphoric and sad. I never held that many bottles of vintage first growth Bordeaux from the 50s, 60s and 70s, each an ancient glass treasure chest holding a little piece of wine history. I had also never seen so many disintegrating corks, stained capsules and stale bottles. Sidney's collection was not maintained or cared for, like so many of his other possessions. Rows and rows of once spectacular wines were slowly decomposing in a dank cellar. Maybe this was all part of his game plan. The man and his wines would rot together in frigid darkness.

"500 thousand cases? Great. Good work boys. I was hoping we'd come in closer to a million, but 500 is a good start. When will they be ready to go?"

I smiled and looked at Karl. Karl looked nervous and his eyes were wide. I think I detected a slight twitch on his bearded cheeks.

"Craig, call the guys at the office. They need to start planning a strategy to move this shit. Get Marvin Shanken on the horn, and call Harvey Chaplin at Southern and my Italian buddies at Peerless. Tell them we got lots of product to start moving," I felt a mild twinge of nervousness, and I was worried we would have to use Sidney's portable defibrillator on Karl. He looked unsteady, and his eyes were getting somewhat vacant and glazed.

"Ah, Mr. Frank, maybe we should wait before we call those guys."

"Wait? Wait for what? Why wait?" Sidney grabbed the cigar out of his mouth and looked at us.

I took a deep breath and looked over at Karl. He was turning pale. "Because we made 500 cases, not 500 thousand." I felt my heart pounding and my ears were buzzing, but I was not going to succumb to the Fear creeping up my spinal cord. I needed to tell him. There had obviously been a massive failure to communicate, and it was my failure. I sent reports, but they were probably intercepted before ever reaching Sidney. This was my project, and this was my responsibility.

Sidney glared at Karl, and it looked like Karl was about to lose bowel control.

"Sidney, it's my fault, not Karl's. I wanted to keep production low to create an artificial market."

Sidney's face was flushed, and the anger was intense and building. He pointed his cigar at me. "Artificial market? What the hell is that, and who the hell put you in charge of sales?"

"No one, Mr. Frank. I thought it was the best move for the brand and the company." I took a deep breath and smiled. I was confident I'd made the right decision. Karl's head was in his hands, and he was rocking back and forth very slowly.

"The brand and the company?" Sidney cackled and stuck his cigar back in his mouth, "I've run this company for 30 years, and became the most successful importer in the world, without your brilliant advice, punk." I noticed he was trying to get out of bed by himself, which was a rare occurrence these days. He finally gave up and settled back against the pillows. I'm not sure what would have happened if he'd made it to his feet, but I'm glad he didn't have the opportunity. I'd never seen him this ornery. "What's the name of the company, smart guy?"

I looked at Karl. He didn't appear to be breathing. "Which company is that sir?" I regretted my response the moment it escaped my lips.

"What company? My company for fuck's sake. What is wrong with you? Craig, call Cornell and verify this schmuck actually went there." Craig picked up the phone and pretended to call someone.

"The Sidney Frank Importing Company?"

"Right. The Sidney Frank Importing Company, not the Seth Schechter Importing Company. I probably should have called you before I sold a million cases of Jägermeister and Grey Goose. You would have set me straight. Probably would have made a shitload of artificial markets and sold nothing. You waltz in here and announce that, in all this time, you and Karl have been jerking each other up in Napa over 500 cases?" Sidney leaned back and closed his eyes. He raised the back of his hands to his shut eyes and rested them there, as if mourning his supreme blunder in hiring me. He remained very still and quiet for several minutes. I momentarily considered correcting our jerking location to Sonoma, but I decided to let that detail go to make a better point.

"Sidney?"

There was no discernible movement. Sidney was frozen in concentration, his mind creating formulas and algorithms to calculate the total costs to terminate and replace us. I looked at Karl, and he looked vacant, as if he'd started crosschecking his mental classifieds for available winemaker positions.

"Sidney, may I ask you something?"

Sidney moved his hands away from his eyes, and barely opened them. He peered at me from his scrunched eye slits, but I could tell he was listening.

"How many cases of Grey Goose did you sell the first year?"

"What?"

"How many cases of Grey Goose did you sell the first year it came out?

"I don't know. Maybe fifty thousand. Can't remember." Sidney opened his eyes halfway and looked at me. "Why?"

"Because if you had produced a million cases your first year and only sold 50,000, you would have had to pay for production, transportation, storage and tax on 950,000 cases that you didn't sell. Your Grey Goose would have been grey paté."

Sidney tried to fight back a little smirk, but he was having difficulty. He was quiet for several minutes. He sucked on his cigar and looked at Karl, then back to me. "So, what's your point?"

"My point is, we under produce the first couple of years. Limited production. A few hundred cases."

"Under produce? Brilliant! You're the best under producer I've ever met." I could tell he wasn't convinced, but at least he was rational and responsive, which was an improvement over apoplectic and catatonic. Sidney was from the old John Barleycorn school of business where success was measured by cases sold each year. Period. End of story. No extra points for designing a sensible, cost-effective, five-year growth plan. One million cases of product sold in a 12-month period ensured platinum status and a top shelf spot in the spirits hall of champions. 500 cases earned a busted brand, pink slip and the scorn of industrial drinkers. Sidney picked up a newspaper and pretended to read.

"Think of it like the hottest nightclub in New York. They only admit a few people, usually celebrities and beautiful girls, and they keep everyone else waiting in long lines out front. And because no one gets in, everyone wants in that much more." Sidney turned a few pages and grunted. "Keeping production small will allow us produce something really special, and we will get some friendly people to do the evaluations." Sidney was very close with Marvin Shanken, the owner of

Wine Spectator and *Cigar Aficionado*, mainly because he spent millions on full-page spreads for Grey Goose and Corazon after they were rated as the "World's Best Tasting Vodka" by the Chicago Beverage Tasting Institute. Marvin's "friends" always seemed to receive higher ratings than they deserved, and a Wine Spectator rating above 95 almost insured wild financial success in the open market. Personally, I found Robert Parker's reviews to be much more credible, although it's clear that even top wine experts can be duped.[13] "If we set our prices absurdly high people will want it more, especially if they can't get it. Then we slowly ramp up production and that wine label will become your personal ATM."

Sidney dropped the paper and leaned back. He put his hands up to his eyes again, but this time he was calculating profits, and he mumbled numbers under his breath, creating some kind of mental spreadsheet. Karl was slowly coming back to life. The color was returning to his cheeks, and his breathing looked steady.

Sidney leaned forward and stared me down. "Ok, alright, charge more and make less. Interesting concept, but we still need more. Make 5,000 cases." Sidney leaned back and picked the paper up again, but this time he was genuinely reading. "Craig, TV". Craig walked in a turned the volume back on, which was our cue that the meeting was officially over.

Karl and I looked at each other. It was well past crush, and now we had to come up with 4,500 more cases of wine. There was no point arguing. Sidney had spoken. And on the bright side, we were still alive and employed.

We wandered out of Sidney's suite in a slight daze, overwhelmed and unsure what to do next. Danny was sitting outside the door at the nurse's station pretending to read a hip-hop magazine, but he'd been listening to our entire meeting. Danny installed a baby monitor, complete with a closed-circuit camera, at the nurse's station so the nurses would always know if the Champ needed anything 24/7. But it also served as an effective eavesdropping device, enabling

---

[13] See *The Billionaire's Vinegar (2008)* by Benjamin Wallace.

whoever was sitting at the station the power to see and hear everything that happened in Sidney's room. There was no such thing as a confidential meeting or private call. Nothing was sacred. Sidney's nurses knew everything. They were the oracles of inside information. They listened to every phone call, every guest conversation, every audible emission from Sidney all day. They could tell you every time the man broke wind in any given hour, which was frequently.

Danny had a wide smile on his pudgy cheeks. He shook his baldhead and laughed. "You boys best be getting yourselves back to work now." He went back to reading.

I escorted Karl to the car. As we were heading up the driveway, I noticed Warren Beatty and Andy Stein walking down. Andy Stein, or Andrew Finkelstein before he changed his name, was the son of Sidney's good friend, Jerry Finkelstein. Jerry was a major New York political power broker and publisher. Andy had been a politician in New York during the 80s and 90s, and he served as president of the New York City Council followed by an unsuccessful bid for mayor of New York in 1993. Andy made news in 2007 by dating conservative politico maven Ann Coulter. In 2010, Andy again made headlines when he was indicted and arrested in connection with an alleged multimillion-dollar Ponzi scheme involving Kenneth Starr (not the Clinton Lewinsky federal prosecutor).[14]

Warren was meeting Sidney to discuss the possibility of casting him in an autobiographical movie that Sidney intended to make at some point. Sidney had narrowed the male lead down to Warren Beatty and Robert Redford. Sidney had been a roguishly handsome man in his youth. He was no Redford. Maybe closer to Beatty or Paul Newman, but those were still a stretch.

---

[14] According to the complaint, Starr and Stein fleeced a laundry list of high profile celebrities. They were charged with five counts of fraud, including wire fraud, fraud by an investment advisor, money laundering, providing false statements to the Internal Revenue Service and providing false statements to a federal officer. Andy also pled guilty to tax evasion.

Sidney, WWII

Warren walked by and gave us a polite nod. Andy didn't even acknowledge us. He was too busy screaming into his cell phone. Warren was still an attractive older man, with a confident coolness and a dignified grace. Andy not so much. He looked like a game show host who'd been left in the freezer beyond his expiration date. But the cherry was his toupee. It was salt, pepper, and unbelievably phony. It

Andrew Stein

looked like he was wearing geriatric road kill on his head.

Andy's melon merkin was fodder for many stories, the most infamous occurring in the Hamptons during the late 1970s. Andy was purportedly courting a wealthy heiress, and they were basking on a private beach in front of her palatial oceanfront estate. The heiress made the unwise decision to take a dip, leaving Andy alone on the beach with his thoughts, his pink Speedo and his non-waterproof wig. Within seconds, Ms. Heiress was sucked into a deadly rip current. She waved her arms frantically and screamed to Andy for help. Andy stood on the beach and pointed at his head. For nearly 20 minutes, Andy quietly watched the wealthy woman drown while gently comforting his skull skunk. One of the gardeners finally dove in and saved her life.

Karl still looked a little frazzled, but I noticed him starring at Warren with a slightly confused look, like he was trying to place the face. I deliberated telling him, but the mystery was keeping him occupied and distracted from our pending wine crisis. I got him in to the town car and waved goodbye.

I turned around and went back to see Chad. Most of the staffers in Rancho Limon were confined in two small spare bedrooms, although there was no lack of space or empty rooms in the sprawling compound. MOF tried to quarantine the human virus in the most minimal space possible, so desks, chairs and file cabinets were crammed into the two staff rooms and you could barely walk through them without bumping into a random cook, nurse or golfer. MOF was also in the habit of turning the lights off in occupied rooms under the pretense of conserving electricity. And using any of the house bathrooms was dicey unless you had a portable HazMat suit handy.

I never knew if Sidney was aware of MOF's antics, or the deplorable conditions and demented abuse his staff was exposed to on a daily basis. When I told people that I worked as a staff attorney for the owner of Grey Goose, I knew they assumed I worked out of lavish offices or luxurious mansions with helipads and *Penthouse* Pet secretaries. Nothing could have been further from the truth, and

I was too embarrassed to enlighten them. A friend who worked in television wanted to make an MTV-like reality show about Sidney's life, but I was terrified that the public would see what was really going on backstage. Sidney's unreal and highly unpleasant world would ruin the harmless deception I was happily perpetuating, and I wanted to suspend disbelief for as long as possible.

Chad had the rare privilege of having his own office, although very little actual work was ever done there. He had all the trappings of a real office - computers, printers, phones, files, and fireproof file cabinets. All of them brand new and barely touched. He also had a birds-eye, unobstructed view of the aberrant genitalia attached to Salvador Dali's 20 foot bronze hermaphrodite *Newton de Gala*, proudly exhibited in the garden area just outside his office window. Chad had his own private bathroom, which was coveted since mystery burritos and suspicious chili were the staff's staple food source. Chad had several conspicuous golf clubs leaning against his desk, and there were large ball-shaped dents adorning most of his office's walls and ceiling area.

Chad motioned for me to shut the door and sit down. He was on the phone, but he quickly ended the call. He stared out of the window, studying the huge bronzed gonads for several minutes before speaking.

"This is big, and highly confidential. We have a major security breach. Check this out." He turned the computer screen my direction. It was the San Diego County Sheriff's Department website, opened to the page listing outstanding warrants. Front and center was an outstanding warrant for someone named Danny Guano. The charges were burglary and drug possession. The warrant referenced Danny's statistics and Pacific Islander ethnicity. There was no photo attached, but it appeared that a Filipino with the same name and vitals as Sidney's Chief of Staff was not only an alleged criminal, but also a fugitive from justice.

"As California counsel, what would you advise us to do?" Chad looked at me squarely and seriously, trying to contain his delight. This was his smoking gun.

"We probably need to notify SFIC security immediately. We need to call Mr. Brown." Chad and I were Sidney's de facto attorneys, although we were more like business advisors and consultants than counsel. Nonetheless, it was our duty to protect our client and his interests, and neither of us liked Danny. In truth, no one liked Danny. He was an arrogant prick who treated the other staffers poorly merely because he could get away with it. He was one of Sidney's favorites and he knew he could do just about anything without accountability or repercussions. He'd been shady from the moment he arrived, but he hadn't posed much of a threat to Sidney's closest advisors, so he was generally ignored. But then, slowly and steadily, like a poisonous spider spinning an intricate death trap, Danny gained Sidney's trust and became Chad's rival for Sidney's affection. And while all of us suspected Danny was a criminal, we now had compelling circumstantial evidence.

Chad turned the screen back around. "I'll print this out. You fax it to Mr. Brown." Mr. Brown was in charge of security for SFIC, and he was definitely the coolest person back at SFIC home office in New Rochelle. He was like a bottle of Febreze in that stale fluorescent shithouse. Brown was a retired FBI agent, and it was a little odd that a former fed was heading up security for a privately held cocktail company, but I didn't scrutinize it at the time. It was a tradition dating back to the Schenley days. Schenley and SFIC had always used FBI agents to protect their companies and business, and no one asked questions. The line separating spirits and state seemed a bit muddled.

"Why am I faxing it to Brown?" I knew why. Chad didn't have the sack to do it himself and I made a convenient flunky if things got botched. I just wanted to hear Chad blow some of his sweet sunshine.

"Because if the company finds out I did it, they'll think I'm out to get Danny. It will look personal. Coming from you, it looks like you're just doing your job." Even Chad was scared of Danny, which was worrisome. If you were going to take a shot at Danny, you would be well advised to take a point blank headshot, and preferably a double because, as Mr. Brown once told me, anyone worth shooting is worth shooting twice. A non-fatal flesh wound could spell imminent disaster for the shooter. Danny had Sidney's ear, and that was a powerful weapon. Once Sidney was poisoned against you, it was extremely difficult to return to his good graces. It happened occasionally, but it wasn't the norm. You had to be very deserving and sympathetic to get another shot at the brass ring, and Sidney had a memory like an elephant. Plus, I knew Chad would throw me under the bus in a heartbeat if anything backfired.

....

Chad almost got me fired during my first month of employment. Chucky Dickstein, the son of one of Sidney's oldest friends, was trying to fundraise for a dreadful movie he was making, and he asked me to arrange a personal meeting with Sidney. Chucky was a small time Los Angeles operator, but he could get past Sidney's normal first line defenders through his dad. Sidney funded Chucky on some smaller projects in the past, and he was back to take another swing at the piñata. Relishing my new role as deputy *consigliere* and hoping to make a good first impression, I called Chad to clear the meeting and make sure that everything was kosher. Chad assured me that Sidney would roll out the red carpet for Chucky.

Chucky and I were escorted to Sidney's New Rochelle bedroom compound. Sidney was in bed smoking a cigar, dozing intermittently, and watching a golf tournament on TV. It was the day after the Jägermeister Million Case

Celebration[15] at the Pierre Hotel, and Sidney looked spent. The party had degraded from a swanky affair featuring Tony Bennett and a swarm of Jagerettes, to a queer bacchanalian orgy featuring top company brass giving body shots and lap dances to other guests. Sidney went to bed before it got ugly, but he toasted more than a few shots during the party and now he was paying the Deutschland piper.

Sidney gave us a quizzical look as we walked towards his bed. I immediately felt uncomfortable, like we'd come at a bad time and Sidney was not in the mood for company. Something didn't feel right, and my gut told me to turn around and walk away quickly.

"Hey Sidney, you look great. Are you working out? You're looking fit, my man. If I was a chick, I'd blow you. Hell, I might do it anyway. And while I'm here, if you have a few minutes, I'd like to show you the treatment for my next project, *Train Wreck*, and tell you about a limited opportunity to get in early on the ground...."

"Jesus Christ, Chucky," Sidney barked, "can't you see I'm trying to watch golf? Sit down, shut up and watch the tournament."

My eyes widened. Chucky was confused. He looked over at me and cocked his head to the side. Sidney didn't want to talk business, and probably had no idea this was supposed to be a business meeting. I started to feel a little shaky, and my lingering Jägermeister hangover wasn't helping the situation. Chucky opened his mouth to respond, but I elbowed him in the ribs before he said anything. He winced and looked at me again. I shook my head. Now was not the time. We sat down and waited.

And for the next very uncomfortable two hours, Sidney, Chucky and I watched some random PGA event in silence. I found out later that Chad never cleared the meeting. Never even mentioned to Sidney that we were dropping by.

---

[15] In 2003, Jägermeister sales surpassed one million cases in a single year, and SFIC hosted a lavish party to celebrate. SFIC was the exclusive importer of Jägermeister.

Sidney was completely blindsided when we walked in to his room. In fact, Chad knew specifically that Sidney didn't want to see Chucky and had no interest in giving him more money. Strangely, this was never communicated to me. Sidney even called Chad after we left, and Chad denied any inkling of the meeting.

I rolled right under the bus, and I was lucky to have escaped with my job and genitals intact. Chad wanted to teach me a dangerous lesson in respect and humility, and he made his point. He was Sidney's right hand. He called the shots and he sanctioned the fights. Any attempt to fondle his cash cow would be met with extreme prejudice. From that moment on, I never trusted Chad again.

....

I thought about my current predicament for a few minutes, and although I hated to admit it, I knew Danny had to be reported. If I were Sidney, I would have wanted to know, and he deserved to know about the alleged unsavory actions of the people who were closest to him. I also knew Chad didn't have the spine to report it. I grabbed the printout and faxed it to Mr. Brown. A couple of minutes later, my cell phone rang.

"Looks like a minor Snafu. I'm flying out there tomorrow. American. Gets in at noon. Pick me up at the airport." The line clicked and went dead. Mr. Brown wasn't clowning around today.

I walked out of Chad's office and started making my way back to Sidney's suite. I noticed more Agamographs covering almost every wall and hallway. Sidney must have had thousands of them. At some point in the 70s after Sidney was excommunicated from Schenley, Agam lured him into becoming his exclusive art dealer. Sidney invested the majority of his savings into a stockpile of Agamographs and sculptures, and he almost lost his shorts when Agam was exposed as more of a fabricator than artist. Agam refused to refund any of Sidney's substantial investment, and they subsequently parted ways and lost touch.[16]

I stuck my head in the golfer's office as I walked past. It was arguably the nastiest little room in the house. It reeked from the seemingly endless flow of JägerBongs and oniony burrito farts. Several golfers and chefs were crammed at a small card table, and they were in the middle of a tense poker session. I could hear a lot of screaming and cursing. One of the chefs had taken down a big pot, and the golfers were not pleased. The chefs had all kinds of tricks and signals, and they would team up against the golfers who were oblivious to everything except the fact that they generally lost. Every once in a while the chefs would throw the golfers a meatball to keep them playing, but they were getting fleeced. The golfers never seemed to tire of parting with their easy earned prize money, and the chefs were more than happy to liberate it.

I tiptoed past MOF's bedroom. Not wanting her artistic talents to be minimized by the Agam conglomeration in her own house, MOF decorated her door with pictures she painted herself. They looked like the product of an emotionally unstable second grader. Her muse seemed to favor fuzzy farm animals equipped with morbidly oversized sex organs.

I passed her zone of danger in stealth mode, and thought I was free and clear when I heard the door burst open and MOF came tearing out. She had a huge glass of Chardonnay in one hand, and she was towing a radio flyer wagon with the other and screaming at the top of her lungs. She galloped down the hall, making a beeline directly at me. MOF was wearing a pair of electric pink cowboy boots and a matching rhinestoned cowboy hat, and little else. Her skin was spackled with some kind of glittery spray, and her sparkling leathery flesh flopped and gyrated in all directions. Amazingly, she didn't spill a drop of wine. I tried to avert my

---

[16] After Sidney became a bona fide, Forbes-listed billionaire in 2005, Agam magically reappeared and begged for money to build the Agam museum in Israel. Sidney agreed to provide support under one condition - Agam would have to consume one of the Agamographs he'd forced Sidney to eat years before. Agam declined the offer.

eyes, but it was impossible to ignore, plus she was closing in fast and I was stuck in the impact zone. As she got closer, I could see that she was pulling the paralyzed dog on the wagon, and the fat cat was riding shotgun. MOF was in an ornery mood, and I was concerned that her intent was verging on homicidal. She stopped just short of bulldozing me.

"Where the hell do you think you're going?" Her eyes were wide and her pupils looked fixed.

I didn't answer. I looked around, hoping for golfers or cooks to use as witnesses if this confrontation went south. This was more entertaining than poker, and there were usually a few loiterers snapping candid shots and emailing the photos to friends with the caption, "You aren't going to believe what happened today at work...."

MOF stared at me for several minutes, never blinking once. "I didn't kill that bitch. They thought I did it. Can you believe it? They all thought I poisoned her. She was unstable, she was a junkie, and she overdosed. Plain and simple. She killed herself, and I had nothing to do with it. I mean, shit, I wasn't even in the country. You know that, right? I had nothing to do with it. You believe me, don't you?" Before I could answer or even speculate as to what she was referencing, she put her glass on a table. She reached into the wagon and pulled the fecal cat out by its neck scruff. She held the cat out to me and hissed, "Want to kiss my pussy?"

....

I ran to Sidney's room, praying that MOF and her freak show wouldn't follow me. He'd just concluded the meeting with Warren Beatty, and I could tell he was in a better mood.

Sidney was in bed, propped up with several pillows and the dogs were napping near his feet. He was reading a book about the JFK assassination. Sidney loved American history, especially war documentaries and conspiracy theories.

He'd been around the block a few times, and he knew people on the inside. He also loved to tell stories, usually involving his high profile buddies. He'd start one by saying something like, "So, I gave Bill Clinton a cigar, but he couldn't smoke it because the Secret Service wouldn't allow him to smoke in public, because of the Lewinsky thing. I told him this was a good cigar and not to ruin it...."

SEF and Bill, 2002

"Seth, come sit down. You did good today. You pissed me off, but you made me think. And I remembered some things too. You are learning, but you still got a long way to go."

"Thanks Sidney, that means a lot to hear you...."

"Shut up and listen. I was thinking about my father-in-law, Lew Rosenstiel, and what he would have done today. Remember him?"

I nodded.

"Lew probably would have had the both of you killed. You and Karl would have disappeared. You would have been hog slop on his farm."

Something made me realize that Sidney wasn't kidding. I felt a cold shiver run through me.

"Lew was a ruthless son-of-a-bitch. He made money the old fashioned way. He was a criminal. Lew and Sam Bronfman smuggled millions of gallons of whisky into the United States. They barged it down from Canada through St. Pierre and Miquelon. Lew then ran small runner boats into New York. The beauty was simplicity. Lew wasn't breaking any law until the boats crossed the three-mile line. If a boat or two got caught, it was a small loss in the big scheme.

"That bastard made boatloads of dough from breaking the law during prohibition. Stupid law, but a law just the same. Let me tell you something. Crime pays. There's a lot that's not in those expensive Ivy League history books your parents paid for. Lots of interesting stories." Sidney looked around the room, as if a little nervous. Old habits died hard. He leaned close to me and lowered his voice. "Want to hear an interesting story?"

"Do I?" I smiled.

"Course you do. Back in the day, bootlegging was wild, and gangsters were legends, almost mythical. They were like superheroes to the kids. Guys like Al Capone and Arnold Rothstein were larger than life. They didn't take any shit, and they made their own success. They weren't gangsters or mafia back then, that came later on. Bootlegging was almost honorable in a way. It was like these assholes were performing a valuable community service. Everyone drank, and they needed a reliable and quality source to get the goods. Smugglers made lots of friends supplying speakeasies and greasing crooked cops and judges.

"Bootlegging was dominated by immigrants. It was a perfect job for a refugee. They could make a fast buck or two, and they didn't need an education or family connections. Off the boat and into business within days.

"Two main groups of immigrants drove the bootlegging trade - Jews and

Italians. Jews had lots in common with them Italians. They looked similar. They acted similar. They shared strong family and community values, and they mainly bootlegged for the money. The Jews formed alliances with Italians in the early days, and many of those alliances are still alive today, believe it or not.

"But when the dough started flowing, the Irish started muscling in. They had relatives in the old country who could supply some the best whisky available. But the Irish were different. They didn't look or act like Jews or Italians, and they didn't associate with them. They kept to themselves, and they were notorious for drinking up their profits and beating the crap out of each other.

"Bootlegging became more ruthless as more players joined the game. It was a rough business, and sometimes things went wrong or someone got greedy and pulled some crooked shit. But there was always honor. Always honor. They were gentlemen, and there were rules and codes to be followed. There were quiet understandings and unspoken respect. They all had to put food on the table, and there was more than enough to go around. Things never got too out of hand. Occasionally, someone crossed the line or was disrespectful. Shipments were ambushed and toes got stepped on. But whisky was replaceable, disputes were settled quietly, and no one rocked the boat or ruffled feathers. There was too much on the line. Too much to lose. Understand?" Sidney didn't wait for me to respond.

"Then sometime in the late 1920s, everything changed. A shipment of some of the finest Irish whiskey ever to leave the emerald isles was on its way to Boston. This was liquid gold, smooth as silk, aged to perfection and treasured by a very close-knit family. The runners went to extreme lengths to get this whisky into the country, and it was for a very special occasion, like a wedding or something.

"But things went wrong. Someone leaked the beans, and a gang tried to ambush the shipment when it got to the states. The occasional ambush happened and fights erupted, someone gave a beat down, someone took a beating, noses got bloody, bottles broke and whisky was wasted, but that was about it. This time, things got ugly. The smugglers were under strict orders to protect their goods.

They were heavily armed and they opened fire on the ambushers, killing 13 unarmed men.

"It was bad. Women lost their husbands. Children lost their fathers. All over some fucking cases of whisky. Turns out the bootleggers were part of a gang working for a guy named Joe Kennedy, and the ambushers belonged to an organization run by Meyer Lansky. I'm assuming you've heard their names?"

"Of course."

Sidney's smile vanished, "Don't give me that of course shit, smart ass. You probably know everything. I'll tell you something, you don't know your ass from a hole in the ground. How about you tell me the story and I'll sit here like a schmuck with my schvantz in my hands and a stupid look on my face." Sidney went from zero to furious in under three seconds, and then returned to quiet and sulky almost as quickly. I wondered what the hell just happened. As I watched his face, his expression slowly morphed from sulky to confusion. "So, where was I?"

"The Kennedy and Lansky massacre?" I can't deny that I harbored some mild concerns up to that point, but at that moment all of my questions and doubts became much more tangible. Sidney was telling me ancient bootlegging stories that sounded both incredible and vaguely paranoid, and he seemed more than a little unbalanced. Was there something clinically wrong with him? Was it just old age and mild dementia, or something more aggressive and nefarious? Why was he telling me all this? Did I really want to know? I thought I wanted to know, but, then again, ignorance was bliss, and I preferred bliss to dread.

"Right, right. Sorry. So, after that bloodbath, everything changed. The honor and respect were gone. Vaporized. Bootlegging became much more dangerous. Men carried guns and used them. The government took heat for lack of enforcement, so they started applying pressure. Gangs splintered off and went underground. Some of the Jews and Italians stuck together, but they kept a wider distance from the Irish. There was still plenty of money to be made, and business went on. Pretty soon that horrible day was a distant and unpleasant memory. But I can assure you that it was never forgotten, and never will be."

I noticed Danny had quietly entered the room.

"Hey Champ, your bridge group is here."

Sidney had a group of card partners, mainly drunk golfers and stoned chefs, who would come in and play bridge with him every day. Danny would stack the deck so that Sidney would win, and everyone knew it, including Sidney. But he still enjoyed playing, mainly for the company.

"Ok, thanks Dan. See you tomorrow Seth. Come by in the morning and I'll tell you more stories.

Chapter 9
Dirty Goose

Mr. Brown was in his mid-fifties, but he looked about mid-thirties and generally acted mid-teens. Not surprisingly we got along well. When he flew in to San Diego I usually picked him up and we'd do extensive brand promotion at titty bars between the airport and Rancho Limon. It's a wonder we ever made it back to the Ranch in one piece.

Mr. Brown was waiting for me at the curb. Today, things were different. His tan face and wrinkly eyes were missing the usual conspiratorial squint. Mr. Brown was in DEFCON mode, all business, and I knew we wouldn't be making any detours on the ride back.

"I spoke to the local FBI and the Sheriff's office from the plane." Mr. Brown was very cool and collected for a guy who'd just disembarked after a five-hour ride, probably in first class with a cocktail or two to pass the time. But he was stone cold sober now. "I need to speak to the office, and check in with Sidney."

"Good. What's the story with the warrants?"

"It's not our Danny. Different guy." I looked over at him. He was sitting in the passenger seat and staring straight ahead. He wasn't even cracking a smile. His cadence was relaxed and his delivery lacked any tells. No wonder feds made great poker players.

"Seriously? It seemed to be him yesterday. Everything matched." I was waiting for the zinger, for Mr. Brown's signature wry smile and dry delivery as he dropped a bomb. I got the bagel.

"Different guy. Everything's cool."

"What the hell? Another Danny Guano with all the same stats? Seriously, what are the odds of that?" I knew that Sidney had influential 'friends' in the Sheriff's department, but I couldn't believe that these friends had seemingly made

Danny's warrants disappear. I also knew the FBI had some juice, but this seemed extreme.

The ride was quiet and tense most of the way back to Sidney's. When we arrived at the Ranch, Mr. Brown went directly into an empty bedroom and had an extended call with the executives in New York. Their decision was entirely predictable. Danny would stay. Disappointing, but not surprising. Sidney loved Danny, and they couldn't just make him disappear without risking extreme unrest and possible depression. Sidney would demand answers, and he probably wouldn't care that Danny was a suspected criminal.

....

A major security concern was that Sidney kept substantial sums of cash handy in a rolling suitcase affectionately known as the Vault. The bills were for tipping and other forms of undisclosed entertainment. Sidney regularly doled out thousands of dollars to golfers, waiters, hostesses, bag rats, and, of course, special gifts to his special friends. He once offered a former Playboy playmate $50,000 in cold hard cash to be his special friend for the night. She ultimately declined, but not without a prolonged internal struggle.

It was an unforgettable experience to be in Sidney's entourage when he arrived at any of his favorite restaurants. He generally sent one of his chefs to the venue, an hour ahead of his estimated time of arrival, to order his food and have it ready and waiting when he arrived. There was something indulgently redundant about sending your personal chef to a restaurant to order food. It was insulting and a boondoggle all in the same wrapper. And when Sidney got there, you knew it. His entrance started a small riot of servers competing for his attention. The golf course was even worse. I once watched two caddies beat the shit out of each other over who would get Sidney's cart.

But when the Vault's contents disappeared faster than normal, there was usually a formal inquiry from Polly. Chad fingered Danny, Danny fingered Chad, and both had their dirty digits deep in Sidney's cookie jar.

I recalled the day I was sorting through the filing cabinet in Chad's office looking for some paperwork. I had only been working for Sidney for a couple of months, and everything was still fresh and innocent. I saw an unusual looking file in the back of the cabinet with a dozen thick SFIC envelopes inside of it. My curiosity got the better of me, and I opened one envelope. I was dazzled by the densely packed $100 bills inside. There had to be several hundred of them. I had never held that much cash in my hands in my life, and I saw there were nine more envelopes in the file. The hairs on the back of my neck stood up, and I started feeling very uneasy. It also occurred to me that the eye in the sky was monitoring my every move. Chad had installed casino-like surveillance cameras in the ceilings of all the rooms in the house after a bad experience with a former golf pro/kleptomaniac staffer who stole everything she could get her sticky fingers on, including many of Chad's golf clubs. She then sold her spoils on eBay. Chad intercepted an eBay listing with a photo of her hands holding his putter. She had a distinctive class ring and manly knuckles. I wondered if she'd ever discovered Chad's slush fund file. Probably not. I closed the file cabinet quickly and decided to occupy myself with something else. But the mental picture was saved in my brain files, and that file was potentially viral and corrupted.

Then there was the time, not long after the filing cabinet incident, when Chad and I were playing golf. We had the exact same black golf bags with a loud company logo emblazoned on them. They were virtually identical, save for our names embroidered on the lower front pocket. I hit a bad shot, and without looking I stuck my hand in a golf bag to retrieve a new ball, and I felt something strangely familiar. It was the unmistakable feel of crisp, clean currency. I pulled my hand out and I found myself clutching thousands of dollars in brand spanking new $100 bills. Chad was away from the cart, although I was sure he would have a plausible explanation for storing thousands of dollars in his golf bag. Maybe his filing cabinet and mattress were full.

Then there was the Windmill incident.

"I need you to drive to the Chevron station on Palomar Airport off the 5, and meet a FedEx agent who is going to hand you a FedEx envelope containing a very large amount of cash. He's white with brown hair, wearing a black polo shirt and tan trousers, and he'll be standing in front of a windmill."

"Excuse me?"

"You heard me."

Allegedly, a large shipment of U.S. currency from New York to San Diego was intercepted by the FedEx security team. For a number of obvious reasons, it's against FedEx's policy to courier cash shipments. Of course that didn't stop Sidney. He'd been advised to keep his bank accounts outside of California for domicile and tax purposes. This inconvenience presented a major obstacle for his lifestyle as he and the entourage generally rolled with the Vault at maximum capacity, usually $40,000 to $50,000, sometimes more depending upon the night's agenda. Thus, Polly routinely couriered cash shipments of up to $100,000 from New York to San Diego, where it was received and logged in. From there, most of it was transferred to Sidney's safe. From the safe, most of the remainder was transferred to the Vault, and from the Vault to other dark and mysterious destinations.

After Chad hung up, I knew something was extremely wrong. And now I was being promoted from skeptical spectator to distraught mule. I was living in a John Grisham novel, and I was now part of the formula. Boy graduated law school. Boy got incredible job. Boy sold soul to keep job and live miserably ever after. I sold my soul to Sidney, and Chad was my odious overlord. I seriously contemplated resigning right then and there, but something inside my head, the grating subconscious, kept me going. It nagged me about my responsibilities, my wife, and my dog that needed hip surgery. The raspy voice of unreason also whined that I'd been given a once in a lifetime opportunity to work with a brilliant entrepreneur, a mentor's mentor who had the treasure map and the keys, and was I really going to flush it all away because I'd been requested to perform a unsavory errand that could get me thrown in jail or killed? It would take more than the possibility of death or dismemberment to deter me. The yellow brick road to everything was paved with a pothole or two.

I drove to the designated meeting place, extremely concerned that I was about to get whacked or, even worse, ambushed by Chris Hansen for a Dateline special on illegal cash shipments. I saw a male Caucasian fitting the description Chad provided standing in front a huge non-functional windmill. The windmill was actually a cleverly disguised Chevron station and effective ruse for luring unsuspecting tourists off the interstate and into their 24-hour convenience corral. One minute they are minding their own business, on their merry way to the Zoo or SeaWorld, when they seize upon the opportunity to double up on family entertainment with a visit to a Norwegian village. Upon discovering they'd been duped and there were no Scandinavians clomping in wooden shoes or pickling herring, the motorists would have to purchase gas, burritos and slurpies to soothe themselves.

The cagey white perp was holding a bulky FedEx envelope. He appeared to be alone, and he didn't look armed or dangerous, but traps never looked like traps. I locked the car doors and pulled up very slowly. My heart was flying and I felt flushed. The Fear was riding shotgun, but there'd be no Chinese fire drill today. I rolled up next to FedEx boy and gingerly lowered my window.

"Are you Seth?" He seemed friendly enough, but my radar was calibrated and my personal threat level was near DEFCON 1.

I nodded and scanned both windows and my rearview mirror, fully expecting to see a violent swarm of vice cops in riot gear storm my car and force me to hump the asphalt.

"Nice to meet you. Here you go....." he tossed a brand new, unsealed FedEx envelope through the window and started walking away. He didn't even wait for a thank you, which wasn't coming anyway. I pulled away, rolled up the window and checked the door locks for the umpteenth time before he was done saying "nice."

I hauled ass down the 5 trying not to look at the unsealed envelope on the seat next to me. It was my guilty conscience, just sitting and staring at me with that disappointed frown on its cover. I worried that it might contain some kind of plastic explosive or paint-bomb, or possibly a tracking device. I scanned the horizon for helicopters. Nothing. I studied the cars in my rear view mirror for nefarious looking tailgaters. None. I appeared to be in the clear.

I pulled off the 5 at Manchester and found a quiet rest area. I waited for a few minutes with the engine running, fully prepared to gun it if some homeys rolled up to jack me. I reached over and slowly opened the envelope. I peeked inside. I saw 10 separate stacks of bills. I removed one stack. My sweaty palms were holding a roll of 100 brand spanking new $100 bills. They were so clean they almost stuck together.

I got back on the freeway and headed for the Sidney's. I realized I had just participated in something very sketchy, even though it seemed mundane and almost matter-of-fact. Two things were very clear. This was not in my job description, and this was not why I signed on to work for Sidney. But there was nothing I could do. If I complained to Sidney, he wouldn't care, but six people would overhear me and Chad would get me fired. If I told Polly, she'd tell Chad and I'd get fired. If I told Danny, he'd be upset that he didn't get a cut of the loot, and he'd demand that Chad cut him in, after which I'd get fired. It was a triple loser. I decided to keep my mouth shut and resume normal business practices.

I pulled up to the Ranch and marched directly into Chad's office. He was on his computer playing a Tiger Woods golf video game, and he didn't even look up. I slammed the envelope on his desk.

"Here's your $50,000."

"Funny." He made no attempt to open the envelope or count the bills.

"I have no idea what that was about, and frankly I don't even want to know. But don't ever pull that shit on me again." I stormed back out of his office, but I turned just in time to catch a parting glimpse of Chad smirking.

....

The next morning I arrived at the house bright and early. It was about 6:30am, and I noticed a locksmith's truck in the driveway. I walked in and saw two SFIC executives sitting at one of the tables in the kitchen. The were dressed in suits, and they both had big glasses of scotch in front of them. They had flown in from New York to visit Sidney at the Ranch, and Sidney insisted that they stay in his guest rooms. One executive looked even more sweaty and agitated than usual. Craig was also in the kitchen making coffee. I walked over to him and grabbed a cup.

"What happened?"

"Care to guess?"

"What did she do?"

"Well, you see that dude who looks a little rattled?" Greg nodded at the executive who was taking a jittery sip from his glass. "I advised him to lock his door last night."

"And did he?"

"Apparently not. At about 2am, he feels something grab his upper leg. He turns the light on, and MOF is sitting on his bed holding his upper thigh in one hand and the remote control in the other. She proceeds to instruct him on the proper technique for using the remote control, in case he gets the itch to watch some TV at 3am or whenever. MOF lingered in her negligee, showing him which buttons to press in which order, and so forth. He finally gets irritated and asks her to leave, and she gets insulted and storms out. The dude is justifiably freaked and he decides he'd be more comfortable, and safer, at a hotel. So he tries to vacate. No dice. MOF locked him in. She had locks installed on the outside of all the guest room doors, in case she's stashing some contraband and doesn't want anyone to have access. The poor guy suffers from claustrophobia, and he has an attack and starts screaming his head off. Of course the rooms are soundproofed, so he was in there for almost two hours before night security was alerted. Security didn't have a copy of the key, and MOF refused to give it up, so they had to get a locksmith here to cut the bolt. He didn't get out until a few minutes ago."

"Wow, that sucks."

"Yep. Should have listened to me."

I grabbed some coffee and rambled to Sidney's suite. "Good morning Sidney." Sidney was in bed reading the paper. I noticed he seemed more tired than usual, like he hadn't slept well. He dropped the paper and looked at me. It took him a moment to register, but he smiled.

"Morning. Care for a Jäger shot? Great way to prime the stomach."

"No thanks, maybe later."

"Right, good idea. How about a bloody then?"

"Ok, sure, why not." That actually sounded good, and the celery and tomato juice made it seem like a healthy option. A spicy tomato smoothie.

"That's the spirit. Pierre, two Bloody Geese."

Sidney picked up the paper and started reading. I watched him for a few minutes, and it was apparent that he'd forgotten about inviting me for more story time. I cleared my throat loudly. He didn't seem to notice.

"So you were telling me about prohibition."

Sidney dropped his paper and glared at me. At first, I was concerned I might be on the receiving end of an ass chewing, but his mood brightened and he put his hands behind his head.

"Right, right. Prohibition. Well, prohibition was stupid, pure and simple. No two ways around it. People are going to find whisky, legal or not. Nothing wrong with drinking in moderation. It's healthy. It kills germs and cleans out of your system. Want proof? Look at me. I'm healthy as an ox." Sidney coughed up a huge brown phlegm ball and spat in his ashtray, causing a mild dust storm. "Prohibition was dumb, but it created opportunities. Take Rosenstiel. He was a colossal schmuck, but I wouldn't say he was stupid. He saw opportunities, and he capitalized on them. He cornered the market on legal spirits even before Prohibition ended. He bought government issued bonds on government stored whisky. You probably thought that feds destroyed all the whisky they confiscated during Prohibition, like you see in the movies. Guys with badges hitting barrels with axes and spilling whisky down street gutters? Am I right? Well, that's bullshit. The government stored the confiscated whisky in warehouses and then issued secured bonds. Bondholders paid the government storage fees, but most of these assholes couldn't afford the fees and never thought prohibition would end, so they abandoned ship. Lew was making mountains of money from bootlegging, and he had friends on the inside. He knew people. Lew bought all the bonds he could get his fingers on. When prohibition ended in 1933, Lew had more barrels and aged whisky than anyone, and the government had aged it for him. Lew bought out Schenley and it quickly became the most successful distillery around. He was years ahead of his closest American competitors.

"Canada was a different story. Sam Bronfman controlled Seagram's, and now after Prohibition ends he's watching Lew take over the American market that he helped build. And he's also got a big supply and demand problem. Namely, lots of supply and little demand. So Sam hatched plans to make a big splash in the states, but Lew didn't want Bronfman muscling in, especially with superior Canadian juice. And, as I mentioned, Lew knew people.

"So Seagram's filed an application to open an American subsidiary, and the U.S. Treasury graciously offered to allow Sam back into the States after paying a little fine of $60 million dollars. Bronfman was pissed off. He and Lew created the game, and now he wasn't allowed to play. So, he commissioned Lew as his exclusive agent for Seagram's in the United States, which was exactly what Lew wanted. He wanted control. He wanted Bronfman to go through him. Lew got what he wanted, and he thought everything was peachy." Sidney stopped and glared at me. "Am I boring you?"

"Not at all."

"You look a little bored. So as it turns out, Sam was no idiot either. He knew what was going on, and he knew some people also. Sam arranged his own meetings with the Treasury Department, and ends up settling Seagram's penalties for a cool million bucks. Substantial savings. Makes you wonder a little, don't it? Sam set up a distillery in Indiana and from then on, Lew and Sam hated each other's guts. They became bitter rivals for many, many years. Lew actually made his office into a war room dedicated to destroying Seagram's. Of course, they would later have some mutual business interests that brought them together briefly, but that's another story for another day."

Sidney was quiet, and I was fairly sure story time had concluded for the day. But I was wrong.

"So take a step back and look at the big picture here. Sam Bronfman and Lew Rosenstiel, two big criminals, both magically transformed into respectable businessmen, like maggots becoming butterflies. Lansky was a different story. He set up his own company and took care of Lew and Sam's more complicated problems.

"Sam was ruthless when it came to business, but he was a decent man. He treated people fairly and took care of his friends. Sam remembered where he came from and he was extremely philanthropic. He did the right thing with his blood money." Sidney hesitated for a moment, and then something else came over his face.

"I can't say the same for Lew. Something was very wrong with him." Sidney's face turned much colder and darker, and his normally low voice got even lower. "He was consumed with greed, and he always wanted more. He'd take a hundred cases of decent whisky and 'blend' them into a thousand cases of crap diluted whisky. He would also 'age' whisky by adding a couple drops of sulfuric

132

acid. Made it taste like it'd been aged in oak for years. Acid would make brand new crap whisky taste like twelve-year crap whisky, but most of Lew's customers didn't know the difference between Dewar's and dog shit. Some of them figured it out. Schenley produced a whisky called Black Velvet DeLuxe that earned the nickname 'Schenley's Black Death.' Lew's toxic blends probably caused severe liver disease, but it was good for business and he could give a crap about collateral damage." Sidney looked straight at me. "Lew was already one of the wealthiest people in the country. He owned 1,200 acres in Greenwich, a swanky penthouse apartment on Park Avenue, yachts, private jets, the best whores money could buy, and it wasn't enough. He poisoned his own customers to make more. He was a sick man." Sidney shook his head and was quiet for a few minutes. I wasn't sure if the story was over, so I sat still. After a minute or two, Sidney perked back up.

"That old pervert tried to fuck anything that moved. And he did eventually succeed in fucking the entire country." Sidney looked straight at me. "Lew was all rotten inside. His core was diseased, and he had poison in his heart. He infected everything around him. Everything he touched." Sidney stared out past me and was quiet for a few minutes. "But I got away from him. I got out before he poisoned me." His brow furrowed and he was silent for several minutes. He stared out past me, lost in bleak memories of shady characters and unforgivable acts. I watched as his eyes turned red and welled up. He shook his head and muttered something I couldn't hear. His breathing was rapid and I was sure he was about to cry. He took some deep breaths, but he was straining.

I considered saying something to ease the tension, but thought better of it and kept my mouth shut. Slowly, the ghost passed and Sidney started breathing easier. His mood lightened a little. He looked at me watching him, and he forced a little smile. "And just look at me now. I could buy and sell Lew's fancy ass 10 times over."

"You sure could, Sidney."

"Shut up and listen. If you don't take anything else away from today, just remember one thing. Lew, Sam and Lansky were all assholes, and they rarely got along, but they worked shit out. They had to, because when it came down to it they were Jews and Jews stuck together. But one thing is dead certain. They all hated the Irish, and Joe Kennedy was at the top of the shit list. "

"Really?" I chuckled. "He seemed like such a sweet guy." Sidney shot me a look that gave me the shivers.

"And the feelings were mutual. Did you ever hear about the kidnapping of Sam Bronfman's grandson in 1975? Sam Bronfman II was abducted and held for a couple of weeks. I think he was about 20 at the time. The kidnappers demanded a $5 million ransom, and his idiot father Edgar wouldn't pay up. They got the FBI involved and it turned into a big clusterfuck. Fortunately, they found the kid alive, and they also found his captors. Guess where they were from."

"Probably not Mexico?"

"Ireland. Fresh off the potato boat. You think it's just a coincidence?" Sidney puffed his cigar.

"Not any more."

"Seth, the things I tell you are not to be repeated, at least not right now. Is that clear?"

"Yes sir. Chrystal clear."

"Good boy. Now get the hell out of here. I need a nap."

Chapter 10
Slippery Nipple

I returned to Sonoma and spent most of the rest of 2003 and early 2004 sourcing as much bulk wine as I could. It turned out there was a lot of California bulk wine available on the open market. The bad news was that most it was crap. Karl and I bought the best wines we could find, and we were able to raise case production to about 3,700 cases. That would have to do.

I was overwhelmed trying to get everything we needed for 3,700 cases of wine. Bottles, labels, corks, foil, boxes, not to mention getting the logistics figured out. It was a monumental task when your entire production is outsourced. And then I started getting annoying phone calls from the corporate accountants at SFIC HQ. They constantly requested additional documentation, like copies of contracts, invoices, spreadsheets, receipts, reports, plans, projections, and forecasts. They wanted updated spreadsheets on a weekly basis, and they wanted backup to backup the backup. They were nervous about all of the money I was burning without actually having anything to show for it. But that was part of the fun in winemaking.

....

Making vodka is easy. Making wine is art. A good wine can take years to get from grape to the bottle, and master winemakers spend those years blending barrels until they achieve perfection. This is assuming a late summer frost didn't ruin the crop, in which case they would have to wait until the next year and start all over.

For vodka, you make it, you bottle it, and you sell it. Making and bottling it are the easiest parts of the process. Selling it is the hardest part, but Sidney had a knack for hustling. If it was in a bottle, Sidney could sell it. He was, without question, a marketing genius. Maybe one of the best natural selling talents ever. If you've ever tasted Jägermeister, you know that it would take a genius to convince consumers it's not poisonous. And yet, Jägermeister became the number one selling liqueur in the country under his control.

Sometime during the early years of Sidney's exclusive distributorship, a damaging article appeared in a small Baton Rouge newspaper. The report referred to Jägermeister as 'liquid Quaalude' and insinuated that it might contain some kind of illicit herbal narcotics, opiates and aphrodisiacs. The outraged writer had the audacity to suggest that this foul German 'love potion' was becoming a cult drink on Bourbon Street, and that it was corrupting the youth of America and leading to carnal acts of depravity, including, but not limited to, blowjobs and orgies.

Sidney read and reread the article several times. A light bulb exploded in his mind. Instead of suing the paper for libel, he made thousands of copies of the article. He posted these copies in the men's rooms of bars and restaurants all over the country, and he placed them directly above the urinal where you were sure to have a man's undivided attention for at least a minute or two. He hired buxom beauties to troll bars wearing Jägermeister outfits that left almost nothing to the imagination. They would giggle and jiggle while passing out the article, along with free ice-cold shots, to enchanted male patrons. Sidney designed flashy Tap Machines that would chill three bottles to ice cold temperatures and dispense shots in little frosty glasses. Jägermeister became the most celebrated and ordered shot in the world, and it tasted like crappy cough syrup.

I was in a Sonoma vineyard when my phone rang. "Morning Mr. Schechter." It was the same SFIC bean counter that called me every week with the same dumb questions. "How's the weather out there? Geez, you're lucky. Sure wish I could live on a lake in Napa. There's a major ice storm here in New Rochelle. Power's been out for days." I think he was expecting sympathy and small talk, so I remained silent. "Well, I was calling because I wanted a progress report on the 2003 vintage." This putz had graduated from Harvard, and he pranced around SFIC in Harvard tee shirts. Most of the Harvard alums I respected didn't advertise it on their persons.

"It's aging. The whites will be ready for bottling soon, but the reds are going to need at least 18 months in oak before they are ready."

"So, we are not selling the 2003 red wines for a while?"

"Yep."

"About a year and a half?"

"That's synonymous with 18 months."

"Right. And you're already signing contracts for the 2004 vintage?"

"We have to get in early to secure the good grapes if we're going to do 500,000 cases next year." There was no way Karl and I could ever make 500,000 cases, but I wanted to zing Harvard and whoever else was monitoring the line. It seemed to work, because I could hear some coughing and papers rustling in the background. They were probably scrambling to figure out how much money it was going to cost to make a half million cases. The wine project was Sidney's baby and his legacy, and we named the brand *Sidney* for obvious reason. The company executives didn't love it so much, and they didn't understand wine or winemaking. They thought making wine was a waste of time and money. Of course, since it was Sidney's money funding the project, they really couldn't do much about it. "Is there a problem?"

"No, no problem. Just need to report to the board, you know the drill." Harvard didn't have a poker voice. I heard some hesitation and stammering. The executive team was probably pacing around behind his desk wringing their hands and pulling their few remaining strands of hair. God forbid the wine budget should cut into their profit sharing performance units. No racehorses for Hanukkah. No new tires for the Ferrari.

"Whatever." I hung up the phone and went back to work. I didn't have time to play with fools. In less than a year, I launched a major wine brand from the ground up. I taught myself how to produce wine from the vine to the bottle. I spent hours each day going through books and manuals, consulting Karl and other local experts, and touring other winemaking operations. I learned more in one year in Sonoma than all my years at college and law school.

The more I learned about winemaking, the more I became aware that our process was flawed, and that massive improvement was needed to compete with top California labels. Our strategy was entirely wrong. We were producing way too much wine for a start-up. We needed to scale back, but I had already floated that biscuit and it was squashed. If we were ever going to do the volume Sidney desired, we really needed our own vineyards and winery. We couldn't control the weather or grape quality, but we'd have much more selection and discretion with our own vineyards. Without vineyards we were at the mercy of grape growers who rarely sold their best fruit on the open market. The two things we could definitely control were equipment and facilities. We were relying on outdated facilities with old tanks and faulty equipment, and our results reflected it. Sidney needed a winery.

"Hello Seth, I was just thinking about you. I was reading the latest reports, and it looks like we are at about 3,700 cases for 2003. Is that right?" He was reading reports now. I guess he learned a lesson also. I couldn't believe he estimated cases from the report numbers. I documented 9,000 gallons under production, and he converted gallons to cases in his head. I knew he'd been doing this for a while, but it was still impressive.

"Yes sir, that was the best we could do." I braced myself and held my breath, waiting for shrapnel to explode in my ear.

"Ok, no problem. 3,700 cases it shall be. I appreciate your work. It hasn't been easy or smooth, but you are doing good." I opened my eyes and took a deep breath. His speech seemed to get slower every time I spoke to him, and I worried he wouldn't be around to taste the inaugural vintage. I knew he'd been having heart trouble on and off for a while now, and the hard partying years were catching up to him. He'd been a legend for his drinking abilities and his stamina, even among the professional drinkers in the business. Sidney could close down clubs and drink into the wee hours of the next morning, and still make it to breakfast meetings fresh as a daisy.

"Sidney, we need to make some changes here. We're making way too much wine. I think we should scale down next year, maybe to a thousand cases."

"No. I'll sell it. Not a problem. Next year we'll make 50,000 cases. You worry about making the wine, and I'll take care of selling it." He was starting to breath heavy, and I didn't want to agitate him.

"Alright, but if we're going to make that much wine, we need a winery."

"A winery?"

"Yes, and a big fucking winery with vineyards to grow our own grapes."

There wasn't the slightest moment of hesitation, "Ok, go buy a winery. Make sure it's nice, but not too nice. And get a good deal." The line clicked off and went dead. I could only imagine the wide eyes of the company executives monitoring that call.

....

In the fall of 2004, I started looking for a suitable winery while commuting between Sonoma, San Diego and New York. I was racking up the frequent flier miles by the thousands, and conjugal visits with my wife were few and far between.

Not surprisingly, Roshambo Winery was on the market. Karl knew the winery inside and out because he designed it. It was a beautiful piece of land with a state-of-the-art winery, albeit filled with goofy artwork and furnishings.

Redecorating would be much more simple than rebuilding. We made an offer on Roshambo at full asking price, which was inflated but Sidney didn't really care. He wanted it, and he usually got what he wanted. Brilliant accepted initially, but then balked and asked for more money. She got greedy and tried to hit the vodka piñata a little harder, but this time it was Kevlar coated. An offer at full asking price was like a handshake to Sidney. He was giving her what she wanted, and more than it was worth. Done deal. And Brilliant basically returned his good faith with a gut shot. She didn't realize that once Sidney got sucker-punched, he usually didn't return for a second helping. Several years later, she was forced to sell the winery operation for millions less than Sidney offered. She then tried to run another innovative wine venture out of a recreational vehicle, but it soured also. Brilliant then decided to quit the wine game altogether and grow super edgy organic vegetables.

So I kept making wine and looking for wineries, all while taking mucky showers and living in the most beautiful place in the world. I would sit on the deck and listen to the river rushing below me. Its rhythm was more constant than the ocean, and it was just as alive. The slow river melodies would drown everything else out, and I would lounge in my chair and mentally drift down the bubbling Russian. How funny that just a short time before, I was dying behind a green computer screen with a dusty desk, plastic plants and a view of a parking lot. I could feel the green monitor draining my soul like an electronic leech, sucking a little more of my life force every day. It seemed like another lifetime. And now I was sitting on the throne of a wine wonderland rising above the rushing waves.

It was during this idyllic period of personal and professional enchantment, when everything was coming together and nothing, except the plumbing, could possibly get any better, that something went terribly wrong. I became aware that I was being monitored. I was not a paranoid person by nature, but I was extremely observant and I noticed small details. It wasn't hard to spot a tail in Sonoma, especially when you lived in a remote area. I began to notice a variety of cheap rental cars pulled over near the dirt road leading to the Barn, and they routinely followed me from a safe distance whenever I went anywhere. Agent 007 wasn't overly concerned about having his cover blown.

I also noticed a persistent echo on the Barn's landline when I made phone calls. It varied in pitch and degree, but it was there most of the time. Cell reception next to the Russian River was nonexistent, so I was forced to use the dreaded yodeling landline for just about every call. I frequently disconnected and called back in an attempt to cease the mind-numbing drone, but the echo endured. It could have been antiquated telephone lines or faulty wiring, but I strongly suspected that the line was bugged. I also detected loud clicks and the distinct sound of breathing at times, but then I second-guessed myself and chalked it up to static interference and my vivid imagination. There were times when I picked up the phone and heard no discernible dial tone for several moments, and then, like an evil spell, the dial tone would return, and with it the maddening endless echo.

One memorable day, Cooper and I returned to the Barn from touring some vineyards, and something definitely wasn't right. His hackles went up and he started growling as soon as we walked in the door. I looked around, and I got the unnerved feeling that we weren't alone. "Hello? Is anyone here?" No answer. I couldn't exactly put my finger on it, but something was different. The Barn was even creepier than normal. I could almost detect a presence, like an unfamiliar odor (not easily distinguished from the multitude of familiar stenches that bunked down in the Barn). I could have sworn that someone or something had been there, or maybe was still there, somewhere. Perhaps the landlord stopped by, but he'd never done that before and I assumed he'd call first or leave a note following. I got a little uneasy, so I retrieved Gary's high-powered hunting rifle from the hall closet. The weapon was not optimal for home security, but it was loads of fun obliterating plastic water bottles and aluminum cans on the deck. Cooper went berserk every time I shot one. He was a true gun dog and hunting was in his blood. I picked the rifle and chambered a shell. I did it loudly so anyone in earshot would know I was ready to party. My adrenaline was pumping. Cooper whined and shivered with eager anticipation.

I walked around the Barn pointing the rifle into closets, behind furniture, and through the shower curtain in every bathroom, half expecting some knife-wielding transvestite to come screaming out. I got nothing, but something had been in the barn. Cooper was sniffing everything and he was on high alert. It was probably just a curious raccoon or porcupine, but it might have been something else. The story Sidney told me about Bronfman's grandson kept nagging at me. Maybe rogue IRA agents were planning to hijack our operations and crucify me on a Cabernet vine as a symbolic message to my superiors. I slept between the loaded rifle and Cooper for the next month.

....

It was a beautiful day in the later part of 2004, and I was touring my third winery of the day. The crush had started a few weeks earlier, and the scent of rotting grape musts and fermenting grapes permeated the Napa air. The smell of crush is distinctive and haunting – it's a smell you never forget. It's a musky, sweet and sour, spoiled yeasty funk, very similar to the odor wafting around a wood paneled frat house rumpus room after decades of jungle juice and beer bong debacles. It's not entirely pleasant, yet not entirely unpleasant either, like strong cheese, aged cigars, leather shoes or your favorite old bird dog.

The winery was a $10 million tear down high up in Calistoga hills. The facilities were old and needed to be gutted, but the vineyards were steep and sprawling and the views of the valley were forever. At these elevations, the Napa floor looked like a patchwork quilt of rolling reds and yellows and greens. You could almost see all the way to Bodega Bay. I was smitten with this little piece of shit winery. This could be the one. My cell phone rang. It was Chad's number.

"Do you know any judges in San Diego?" No hello or how are you. Not even a thinly veiled gratuitous pleasantry.

"Hey Chad, nice to hear from you."

"Do you or don't you?" I could tell something was bothering him. He was more of a dick than normal.

"I used to work for one. Why?"

"We have a situation. Fly here as soon as possible."

I drove back and packed up, not realizing it would be the last time I would ever see (or smell) the Barn. I flew back to San Diego with Cooper. I hated having to crate him and check him through as baggage. I'd heard awful stories of airlines sending dogs on the wrong flight and losing them. Even worse, I'd heard of dogs perishing due to extreme heat, cold or sudden loss of oxygen and pressure. Even in the best scenario, I'm sure it was the ride from hell. But that was Cooper's small sacrifice to share enchantment. Little did I realize this fairytale was heading south.

Chapter 11
Fuzzy Navel

I parked my crappy Audi on the steep driveway descending into Rancho Limon. It was burning oil, and I rolled in a perpetual iridescent cloud. There were about 20 cars already parked on the narrow driveway at various angles, and getting in and out was always a logistical nightmare. I noticed a gleaming silver Bentley GT parked next to the front door. Inside the Bentley I could see a pastel pink cashmere sweater, mirrored Maui Jim sunglasses, and a recent issue of the *DuPont Registry* on the passenger seat. In the rear was a child's car seat on one side, and a toppled sippy cup surrounded by a pool of warm milk on the other side. The milk was slowly absorbing into the buttery leather seat, creating a dark cream nucleus surrounded by a concentric evaporation rings in lighter shades of tan. Chad had a new ride.

I walked into Chad's office and sat down. He was on the phone with an attorney, and he had his hand in his hair and a pained expression on his face. He was wearing a pastel green, double-mercerized golf shirt, silky trousers, and pointy Italian loafers. Chad was also sporting a new platinum Patek Phillipe, and I realized it was the first time I had been in his office when he wasn't playing video games, slamming golf balls into the walls, or browsing magazines. From what I could piece together from Chad's half of the conversation, he was being investigated by the California Fair Political Practices Commission ("CFPPC") for violating the Political Reform Act. In laymen's terms, Chad got popped for an illegal campaign contribution.

"Unfuckingbelieveable." Chad was accused of orchestrating a $5,000 contribution to the incumbent Sheriff of San Diego. The problem was that the contribution limit in San Diego was $500 per individual donor. Sidney allegedly wanted to do more for a buddy who'd done him some solids, like quietly overlooking the time officers found him intoxicated and passed out in the driver's seat of his little Mercedes coupe. The car was also parked in the middle of a neighbor's Rancho Santa Fe orange grove, and it was upside down.

Sidney allegedly instructed Chad to make the large contribution, and Chad concocted a foolproof scheme. He purportedly instructed 10 staffers to write personal checks to the Sheriff's campaign for $500 each, following which he handed them envelopes containing $500 cash. None of them wanted to be involved, but Chad supposedly applied torque and they relented. And this cockamamie plan might have worked if Chad hadn't fired one of those pesky participants a few weeks later for insubordination. Mr. Insubordination quickly became Mr. Whistle Blower.

And when an official-looking agent from the CFPPC made a surprise visit to Rancho Limon and flashed his intimidating plastic badge around, most of the donors spilled their guts and told him exactly what he wanted to hear.

"And Mr. Harmony handed you an envelope containing $500?"

"Yes."

"And Mr. Harmony informed you that he was reimbursing you for the contribution you made to the Sheriff's campaign?

"Yes."

"And you understood that this was reimbursement for the donation you made to the Sheriff's campaign?"

"Yes."

"And Mr. Harmony was aware that you were aware...."

It was a turkey shoot. Chad slammed the phone down and grabbed a 7 iron that was leaning next to the door. He bashed it against his desk, sending papers and his computer flying. Small splintered wood fragments shot out in all directions. I was caught completely off guard by the intensity of his rage. I rolled my chair back and observed the demolition, ducking whenever desk particles breached my no-fly zone. The desk obliteration seemed to relax and calm him. He even flashed an inappropriate smile when he drove a steel coffee thermos through a plate glass window.

MOF opened the door and surveyed the crime scene. She shook her head and made a few disapproving grunts.

"Get the fuck out!" Chad was immediately in her face and screaming at the top of his lungs. I was mortified. I'd seen Chad and MOF go at it, but he'd never been this disrespectful. I was sure she was on the verge of hysteria.

MOF didn't even flinch. If fact, she seemed to be smiling and humming to herself. She walked in and started picking up scraps of desk and other debris, making tidy little piles on his floor. After making five or six piles, she bowed and exited, giggling and turning off the lights.

Chad slammed the door shut and flipped the lights back on. He kicked every pile MOF made, until his floor was again coated with chunks of former furniture. He sat down on an ergonomic desk chair that resided behind his now missing desk.

"I'm fucked."

"What's going on?" I knew what was going on from listening, but I didn't know all the gory details.

"They are going to crucify me. For a lousy couple of $500 donations to the Sheriff, I'm going to get disbarred, and Sidney will probably go to jail. Can you believe it? That old Jew in prison? He won't last a day. And all because of these fucking idiots. All they had to say was that they didn't get reimbursed. $500. Just tell him they didn't get reimbursed, or they can't remember, or something. And what do they do? All 10 of them insist that I forced them to donate and to accept the reimbursement. Motherfuckers." Chad started swinging the club again, but he was defeated and there wasn't any desk left to destroy. He hit a few stray books and then sat down again. The staffers were disloyal because he treated them like shit, but it wasn't the opportune moment for a reality check.

"We're going back to New York tonight, and you're coming with us."

"To New York? Yeah, right." I forced a little smile. I'd been living in

Sonoma in relative peace and tranquility, notwithstanding a few minor inconveniences like bathing in sludge, tenacious ticks and monitoring by IRA assassins. I'd visited Sidney and the traveling staff circus a few times in New York and California, but I'd never been invited to fly with them. Chad wasn't smiling back.

"Dude, listen to me, we have to bounce, and you have to escort us. We need California counsel, for Sidney's protection. You're the best California licensed attorney we have on staff." Chad finally grinned. We both knew I was the only California attorney on staff. Chad was only licensed in New York. "And we're never coming back to California." Chad slammed one of the last recognizable pieces of his desk for emphasis. "They're getting the plane ready to go. We have to go intercept Sidney, and you have to stay with him from the time we get him until the plane takes off. Those jerkoffs from the Commission might try to detain him if they suspect he's a flight risk." Chad really seemed to be overreacting for a $5,000 misdemeanor. I knew Chad had a penchant for exaggeration, but this seemed excessive.

"Where is he?"

"He's attending a private offsite meeting." Chad grinned again. He was privy to an inside joke, and I was clearly on the outside. "Let's go reel him in."

We walked back through the house, and I could see that Chad was still fuming. He stumbled over Meisty, who'd been fast asleep in a sun puddle near the front door, and she yelped and took off faster than I'd ever seen her move, other than the times she raced Jagey to get to Barry's Burrito Tree. The Burrito Tree was named after one of the cooks whose creative delicacies frequently ended up stuck to its trunk or hanging from its branches. The Burrito Tree was located next to the staff's outdoor dining table, and mealtime amusement consisted of launching leftovers into its braches and watching the dogs bump the trunk with their massive flanks and tussle over dropping treats.

The sight of some of the staffers who'd snitched set Chad off again. He stuck his head into the golfer's office and started screaming "We're going to New York tonight. Go home and pack." The golfers and cooks who'd been playing cards froze and looked at each other, wondering if Chad was kidding. "I'm not kidding idiots. Go get packed, unless you spoke to that asshole Commission agent, in which case you're fired. And don't even think about suing me. I'm a lawyer." They all looked dazed as they walked out of the office. Chad walked over to the main house intercom and pushed the on button, "Good morning assholes. Everyone go home and pack your shit. Most of you are coming to New York tonight, and a few of you, and I think you probably know who you are, can go fuck yourselves."

We walked outside and Chad unlocked the Bentley and looked at me. "Like it?"

"It's dreamy. Do they make these for men too?"

"Whatever. Get in." Chad was in no mood for derisive banter. He was usually good for a nasty quip or insulting comeback. I'd seen him moody and compulsive, but never this far down. I had serious doubts about riding shotgun.

I climbed aboard and buckled up. This was my first ride in a Bentley, and I had to admit it was luxurious. I could only compare it to being in the passenger seat of a private jet, or in the back of one of Sidney's Maybachs. Very sophisticated, refined, elegant, and overstated. It had all the bells and whistles, but none of the ringing or whistling that accompanied my Audi commutes. The finest wood trim, the best leather, hand-built quality craftsmanship and attention to every detail. It had a grace and a presence, and it felt very solid and precise. It was a lovely car, but not a very cool car. There were about a thousand cars I would have bought before a Bentley. It was the ultimate poser car for someone who had serious shortcomings and insecurities. It was perfect car for an old man with a neatly trimmed mustache, tweed cap and fingerless leather driving gloves, or a hot soccer mom with long shiny nails, a big shiny rock and a yapping, sweatered poodle in her lap. It was an interesting choice for a 30-something metrosexual male with messy toddlers.

As we cleared the driveway, Chad punched the gas and the Bentley's 600 horses roared to life, pinning me to the back of my seat. The acceleration was surprisingly smooth and frighteningly powerful, and we hit 100 mph in seconds.

The hamlet of Rancho Santa Fe was a rural and quiet sanctuary where hermit moguls, trust funders and hedgehogs could buy a big slice of peace and tranquility just outside San Diego's manic beach communities. Long, tree-lined, serpentine country roads separated magnificent horse estates from sprawling citrus groves. Bentleys, Ferraris, and Lamborghinis were a dime a dozen in the Ranch. Maybachs were less common, but you would see them touring the country roads on occasion.

Rarely seen were two idiots screaming 160 mph down the perfectly manicured lanes of Via Fortuna, or getting into a four-wheel power slide on the corner of Paseo Delicias and Del Dios. The casual bystander might also have seen demonic rage in the eyes of the driver coupled with unbridled terror in the eyes of the passenger, but the driver was wearing mirrored sunglasses and passenger's eyes were shut tight.

In truth, I was less concerned for my own safety, and more concerned about impaling a stray horse or cow, or pulverizing a hobbling, hunchbacked old woman, or even worse a mother pushing a baby stroller. You never knew what might suddenly pop out of a driveway on a narrow country road, and I really didn't think it was too prudent or responsible to break 180 mph on the straight 1/4 mile stretch of Las Colinas, even though it was exhilarating. I'd probably hit 120 mph on the freeway a few times in my Audi, but I slowed as soon as the speed wobbles became seismic. I was amazed that even at close to 200 mph, I barely felt a ripple in the Bentley. We could have been sitting in the garage, except the world outside and my life were both flashing by in a frightening blur. Outside scenery seemed to move slowly when driving that fast, like some kind of optical illusion. Your peripheral vision can't keep up with your brain, so everything slows and gets quiet, calm and peaceful. I'm sure a pilot experiences this same serenity just before his diving airplane vaporizes into a crater.

"Open your eyes and get your claws out of the leather. Damn, your fingernails are blue and you're going to ruin the upholstery." Chad was laughing and going through his CDs, holding the steering wheel with his knees.

"Jesus, watch the fucking road." The car was swerving very close to a row of telephone poles and eucalyptus trees. Chad looked up in time to narrowly escape a lethal collision, but it was really damn close.

"Hey idiot, Jesus isn't allowed in my Bentley. I'm an excellent driver, so shut your pie hole and enjoy."

Chad put a rap disc in the player and turned the volume way up. We slowed and rolled up to a stoplight in the center of the utopian village of Fairbanks Ranch. Chad revved the engine and rolled the windows down. I opened my eyes and took some deep breaths, and I noticed two girls standing near the car and giggling. Chad and I were dorky white dudes in a Bentley blasting gangsta music and looking painfully stupid. The light turned green and Chad gunned it, adding more insult to injury.

We drove to the coast and pulled up to an oceanfront estate. There was an impressive iron gate blocking the driveway and my view, but I could see it was an incredible property. It was modern and made of wood, stainless steel, concrete and glass.

"Where are we?"

"Sidney's house," Chad loved the fact that I was completely out of the loop when it came to much of Sidney's life.

"What are you talking about?"

"Well, Sidney technically owns the house, but he doesn't spend much time here." Chad punched a code into the keypad and the gate slowly opened. We drove up the driveway and parked near the front door. Chad opened his car door and looked over at me. "Welcome to Sidney's crab shack."

We walked up to the massive door. Chad waved a key fob in front of a security box, and the door opened automatically. Chad looked at me, and I couldn't hide the fact that I was impressed. He had obviously been here before. We walked in and looked around. The house was unreal. The entrance led past enormous windows looking out at the beach and ocean, and the water was so close that it seemed like the waves were almost breaking against the windows. The floors were a cool brushed concrete with inlaid tiles. The walls were painted in warm neutral colors, and the artwork was slightly modern Asian, but not overdone. The furniture was actually inviting and comfortable looking. There were huge LCD TVs in almost every room, and a bar area filled with Grey Goose and Jägermeister products. Someone had hired a designer to decorate, and that person had done well to keep things simple and masculine. It was a seaside man-cave, textbook beaver trap. I estimated the house was worth between $10 and $15 million, maybe more.

I wondered down the main hallway, intrigued and baffled that Sidney owned it. It was so different than his other houses, which were all in various stages of disarray and decomposition. This place didn't have the same feel. There was no rotting clutter, obese pets, or putrid burrito parts. No mysterious odors, loitering staff, stained carpets, or pickled witch screaming at her shadow. I never thought Sidney cared about his surroundings, but someone else obviously did.

Chad saw me marveling. "You should see Sidney's penthouse in Manhattan. It makes this place look like a trailer." I'd heard rumors that Sidney had a love nest on Central Park, but it was kept highly confidential. Staffers who went there had to sign a NDA.

We walked into a den area off the kitchen and encountered our first loitering staffer. Danny was reclining on a chaise in the den, watching WWF wrestling on a huge TV and smoking a cigarette. He was wearing his standard tight black pants, but he replaced his standard skin-tight black tee shirt with an even tighter black tank top. He looked bloated and uncomfortable, like the outfit was cutting off his circulation.

"Hey D." I nodded, trying to be friendly.

Danny barely acknowledged our presence. He grunted and shifted slightly on the chaise, seemingly annoyed about something.

Chad and I walked upstairs to the master suite. We came to a door and stopped. We could hear giggling, grunting and bed squeaking coming from inside the room. Chad looked at me and grinned, and then knocked loudly.

"Go away Dan. The injection is working, and I don't need the pump tonight. You're off the hook." Sidney grunted and coughed from somewhere behind the door. I detected more female giggling also.

"It's not Dan, sir. It's Chad, and Seth is with me. We need to come in and get you. You need to come with us."

"Goddamnit, I'm busy. Come back in two hours."

"Sorry sir, no can do. We need to get you out of California, pronto. We need to hurry before they lock you up in the pokey. The BBJ is waiting." Chad had a big smile on his face and he was clearly enjoying himself. It seemed to take his mind off the contribution fiasco, and he was sharing some grief with the alleged perpetrator.

"For Christ's sake. Hang on." I heard some rustling and Sidney trying to whisper in a hushed grunt. I heard a hard slapping noise and more feminine laughter.

"OK, come in"

Chad opened the door and we entered the expansive master suite. There were enormous fish tank windows looking out over the coast, but Sidney's blackout curtains were covering them, which was a crime because I was sure the view was stellar. The huge LCD TV mounted on the wall was broadcasting an old porn movie with the sound turned down. Big oily breasts were bobbing on a large purple penis, and the accompanying superfunk music was almost comical. The walls were adorned with huge poster sized photographs of Sidney from different stages of his life. It was like a Sidney shrine, maybe even closer to a memorial. The idol himself was reclined on the bed in full glory with his erection proudly in one hand and a big smoldering cigar in the other.

"Now you know why they call me the cocktail king." Sidney laughed, and it seemed like he was in a pretty good mood, considering the circumstances. I think I knew why. The door to the adjoining master bathroom was cracked open, and I could see a woman applying makeup in the mirror's reflection. She was stunningly beautiful. I'd guess she was in her late 20s or early 30s, but it was difficult to tell. She had blonde hair, flawless features, long legs, and what appeared to be a perfect body under a very sheer nightgown. She was a pro, no doubt about it. I'd seen lots of them, but she was by far the best.

"Mr. Frank, you need to come with us now. Seth and I will be escorting you to New York, and he needs to be with you at all times. Where are your clothes?" Chad tried to cover Sidney with the bed sheets, but Sidney kept playfully brushing them off and exposing himself.

"What's the rush? We have plenty of time. Stop worrying so much. Danny just gave me an injection and I don't want to waste it." Sidney was laughing and foiling Chad's attempts to conceal his virtue. The 'injection' allowed Sidney to maintain an erection, and it was administered directly in to his main vein. Viagra was no longer effective, and he needed extreme measures to fornicate. The thought of it made my testicles recoil up into my stomach.

"Seth, go find his pants." Chad was frustrated, and Sidney was now crawling around the bed on all fours looking for the cigar he dropped. It was a freak show, but impossible to look away. Sidney was laughing and grunting, and Chad was trying to lasso him with the sheet whenever he had a clear shot.

"Hey, I got an idea. Why don't you two have some fun with my gal? I need a few minutes to have a smoke and catch my second wind." I'd heard rumors that Sidney allowed one of his former golf pros similar liberties, but I chalked it up to drunk golfers and urban myth.

I scanned the room for Sidney's trademark stained sweatpants and torched sport shirt, and finally spotted them draped over a chair. As I was walking to the chair to retrieve said clothes, the bathroom door opened and the goddess appeared. She made a beeline straight for the bedroom door, but I was directly in her path.

I opened my mouth to speak, but I froze and the only sounds that emerged were low guttural squeals. It didn't matter because she blew straight past me. The silky nightgown clung to her like a car cover. Her perfume was like musky lemonade poured over cinnamon saltwater taffy, and it made my reticent testicles drop and twitch. I was bewitched. I stood staring at the door she exited, entranced and oblivious.

"Nice ass, right?" Sidney was looking directly at me and smiling. I couldn't hide a mild blush.

"Yeah, not bad."

"Not bad? You seen better?"

"No, actually I haven't"

"Yeah, didn't think so. Shit, for 20 grand a pop she better be not bad." Sidney was not the least bit shy about his indulgences. He frequently disclosed the exorbitant prices of the Waygu steaks and vintage Bordeaux he served to dinner guests. Not to make them feel guilty or grateful, but more because Sidney wanted them to know they were consuming the best of everything. Everything was a commodity, and everything had a price.

"Looks like she's worth every penny." I smiled as I helped Sidney get his clothes on, which was not pleasant. Chad turned the video off and now was pretending to read some imaginary emails on his Blackberry. I knew he wasn't going to help, and Danny was useless.

Sidney nodded toward the door. "You should give her a try sometime."

"Thanks Sidney, but I don't think my wife would approve." I managed, by some Herculean effort, to clothe him, but was still struggling to stuff his block feet into his white sneakers.

"Sounds like your wife doesn't understand men. You need to train her better." Sidney laughed again which sent his thick legs into involuntary spasms, nearly braining me as I tried to tie his laces. "You know what? I love Marian, even though she's crazier than a shithouse rat. You know why? She understands my needs and gives me my freedom. She don't ask questions, and she don't give me too much trouble. Besides, I can't get rid of her, and I've tried. She keeps coming back, like herpes." Sidney roared, and his lungs joined his legs in synchronized spasms. Fortunately, I was finished dressing him.

I heard the intercom crackle and Danny's chipper voice chimed on.

"You alright Champ? You need anything Champ? Halls? Evian?" The repetitive champs from Sir Chumpsalot were getting old. Danny was so blatantly insincere that I was embarrassed for him. I wondered if Sidney ever saw through his phoniness. He must have, but I'm sure he liked all the fawning and attention, and he needed Danny. Who else was going to administer injections, operate the Swedish vacuum pump, or change his dirty diapers.

"I'm fine, Danny." The spasm was subsiding and Sidney was calming down. It was terrifying to see him hacking up chunks of lung and phlegm ribbons.

"Ok, Champ. Buzz me if you need anything."

Chad hit the intercom button.

"Yes Champ?"

"Danny, this is Chad," as if clarification was needed. Chad put his Blackberry away and assumed his serious look. "Gary is coming with the car. Seth and I could use help getting Mr. Frank downstairs." Stairs were always a tricky proposition with Sidney, and the more manpower we could muster the better.

"Wheelchair's in the closet. I'll go meet Gary and prep the car." Danny was irked that Chad was taking charge of the rescue and recovery operation. We all knew a wheelchair was not an option, and that no prep work would be necessary for the car, but I'm sure Danny was all smiles as he walked outside to smoke another cigarette.

"Thanks, Danny." Chad rolled his eyes and coughed "asshole" into his fist. I nodded. We had to get the big man down the stairs without killing him or ourselves. I quickly dismissed the idea of asking Sidney's special friend to assist, although I enjoyed the thought of it.

"Are you ready to go sir?"

"Hell yes, I've been ready to go for the last 20 minutes. I told you that injection worked. Is she coming back in?" Sidney started removing the clothing I had just packed him into.

"No Mr. Frank. We're going to New York."

"New York? Why?"

"Because there is a very real possibility you will be arrested if we stay here."

"Arrested? What the hell for?"

"You remember the contribution to the Sheriff? For that."

"Oh yeah? Jesus." Sidney shook his head and chuckled a little. "What is this world coming to? Back in the old days, a briefcase full of bills solved all of your problems. These days, you can't give a few grand away without some idiot blowing his whistle up your ass. Ok, let's go."

Chad took one arm, and I took the other, and although the going was painfully slow, we managed to get Sidney down the stairs and out to the waiting Maybach without dual hernias. I thought I saw Sidney's special friend poke her head out of another bedroom door and smile as we escorted him down, but it was probably a mirage of fairy dust and cigar smoke. Gary and Danny were standing by the front door.

"Gary, we need to get to the private terminal pronto. I'm riding with Sidney," Chad announced as he breezed past Gary and Danny and left me bracing Sidney. Chad tried to open the car door, which was no easy feat as it was reinforced with heavy armored panels made out of steel, Kevlar, titanium and windows that were thicker than aquarium glass. Sidney wanted the only bombproof Maybach on the road, and he got what he wanted. He bought the Maybach for half a million dollars and spent another $250,000 customizing it to his high security specs. Maybach would eventually use Sidney's modifications to produce their own armored model for the overseas market, particularly popular in Russia and the Middle East.

"Slow down there Chief," Danny grabbed Chad's arm and slid between him and the door handle, "I'll ride with the Champ, just in case he needs any medical assistance." Danny took a final drag on his cigarette, flicked the butt, and prepared to enter the car.

Sidney cleared his throat. "Seth will ride with me. You two follow in another car."

Nobody saw that one coming, least of all me. Danny and Chad were like toddlers excluded from the zoo field trip. My knees felt unsteady and I got lightheaded, which was suboptimal since I was keeping Sidney upright.

The Maybach was a decent car to drive, but it was designed to be driven in. The back seats were incredibly soft and ergonomically perfect. They reclined all the way to flat, and they had more positions and adjustments than a Craftmatic bed. Sidney usually didn't talk much during rides. He read reports on his products and investments, watched the news, or shot the bull with Gary. But tonight, things were different. He raised the bulletproof privacy divider so Gary couldn't hear our conversation, and he studied me for a few long minutes. I looked at him and smiled a little uncomfortably. I could sense that he wanted to talk about something.

"So, she was pretty."

"Yeah, she's alright. Bad attitude and not too bright, but she's not my accountant. And what a set of cans. She got tits like a Da Vinci. Listen, I need to tell you something. The company has been keeping tabs on you for a while, but you probably know that by now. Wasn't my idea. The boys were concerned about all the money we were pumping into a couple thousand cases of wine without seeing any product, but that's the wine business I kept telling them." He smiled and patted me on the hand reassuringly. "So we tailed you, we broke in your house and went through the files, we broke in the crush facilities and took inventory, and then we had everything examined and re-examined and rectally examined by forensic experts. And you know what? We couldn't find a goddamn dime missing. Not a fucking nickel!" Sidney roared and hit me on the leg. "Everyone steals from me! You think I don't know that? You think I'm an idiot? Of course I know. Polly, Danny, Chad, all my executives, they all have their noses in my ass and their hands in my pocket. And to be honest, I don't really give a shit as long as they don't steal too much. I'm an old man and I don't have much time left, so what am I going to do? Die with it? I'll tell you what I'm going to do. I'm going to do whatever the fuck I want to. I'm going to enjoy all the time that's left. Every second." Sidney pulled a cigar out and put it in his mouth. "You got a light?" I pulled out a lighter and torched Sidney's cigar. "Thanks. So I asked myself, what the hell is up with this kid? Either he's too good to be true, or he's just really good at hiding shit." Sidney blew a big cloud of smoke in my face. "So which is it?"

I looked at Sidney's face and couldn't contain my smile. "Too good to be true?" He was wearing a pair of funky wrap sunglasses and his permagrin was plastered across his face, but I knew he was reading my reaction like a polygraph. He was looking for the slightest flinch or hesitation. He was watching to see if I perspired, flushed, my pulse quickened or my pupils dilated. Many poker players wore mirrored sunglasses to hide their pupils. I was not worried because I was telling the truth, and I knew that he knew it.

"You're not the smartest lawyer I ever met, and you don't know you're ass from a hole in the ground when it comes to moving product, but I think you are honest and probably one of the few people I can trust. And to me, loyalty is more important than anything. You understand?"

I nodded. I was not sure where this was going, but I knew for damn sure I wasn't going anywhere.

"I don't trust many people on this world, and I give people more chances than they deserve. And no matter what, they usually let me down. I can't even trust my own goddamn family. Can you imagine that? Not trusting your children? Your flesh and blood?" He looked out the window, and his breathing was getting more rapid. "Something is wrong with them." Sidney stared straight ahead, barely moving. He slowly removed his sunglasses and looked me squarely in the eyes. "I've had good luck and successes in life. I realize that I've been blessed." He was breathing heavy, and the words were not coming easily. "But I had some failures also. My greatest failure in life..." Sidney took a deep breath and lowered his head. I knew this was difficult for him. This was a man who didn't admit or accept failure lightly. But I knew he wanted to tell me. He raised his head and his eyes were red and watery. "My greatest failure in life is my children."

Sidney replaced his sunglasses and sat back in his seat. I watched a single tear moving slowly down his cheek from under his sunglasses. He was very still, and I thought he might have dozed off. I was not sure what to do, so I kept quiet and waited. After several moments, he wiped his cheek.

"When your family turns on each other like a pack of wild dogs, you realize something terrible has happened. You might have everything you wanted in life, all the money in the world, but it's a mirage. It's a big fucking illusion. I should've done shit differently, but by the time I noticed it was too late and they were deep in their disease. I lost my family, and that was the lowest point in my life. I was despondent. I had almost five long years when I couldn't see any beauty in life or any reason to live. I could look at a Renoir or Picasso and not even notice it was there. Beauty vanished and I couldn't see anything but pain and despair. I had no hope. I didn't want to get up or face the day. There were weeks and months that I just laid in bed and waited to die. I wanted to die. I accepted and embraced it. I sunk into a dark hole, and I never thought I'd crawl out." Sidney looked at me. "I hope you never have to endure that kind of pain. It can ruin you.

It can destroy you. There is no cure for it. There is no medication, and I tried everything. Pills, booze, shrinks, women, anything and everything, and nothing worked. Some of those things distracted me, but the pain was still there, always there, hollow and cold, constantly gnawing at me. It would not stop. There were some days when I would have given anything to just make it stop." Sidney looked at me and smiled kind of sadly. He touched my hand. "Look, I realize it wasn't all because of my children. There were other issues in my life, and a lot of my pain I brought on myself. I'll accept that. I wasn't a model father, and I'm probably responsible for making my children what they are today." Sidney paused and took a long look at me. "Useless." Sidney was quiet and reflective for a few minutes, and I thought he might be finished, but he wasn't.

"But it's not all my fault either. They have poison in their cores. Sometimes I look at them and can't believe they came from me." Sidney looked at me squarely. "I'm sorry to have to tell you all this, but I don't want to see anyone make the same mistakes I did. I don't care how much money you have or what resources you can provide. You must make your children work. Make them earn a living. Make them appreciate responsibility and accountability. Let them learn how to form relationships, communicate, influence and earn respect. If you don't, they won't learn how to deal with people, and they will never achieve anything on their own. Don't let them invent fairytale excuses for not working. It's a load of bullshit."

I tried to recall if I'd ever actually met Sidney's children, and I really hadn't at that point in time. He had a daughter who was some kind of artist in Seattle, and a son who lived near Stanford. Both were from his marriage with Skippy, and neither of them had worked a day in their lives as far as I could tell. I'd heard his kids' names in passing, but that was about it.

"They have their grandfather's blood. Lew Rosenstiel was a maniac. He didn't respect anything, not the law, not women, not even his own mother. He would have traded her for a hot tip on a horse." Sidney took a long drag on his cigar. "I didn't like him, and I didn't understand him, but he knew how to make fortunes and build empires." Sidney grinned and took a drag on his cigar. He blew out some intricate smoke rings and sat back admiring them. They were almost perfect little circles. They danced in the light momentarily and then vanished.

"That old bastard didn't trust anyone, especially his family. Shit, you don't go through five wives without a healthy dose of skepticism. He bugged his entire house. He bugged his own bedroom and bathroom. His own bathroom for Christ's sake. Bugged his children's rooms too, sick bastard. But I'll tell you what, he sure as shit figured out what was going on around him." Sidney winked at me. "I'll tell you a funny story. One night, Lew calls all his top brass and tells them he's not feeling well. He asks them to come up to his house to see him. It's late, and these assholes slowly begin showing up. But when they arrive, they are ushered into a waiting room with several doctors and nurses, and they are told that it's worse than anyone realized and that the old man is on his deathbed and not seeing visitors. A while later, one of the doctors comes in and announces that Lew crapped out." Sidney grinned and shook his head fondly. "The resulting celebration was recorded by hidden cameras and microphones. I suppose you probably could have heard a pin drop when Lew walked into the room and announced that the report of his death was mildly exaggerated." Sidney chuckled. I could sense twisted admiration for his former father-in-law. Sidney probably idolized him in a disturbing way. He had many of the qualities that Sidney held dear. Fabulously wealthy, enormously powerful, shrewd and feared. He also had some considerable flaws.

"Lew just wasn't right. Something was missing from him. He could be inhuman. He could be a monster. Some of the things that he did...." Sidney paused and looked at me. "Some things he did I will never accept. Never."

"What did he do?"

Sidney shot me a look that made me sorry I asked. Sometimes it was better to keep you mouth shut and listen.

"He did some things that are unforgiveable." This meant a lot coming from a man who had forgiven most of the betrayals in his life. He still took care of Lew's fourth wife Susan, the woman who he sometimes blamed for his fall out with Rosenstiel. Sidney even agreed to a reconciliatory meeting with the Bronfmans to discuss Israeli philanthropy, an act of such high treason that Rosenstiel was likely doing cartwheels through the underworld.

I'd completely lost track of time, but I noticed we were pulling into the private terminal area, and Sidney's Boeing Business Jet was waiting. This would be my first flight on a private jet, and I was starting at the top. The BBJ was the biggest and sweetest private aircraft on the market, and the Maybach was permitted to pull directly up to the ramp so Sidney could board without any screening. Wealth and FBI security have their privileges. Private air transportation will absolutely ruin you when it comes to flying commercially. The prospect of standing at the end of the C group cattle call on Southwest Airlines, knowing you are destined to get the last row, non-reclining middle seat situated directly between two obese garlic farmers and across the aisle from a ripe lavatory, now seems almost inhumane.

Sidney was whisked out of the car and into the plane. I was detained for a brief security check, but was walking up the ramp minutes after Sidney. I was considering the phone call I would have to make to my wife who was still expecting me home for dinner. I had just flown in from Sonoma and now I was boarding a plane to New York with no clear indication of returning, and could she please feed the dog and FedEx some clothes and clean underwear. It was no wonder she was starting to hate me. I was starting to hate me also.

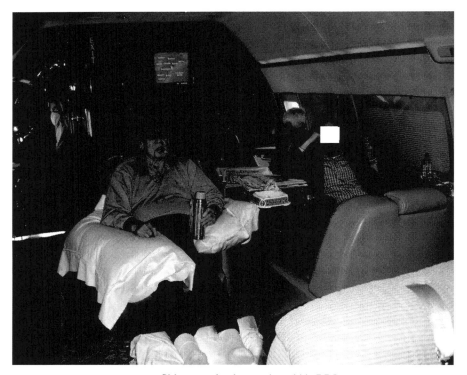

Sidney on the throne aboard his BBJ

The plane was already bustling with activity when we entered. The chefs were storing trays of food and coolers full of drinks in every conceivable space. The golfers were concealing cocktails and jockeying for seats as far away as possible from MOF, and she was busy abusing two attractive flight attendants who were trying to stow her cartoonish luggage, accusing them of damaging the ridiculous crap she packed. The dogs were burrowed under Sidney's throne, a heavily cushioned recliner (with several added pillows) positioned directly in front of a large LCD TV that broadcasted his favorite movies non-stop. Sidney's staff exercise therapist, a petite blonde who strutted around in short skirts and padded bras for Sidney's amusement, was busy rubbing his back and shoulders. On rare occasions she coaxed Sidney to go swimming, or more appropriately, floating.

164

She would wear a bikini and guide him around the pool like a tugboat while he floated on his back. This popular event always drew an enthusiastic crowd of male staff spectators.

Sidney was seated on the throne and still wearing his sunglasses, and I noticed he was watching *Shawshank Redemption* as I walked up. He had a double Grey Goose bloody Mary on the tray next to him, even though his cardiologist had cautioned him about the health risks of drinking on airplanes and sudden changes in cabin pressure.

Chad was occupying a slightly less opulent seat next to the throne, trying to go over some financial reports. He was prepared to hunker down and get some work done during the flight. Sidney was trying to ignore Chad by throwing large chunks of smoked salmon and cream cheese to the dogs. The dogs were like trained seals, snapping at the flying food and bobbing their heads up and down. Chad was frustrated by Sidney's lack of interest, and so he placed several reports on Sidney's tray. Sidney playfully bumped the reports off, sending Chad scurrying for flying papers. The cabin was quickly filling up with smoke from Sidney's cigar. I assumed that smoking was prohibited on all aircraft, but then I remembered that Air Sidney was an unregulated outlier. Sidney looked up and noticed me standing.

"Seth, come sit." Sidney pointed the claw at Chad's seat. It was Sidney's way of dismissing Chad. Chad was stupefied. He stood up stiffly, walked to the next seat and evicted a golfer from a prime window location.

I sat down and almost immediately experienced another intense wave of *déjà-vu*. I had been on this plane, sitting next to Sidney and his fat dogs even though my rational brain knew I'd never been near a BBJ. It seemed so familiar in a very vivid and peculiar way. After that passed, I started feeling highly exposed, like I was naked at my first day of school. Everyone was watching me, wondering why I was seated next to his majesty. I had always been Chad's underling, and now I had usurped his authority. Danny, who was pretending to attend to Sidney's baggage and other inconsequential tasks, eyed me suspiciously. The chefs also looked perplexed, and the golfers were intermittently flipping me the bird between covert slugs from their cocktails.

This was my inaugural flight on Air Sidney, and I had already been upgraded to ultra-premium class. My seat was arguably the second best seat in the house. From this vantage point, one could fully savor Sidney's sycophantastic circus. This was the pure, distilled essence of Sidney's martini wonderland, and the power was intoxicating. Everyone wanted to be as close as possible to the mush pot. The chefs relentlessly filled his plate with rich delicacies and indulgent delights. Sidney's cigar was perpetually smoking, and his drink was continually fresh. The golfers pestered him to play cards or discuss their golf scores, swing adjustments, whether Tiger could beat Jack in his prime, or the flight attendant's tits. MOF stopped raving just long enough to blow a crusty pink kiss and flash her lipstick stained teeth in Sidney's direction.

It was a special treat to be invited into the Maybach or the BBJ, but it was a very rare honor to watch the munchkin parade directly next to the Wizard of Booze. But with that reward came risk. The catbird seat in Sidney's circus was generally in the crosshairs of another Bozo's sights.

"Sidney, this is great. I thought the Maybach was nice, but this is unbelievable. Really special. So, it looks like you're safe and out of harms way. You'll be in New York before you know it. I was wondering if it might be possible for me to go grab a few things at home? I could catch the redeye and meet you in...."

"No." Sidney didn't look at me or move a muscle. Not a flinch. Only his mouth moved. Barely.

"No?"

"Shut up and watch the movie."

And that was that. Not up for discussion. I had my answer. I was to remain with him as his legal security blanket, lest the plane be intercepted in Iowa and require counsel to clear up the California clusterfuck. Once we were in New York, Chad would become Sidney's custodian and I could fly home.

We watched *The Shawshank Redemption*, part of an Eastwood western, and several segments of a Winston Churchill documentary. Sidney napped intermittently for most of the trip, and I alternated between watching the television and ignoring all the inbound stink eye.

Chapter 12
Long Island Ice Tea

Another black Maybach, almost a clone of Sidney's San Diego car, was waiting at the airport in White Plains. Sidney insisted that I accompany him on the ride back to the New Rochelle house, which was another dagger in Chad's already ruptured heart. Sidney was quietly reading a report that had been delivered to him at the airport. I wondered whether he was still partially asleep.

Sidney grunted and handed the report to me. I scanned it. My eyes widened. It was a confidential offer sheet from Bacardi.

"Bacardi is offering a billion dollars for Grey Goose." Sidney was very matter of fact, like he was telling me the score of the Yankee game or the weather forecast.

"Holy shit," I couldn't even conceive of that amount of money for one brand.

He smiled. "Yeah, not bad for seven years of work."

"So you're accepting?"

"No."

"No?"

"No."

"Why not?"

"Because, they will pay two." I looked at Sidney. He was completely straight faced.

"Two billion? For Grey Goose?"

"Yeah. Maybe more. I have a project for you."

"A project?"

"Yes."

"For me?"

"Do you see anyone else in the car?"

My mind was racing. I still hadn't processed the fact that Sidney was going to refuse a billion dollar offer for a single vodka brand.

"I want to buy an island."

"An island?"

"Am I mumbling? Yes, an island for Christ sake."

"Ok, yes sir, an island." I waited for more information. Sidney was quiet. "Any particular kind of island?"

"A big fucking island." Sidney took a long drag on his cigar. "I'm going to build a golf course."

I was silent, watching him. I hoped more details would be forthcoming, but I wasn't about to ask.

"I'm going to build the world's most challenging and beautiful golf course. Every hole is going to be on the ocean. I'm going to hire the best course architect to design it, and you're going to make it happen."

"Me? But I don't know anything about building golf courses."

"I know. You are perfect." Sidney smiled, amused with himself. "When the old bastard hired me at Schenley, I knew squadouche about making sauce. I turned his entire company around," Sidney took a drag on his cigar and blew small bubbles. "I made that meshuga cocksucker a fortune." Rosenstiel was one of the wealthiest men in the world when Sidney met him, but I didn't say anything. "And then he had the gratitude to fire me." Sidney looked me squarely in the eyes. "Do you want to know why he fired me?"

I didn't respond. I didn't even blink.

"Because I was nailing his fourth wife, Susan." Sidney laughed loudly and slapped me on the leg. I had never seen him so animated. "I figured, why not, everyone else was. So I schtuped her also. And what a piece of ass she was. And the fact that she was my mother-in-law made it even more interesting, although she was only a few years older than me. And she was a prostitute, did I tell you that?"

"No sir." I tried to contain my smile, but it was difficult.

"Well, it's the truth. She was a pro. One of the distributors hired her to pop out of Lew's birthday cake as a joke. And then Lew married her. Joke was on them I suppose. Want to hear a funny story?" Sidney had the toothy smile and familiar glimmer in his eyes. I knew he has something good stashed away.

"That old pervert caught us red handed. Like I told you, he had bugs and cameras in every room. Every room, even his own bedroom. Unfortunately, I didn't know that until it was too late. He got the whole thing recorded. There was no denying it. She's screaming my name. I'm slapping her ass. All recorded on tape. Lew plays the tape in front of his executive team. It was great. Then he fired me. Which was not so great. But after a while he hired me back. I think he realized that whore wives are replaceable, but good salesmen are like gold. He divorced Sue in Mexico and she barely walked away with two nickels to rub together. She still lives in New York, one of those nutty Upper East Side shut-in's with an apartment full of cats and an attic full of bats. And I give that crazy bitch money, even though she's too proud to ask for it. I pay her hotel bills, and deliver a couple of cases of Goose to her every month to keep her quiet. I feel bad about what happened. She seduced me, but I didn't put up much of a fight."

Sidney smiled and fell silent for a few moments.

"So, what the hell were we talking about?"

"An island."

"Right. Go find an island. And make sure it's a nice one, but not too nice."

"Any particular location?"

"Surprise me." We rolled into the driveway at the Hillandale farmhouse, and before I knew it, the doors opened and four security guards whisked Sidney away to his bedroom suite. I sat in the car for a few minutes looking at the empty seat next to me.

There was a small motorcade of rental cars waiting for us at Sidney's house. Polly had sensible rental cars delivered to the house for our convenience, and to keep us from selecting expensive rides. I walked towards the vehicle Polly picked for my driving pleasure. It was a tiny subcompact, and as I opened the door the stench of failed air freshener and homelessness hit me like a living wall of stink. The car model was an Aspire, which was fitting because it aspired to be a car. It also made my ass perspire when I drove it. I smiled to myself. It didn't matter. I would simply drive it directly to the rental company and trade it for an Escalade or something equally obnoxious.

Polly truly enjoyed irritating the staff and making our New York stays as unpleasant as she possibly could. She picked the worst New Rochelle hotels, reserved the crappiest rental cars, and eliminated random items from our expense reports without any notice or explanation, just to aggravate us.

Polly resented the fact that she was doing grunt work, albeit cushioned by the fact that she was the highest paid secretary in history. In her mind, she toiled all day in fluorescent offices with funky Jägermeister crap all over the walls. All the while, Sidney's staffers jetted around the world playing golf and buying islands. We sent her the bills, and she did her best to avoid paying them. It became a petty and juvenile game, but it kept her simple mind occupied between cat videos and blazer bonanzas.

Chad walked up and knocked on my window. I tried to roll it down, but it resisted my efforts with a loud screech, probably due to all the accumulated dirt and what might have been dried blood stuck in the window jam.

"Sweet ride." He chuckled and dangled his key chain in my face "Denali baby. Want to trade?"

"No thanks. I love this car." I started my Aspire and it squealed to life. We both grinned at each other. Chad was Polly's snitch. He ratted out all of the other staff members to Polly and her minions. He was her eyes and ears when it came to staff issues, and Polly always made sure Chad had the best car and hotel room available.

"So, what did you and Sidney discuss?"

"He wants me to buy an island."

"Seriously, what did you two talk about?"

"The island he wants me to buy."

"Whatever asshole." Chad strutted over to his shiny black Denali, got in and slammed the door. He started it, gunned the engine and peeled out of the driveway, burning rubber and accelerating for about a quarter mile down Hillandale Drive, directly in front of the uniformed New Rochelle police officers stationed outside of Sidney's house. The officers didn't even lift their heads.

I drove the Aspire to the Marriott Residence Inn in downtown New Rochelle where the staff was housed. New Rock City was a rough place. It had supposedly been nice back in the day, but that day had been gone a while. The hotel was in the heart of urban metro sprawl, and it was extremely dangerous to venture out alone after dark. The train station was a half-mile away, and when necessary I sprinted to and from it faster than Usain Bolt.

I tried to spend as little time in the Marriott as humanly possible. I could feel my essential life force draining away every time I entered the lobby. There was always some mysterious rotten corpse or chemical cleanser odors wafting through the hallways. Every room was moldy from faulty AC window-units that constantly perspired on the carpets. One time I came home to find a pond in the middle of my room, and some of the golfers tried to bodysurf through it. I flew Cooper out to New York to spend the summer, and he was more traumatized by the hotel stay than the flight. I would come home and find him curled in a little fetal ball in the bathtub or behind the toilet, violently shaking and inconsolable. Dogs have a sixth sense, and there was an evil Residence Inn energy that tried to possess him. The icing on the cake of that hotel was the day Cooper bolted down the hall and disappeared behind a chair near the elevator. As I caught up to him, I noticed he was busy devouring the regurgitated chunks of someone's Taco Bell and tequila infused smorgasbord. I almost fainted.

Chapter 13
Golden Goose

It was June of 2004, and I was in Fiji passing a big mug of cava within a circle of natives and feeling pretty groovy. I had been looking at islands nonstop for almost six months. I had spanned the tropics looking for a suitable venue for Sidney's vision, and I decided the logical way to proceed would be alphabetically. I'd been to Anguilla, Antigua, Aruba, Bahamas, Bali, Barbados, Bermuda, Bora Bora, British Virgin Islands, and British West Indies. And now Fiji. I realized Fiji didn't fit the pattern, but I made a special exception for islands with good waves.

I hadn't seen Laurel in what seemed like forever, and I could feel us beginning to drift further apart. She rarely wanted to talk about my travels or hear my stories when we were together. She was getting tired of being alone and responsible for running the household while I chased improbable dreams. I understood and I felt terrible about being away, but there wasn't much I could do about it. We needed my paycheck, and I was pretty certain there was a pot of everything at the end of the rainbow. But I was getting fatigued from traveling and searching, and it seemed like the more I looked for islands, the more I felt like I was already living on one.

In spite of my weariness, I was thoroughly enjoying Fiji. It was tranquil and magnificent. The sand was pure white, the water was clear and warm, and there were thousands of tiny little islands scattered up and down the chain. The native Fijians were some of the nicest people I met during my travels. They were huge and happy, and they followed me around like puppy dogs, fascinated by the trappings of modern life. My clothing, sunglasses, satellite phone and iPod kept them immensely entertained. They lived in a utopia with minimal needs and few possessions. They all wore skirts, and they fished, dove and surfed all day. They didn't need much more to be content. They lived in close-knit family units, and they exuded such genuine warmth and kindness that I hated the thought of tainting their world with Sidney's sideshow freaks.

I looked at a few completely uninhabited islands around the main Fijian island of Viti Levu. It was kind of crazy to land on an island and realize that there were no other people there besides you and the pilot. In some ways it was very thrilling and romantic. We were intrepid explorers boldly going where no sane person had dared or cared to go. It was exciting, but it wasn't going to be easy. We were going to create our own new territory - Sidney's Island.

The main problem would be infrastructure. On an uninhabited island, I would be starting from scratch. You realize how much you take for granted living in a civilized, industrialized and commercialized area when formulating a development plan for an uninhabited island. On an island, you need to build everything. First comes roads, because without roads and transportation there is no progress. After roads comes power, because without utilities there are no structures, airstrip, sewage, and on and on. On some primitive level, it was amazing to be able to do anything I wanted. But it would be a long and bumpy road to get things up and running. And, to be honest, up and running was really just the start. The greatest challenge would be maintaining and sustaining.

Chad occasionally joined me for a few days, but only if there was a fluffy boutique hotel and championship golf course close by. He was fairly useless, but he did provide some minimal amusement. At least he opted out of the Fiji trip, for which I was thankful. There weren't any good golf courses around, and I would have had to listen to his bitching about the rustic accommodations and ugly native women.

My satellite phones rang.

"Did you hear the news?" I detected a sharp note of glee under all of the raspy phlegm.

"Yes sir. Chad called me about an hour ago with the good news. You got a lot of money."

"A lot *more* money." I heard him laugh and cough, and blow smoke into the receiver. Even 8,000 miles away I could almost smell the stinky cigar.

Bacardi agreed to pay the astronomical price of two and a half billion dollars ($2,500,000,000), plus residuals, for the Grey Goose brand.[17] Not bad for seven years of light work. The jackals and hyenas would snap up a big chunk of the carcass, and the remaining buzzards picked at the Golden Goose's skeletal remains, but Sidney still was very comfortable considering he grossed about 70% of the overall proceeds from the transaction.

"Lots of money, little time. How's Fiji?"

"Perfection. Beaches are white sand and clean. Water is like a hot tub and so blue it's almost green. They also have a drink here called cava. They make it by grinding up roots in a bowl. It reminds me of Jägermeister. Tastes like muddy water, but if you drink enough your body goes numb."

"Yeah? Sounds good. How long did it take to get there?"

"To Fiji?

"No, to Uranus."

"About 14 hours."

"Too far. Come on back." The line clicked and went dead.

Come back? I was in fucking Fiji. I could get away with spending a day, but if I dragged ass he'd know. I jumped on a dive boat and did the most amazing dive of my life. I dropped into a long dark tunnel made out of lava, and popped out on a thousand foot wall of soft white coral. The coral waved in slow, synchronized formations as I floated over it on warm currents. I felt like a butterfly gliding over a huge field of white poppies, or like a stray astronaut soaring through outer space, utterly lost yet completely tranquil and prepared to drift aimlessly and indefinitely into infinity. I never wanted to come down.

---

[17] Bacardi bought both Grey Goose and Blue Goose - a premium gin that Sidney was developing in England. They killed the Blue Goose brand to eliminate competition with Bombay Sapphire, their top selling gin brand.

Chapter 14
Harvey Wallbanger

I spent the next few months commuting between New York and tropical locations that started with the letter C. I started with the Caymans, which were really nice and their banking laws were appealing to high net worth individuals with cash to stash. I was also trying to spend as much time with Sidney as possible. I monitored the wines from a distance, but felt guilty that I couldn't be there to help Karl. I knew he was probably overwhelmed and distressed, but I was caught in Sidney's web and it was difficult to extricate myself, even for a day or two. The winery acquisition was on hold as the island acquisition took precedence.

I tried to call Laurel when I could, but some places were so remote there was no phone service. I started to wonder what the hell I was doing, and whether it was really worth it. I missed my family. I missed my wife desperately. I missed her big blue eyes, warm silky hair and her soft skin. I missed having a warm body next to me in bed. I missed companionship, even if it was sometimes hostile. I also felt bad for Cooper. I wandered if he was getting walked or taken to the beach. I had ridiculous fears that he wasn't getting fed regularly, or that his water bowl was empty during hot summer days. I worried that he was just sitting and staring at the door, waiting for me to come home.

One day in the late fall of 2004, I arrived at the New Rochelle compound and noticed a procession of long, black town cars parked in the driveway. A gathering of town cars was usually a bad sign. It generally meant the corporate rubes were paying their monthly respects. I walked in and immediately knew something was different. I sensed electricity and mirth. There was a presence even greater than Sidney in our midst that day. All the golfers and other assorted kitchen rats were tense and alert, but no one was talking. I walked up to the bedroom compound and opened the door.

The room was filled with people and smoke, and one interesting specimen. Harvey Weinstein, the co-owner of Miramax, was sitting on Sidney's bed smoking a cigarette while Sidney chugged away at his cigar. Harvey's entourage of young Hollywood insiders were swarming around the room on their blue tools barking out orders to production assistants scurrying through San Fernando Valley. Other industry loiterers lurked in the hallways, looking uncomfortable with the surroundings. Most of Sidney's staffers were also in the room under various false pretenses. My radar was transmitting strong warning indications. Weinstein could only be here for one reason. He smelled blood.

A few weeks earlier, Sidney had attended a fundraiser for the Robin Hood Foundation, a clever moniker for a New York charity that seduced it's uber-rich patrons into pledging hedge fund payouts to support Harlem. Their cause was entirely noble, no question about it. Their methods were a little more fringe. Robin Hood threw huge galas in the city with A-list celebrities and entertainers who pandered to billionaires so enraptured in their glorious deeds that they failed to notice life was imitating art, and Robin Hood was liberating them of their loot. In some sense, it was a victimless crime. Fat cats with big cheese were helping to fund programs for disadvantaged, inner-city youth with limited resources and few opportunities. The star-studded board of merry men and wanton wenches stalked drunk and foolish noblemen, and then shot blazing arrows with pinpoint precision.

In order to impress Gwyneth Paltrow, one of Harvey's minions who'd been planted at his table, Sidney pledged a whopping $10 million to Robin Hood. Generally, the men in designer green tights were happy if they could bleed a few hundred G's out of a whale like Sidney. But this was awesome by any measure. $10 million was a trophy pledge, and it made an impression.

Gwyneth was on the phone with Sidney almost every day for several weeks following the whopper, teasing, cooing, giggling and cajoling. She referred to Sidney as her boyfriend. She invited him to London to visit her on set of some new Miramax video. I listened to a few of their calls. She was a convincing actress, but she was only the chum, and Weinstein was now Ishmael. Weinstein didn't have nice tits or a cute ass, so he took a much more direct approach.

Gweneth Paltrow with Sidney at the Robin Hood Gala
(Harvey Weinstein in background zipping his fly)

"Sidney, bubbie, I love what you've done with the place." Weinstein surveyed the scene, no effort to conceal his contempt for the set decorations. He shot some glances around the room, probably making a mental record of the assorted freaks and oddities. The camera pans the room slowly, allowing the audience an intimate appreciation of the bizarre scenes inside the goldmine asylum. Cut to obese wheezing octogenarian with a fat wallet and a weakness for waifish blonde starlets. Seated next to the beached whale on the huge hospital bed is the slimy producer smoking a cigarette and processing the buffoonery.

Weinstein leaned over and ashed his cigarette into the huge Jägermeister ashtray sitting on Sidney's chest. I detected a slight furrow in Sidney's brow, as if he was mildly irritated that Weinstein violated his restricted ashtray airspace.

"So I brought some beautiful trailers for you to see. These movies will be fucking cash cows, bigger than Grey Goose, and I am giving you a sweetheart opportunity to get in early, before anyone else. Friends and family only. That's it. Actually, fuck family. I wouldn't even let my own mother into a deal this good. She would disown me and start ripping her schmatas if she knew what she was missing." Harvey turned to one of his entourage. "Stuart. DVD."

Stuart, a slender man sporting a faux hawk and chunky plastic glasses, emerged and opened a Gucci man purse. He produced a single shiny DVD and presented it to Weinstein who held it aloft, like the Holy Grail, for all to crave and covet. Behold, a Weinstein Company Production!

Sidney was not impressed. Harvey should have known that a consummate salesman can smell another salesman's foul wind from a country mile. Weinstein assumed Sidney would be a blockbuster piñata, but Sidney had industry connections and he knew how the movie business worked. Motion pictures are, notoriously, the worst possible investments for outside investors. Producers do not need special effects to make net profits disappear. A movie can make a titanic amount of gross revenue, and still show a negative net. It would be highly unusual and inefficient for a movie to show high nets.

Sidney made no effort to accept Weinstein's gift. He stared at the DVD in Harvey's hand for several moments, took a long draw from his cigar, and exhaled in Harvey's direction. "Danny, put the *Brown* video on." There was an audible gasp in the room, and the air was suddenly even thinner and colder than normal. He was going to play the Brown video, and for Harvey Weinstein no less. I felt a chill run down my spine. This weird scene was becoming weirder by the moment. The Brown video was a roughly shot home movie documenting Sidney's appearance at the Brown University commencement after he gave a colossal donation and became their all-time most generous private benefactor. Sidney wanted to ensure that Brown students would never be forced to withdraw due to inability to afford the steep tuition, as he claimed happened to him, so in September 2004 he created a scholarship program with a $120 million donation. Brown rolled out the red carpet for him. They invited him and the entourage to attend the commencement, and they drove him around in his own personalized Hummer golf cart as crowds of students and faculty cheered for him like he was a national hero. Sidney waved and cried the entire time, and gave an emotional, Lou Gehrig inspired speech about how it was the greatest day of his life, and how he was leaving everything to his foundation, and how his daughter would carry on his legacy and take care of everything. And it was all captured on video - possibly the most nauseating amateur video ever made. It looked like Katherine Hepburn filmed it after a triple espresso. And Sidney was about to preview it for Weinstein. The man who brought us Lord of the Rings, the English Patient, and Shakespeare in Love was about to preview Shaking in Providence.

The video came sputtering and coughing to life, and it was impossible to watch. Literally. Weinstein forced a smile and lit up another cigarette. Sidney was loving every sickening moment, and he abruptly moved his ashtray out of Weinstein's reach. Weinstein, upon noticing the absence of an ashtray, opted to tap on the carpet. It didn't really matter. The brown shag swallowed the ash without any trouble.

Weinstein's entourage crowded in for a closer view of the video earthquake. I casually made way over to the bar area.

Danny and the Donger were already standing at the bar, and the Donger was holding a diet coke and dealing with a different crisis. The Donger was a chubby Asian golf pro, and he was Sidney's favorite. He drove Sidney's golf cart almost every day, and he'd become the de facto manager of Sidney's golf group. When the team grew to include four professionals and eight amateurs, the Donger would create the daily line-ups and decide who would be golfing with Sidney on any particular day. Golfers fell in and out of favor constantly, with little rhyme or reason. One golfer was let go for wearing sweat pants on Sidney's jet.

"Danny, you are supposed to take this drink to Weinstein," the Donger held the diet coke out to Danny.

"Fuck you, Donger. I may be Filipino, but that doesn't make me the house Negro."

The Donger looked like a deer in the headlights. Delivering the beverage was clearly Danny's duty as chief domestic officer, but it was clear that Danny wasn't going to do his job. The Donger wasn't comfortable performing the task either, and they were locked in a tense standoff. None of the assembled spectators were offering assistance.

Thankfully, MOF broke the tension when she made her grand entrance. She burst into the bedroom wearing knee-high rubber boots and a transparent negligee that didn't leave enough to the imagination, and she accessorized with some kind of hat and veil that made her look like some kind of boudoir beekeeper. She was also pulling Jagey on his fecal gurney. MOF was convinced that this was her best opportunity to get discovered, and she scooped the diet coke out of the Donger's hands.

"Mr. Weinstein, here's your cocktail." She giggled and placed the drink between his legs. The dazed expression on Weinstein's face was pure Hollywood magic. He had no clue what horror had just bombed his romcom. MOF sat down on the bed next to him and placed her hand on his thigh, alarmingly close to the danger zone. Weinstein froze, speechless for the first time since entering the scene. He alternated between staring at MOF and the grim beast grunting on the shit trolley.

"Mr. Weinstein, may I call you Harvey? I have something special, just for you. But first close your eyes."

"What?" Weinstein looked around the room, hoping someone would let him in on the joke.

"Close your eyes."

"Okay." He smirked and shut his eyes. Big mistake. MOF leaned in and kissed him directly on the lips. Weinstein sat paralyzed.

MOF finally unclenched, Weinstein opened his eyes and he had a look on his face like he'd just been French kissed by his grandmother. "Let's do lunch. Call me." MOF giggled and curtsied and made her grand exit, diarrhea dog trailing and attempting to wag his crusty tail.

Sidney, who had been quietly reliving his glory days at Brown and ignoring the impromptu freak show next to him, yelled at Danny to turn the volume up. He finally looked over at Weinstein.

"Harvey, you alright? Look like you seen a ghost"

Harvey was still in distress, wondering what the hell was going on in this house of horrors and whether he now needed a course of antibiotics and a tetanus shot.

"So, Harvey, who's going to play me?"

"What?" Harvey coughed and picked up the diet coke. He sniffed it a few times.

"In the movie?"

"What movie?"

"I have it narrowed down to Warren Beatty or Robert Redford."

"What the hell are you talking about?"

"The movie. The movie you are going to make about me. I am the world's greatest story. I am the most interesting man you'll ever meet. Isn't that why you're here? To make a movie about me?"

....

I left Sidney's room and made my way downstairs. As I passed the window to the backyard, I could see MOF outside. She was seated at a small table, and she appeared to be having a tea party with Jagey and two large stuffed animals – a gopher and a beaver. MOF was pouring tea into their cups and chatting away. I cracked the door open.

"Two lumps? Mrs. Pettigrew, you have such a sweet tooth. So, as I was telling you and Mrs. Crabtree before we were so rudely interrupted by Jagey's bowel movement, Harvey has invited me to Hollywood to test for one of his upcoming projects. It's for the lead in an independent film about a brilliant woman who was born with two brains. The brains spoke to each other in different languages, but they understood each other perfectly and had very few tiffs, except when one forgot where the other one buried the bullion. The brilliant two-brained woman married a beggar but her brains enabled them to become rich beyond their wildest imagination when she created an enchanted drink that caused people to grow a second brain that could speak to them in Chinese. So exciting, I know. Nudity? Well, maybe some, but only brief and tasteful. Who wants more tea?"

....

Several weeks later there was another cavalcade of black town cars in Sidney's driveway, and I was concerned that Weinstein had returned for another swing, although that seemed unlikely.

Sidney was sitting at the conference table with one person of interest, and they were discussing something to do with golf resorts and development. I assumed Sidney was telling him about our Bahamas project. Enormous bodyguards surrounded the table, but these guys looked a little rougher than the standard issue security. I also saw Mr. Brown and some of Sidney's security team stationed throughout room. I walked over to Mr. Brown. He didn't say anything, but he handed me a business card. The card belonged to a John Magglioco, and it identified Mr. Magglioco as the owner of Peerless Distributors, a large beverage distributorship in New York/New Jersey area.

The card did not disclose that Mr. Magglioco was also a made member of the Profaci/Colombo family, one of New York's Five Families. Mr. Magglioco was pure, red-blooded Cosa Nostra.

"Sidney, have you ever considered building a golf resort in Sicily?" Magglioco had heard about our concept, and he was trying to pitch Sidney on Sicilian golf and real estate development. He had a professional prospectus for a golf resort he was building in the mafia's birthplace, and he was looking for partners.

I almost expected Luca Brazzi to come limping through the door holding a bloody Big Bertha. Sidney needed to maintain good relationships with distributors, but this deal was clearly outside normal business and an offer he could easily refuse. I was a little disappointed he didn't want to send me to Sicily for research, but I was thankful we didn't have partners who would fit us with custom concrete golf shoes if things went south.

....

Sidney wasn't feeling well. He'd been to see some cardio and respiratory specialists, and it was apparent his condition was deteriorating.

I walked into the room. He was playing bridge with some of the golfers, but he seemed frail and in need of sleep. He looked up from his hand, saw me walk in, and perked up immediately.

"Everyone, out." Sidney threw his cards down. "I need a minute."

The assembled crowd quickly vacated, and I was sure that Danny was outside glued to the baby monitor.

"Seth, I want you to go see someone." He handed me a note with a name and a number. It was not a phone number, and it had many zeros.

"What's this?"

"The name of an old friend. I want you to find him, and give him a check. Polly will have it ready for you."

I looked at the paper again. "Is that the checking account number?"

"No, genius, that's the amount of the check."

I drove to the office and Polly was waiting with a check and a crappy rental car. The rental car was an old Nissan SUV, and it was even fouler than Polly's standard selections. I was assigned to deliver it to Sidney's granddaughter at Cornell. She was already driving a company owned Volvo, but she was apparently unhappy with it, so I was bringing the Nissan to swap out. I could not imagine anyone being happy with the shitty Pathfinder I was delivering, but I was only following orders. By happy coincidence, Sidney's soon to be extremely wealthy friend also lived in upstate New York, very close to Ithaca. My mission was to deliver the Pathfinder to Sidney's granddaughter, take the Volvo, and then deliver the check to Sidney's friend on the way home.

My crusade to Cornell was much different this time around. It was the first time I'd gone back in over 10 years, and even though I didn't quite have everything I'd hoped for, I was probably much closer than I thought. I took Cooper and we stayed in the Statler Hotel on campus. The Cornell campus is dog friendly pursuant to the dying wishes of a dog-loving whale donor, and Cooper took full advantage. He loved running around the quad chasing squirrels and other dogs. Fall was just starting, and Cooper had never seen piles of leaves. They weren't piles when he got done with them. He also managed to attract the attention of a few cute coeds, which didn't bother me in the least. I kicked myself for not getting a dog the first time around.

I made the car swap with Sidney's granddaughter, and the Volvo was much nicer than I expected. It turned out to be a speedy turbo charged sedan, and besides a few conspicuous dents in the front right bumper and hood, it was a peach. I felt bad when I saw the look on Sidney's granddaughter's face when I rolled up in the exchange vehicle, but I was only the messenger. I wanted to explain that I had no participation in the selection process, but the point seemed moot so I kept quiet and handed her the keys.

188

Cooper and I drove from Cornell to meet Sidney's old friend, who was extremely happy to see us, and then we zipped back to New Rochelle. I could not figure out why Sidney's granddaughter was unhappy with the Volvo until Chad explained the dents. Before the granddaughter acquired the car, one of Sidney's drivers was racing the Volvo through Manhattan when he clipped a pedestrian who was blabbing away on a cell phone, totally absorbed and unaware that he was crossing on red and about to die. Sidney's driver was ultimately exonerated, and the company attorneys breathed a collective sigh of relief. Nonetheless, the Volvo was a killing machine, and the granddaughter had not been made aware of the car's bad mojo when she took delivery. The dinged death-ride was a deal breaker, so Polly crammed her ungrateful backside into a crappy Nissan to show her who the real boss was.

Chapter 15
Banana Daiquiri

In early 2005 I flew back to the Bahamas to look at a property that blipped on our radar. The Cotton Bay Club on South Eleuthera was for sale. Our strategy had evolved from developing an uninhabited, undeveloped island to purchasing a large undeveloped tract on a developed island. Eleuthera was a huge island just south of Nassau with limited development. It had airports and utilities and infrastructure, although much of it needed major upgrading.

The Cotton Bay Club was built on land that had once been part of the empire built by Arthur Vining Davis, the great aluminum industrialist and founder of Alcoa. It was subsequently acquired by Juan Trippe, then the head of Pan Am. Trippe built a pimping beachfront hotel and golf course, and it was a swanky place for many years. Rumors of high society scandal and rum soaked orgies with jetsetters and wanton flight attendants abounded. It was a beautiful piece of seaside property, with white sandy beaches, hot tub water and a classic Robert Trent Jones golf course running straight through the middle of it. The property slowly declined after Trippe passed away, and it was never well maintained or cared for by subsequent owners. The hotel and golf course were eventually sold to a billionaire Colombian banker named Luis Carlos Sarmiento-Angulo[18] in the early 1990s. Sarmiento had some connection to Prime Minister Lynden Pindling, godfather of the Bahamas and the Tony Montana of island politics. Sarmiento was expected to rejuvenate the aging property, and the government was happy to let him have a crack at it. But for the next 15 years, very little redevelopment was done.

The Bahamian government wasn't pleased with the situation, but they

---

[18] Sarmiento is now the wealthiest man in Colombia with a net worth estimated at $12 billion as of 2012.

weren't about to make any trouble for an extremely well connected Colombian. They were absolutely thrilled that Sidney was sniffing around Cotton Bay, and it seemed like a perfect fit. It had everything he was looking for. It was close to New York, and it had a nice airport with an extra long runway for big jets (thanks to Trippe). It had decent infrastructure and everything seemed to be in working order, albeit in need of updating and renovation. The buildings would need to be bulldozed and the golf course completely overhauled, but at least we weren't starting from scratch.

We tried to buy the Cotton Bay Club quickly and quietly, and Sarmiento seemed motivated to unload it. We formed a separate entity to keep the transaction confidential. We brought in all our big legal guns, including the Negotiator, the Closer, and the ever-important Bag Man. We agreed on a fair price and the paperwork was ready to be executed. We were in the red zone and sniffing the goal line when Sarmiento's attorneys started to delay. They would ask repetitive questions and make excuses. Meetings were canceled and rescheduled. People with decision-making authority were traveling or busy. I suspect they'd identified Sidney as the buyer, because they reneged on the selling price and demanded a $10 million premium. It was eerily similar to the Roshambo negotiations, but Sarmiento's people were much more polished and macho. We didn't counter. They wasted many thousands of Sidney's dollars and valuable hours of my life, and I was frustrated. The Sarmiento experience was a total loss, and just when I thought it couldn't get any worse, I met the Kingsnake.

Franklyn "Kingsnake" Wilson was a legend in the Bahamas. He was an imposing figure, more like a linebacker than a politico. He had movie star good looks, a successful career as a businessman and land developer, and he was very well connected up and down the Nassau government food chain. Wilson was the godson of Sir Lynden Pindling, Prime Minister of the Bahamas from 1969 to 1992. Pindling is generally regarded as "Father of the Nation" despite serious allegations of corruption during his administration. Sir Lynden had been heavily involved with Colombian Carlos Lehder[19], co-founder and kingpin of the Medellin Cartel who ran a multibillion-dollar cocaine logistics empire from Norman's Cay in the Exumas. Although Sir Lynden denied multiple accusations that he accepted bribes from Lehder in exchange for sheltering his operations, he failed to offer any credible explanation for $60 million in undisclosed income discovered in one of his bank accounts by an internal commission investigating governmental corruption.

Wilson appeared to be cut from the same clothe as his godfather. You don't earn a nickname like Kingsnake being an eagle scout. He was part of an investment group that acquired a considerable amount of prime real estate on Eleuthera. And it had clear title, which was a huge bonus. Title issues are a very nebulous and sordid affair in the Bahamas. The pirates, shipwreckers, and missionaries who'd established the Bahamas stole most of the land from the natives, and it's difficult at best to establish a clear chain of clean title to any parcel of land, particularly sizable oceanfront parcels. Good government connections can definitely help sanitize and expedite the process.

During our Sarmiento negotiations, Wilson was tipped off that an American billionaire was interested in acquiring the Cotton Bay Club. He slithered over and tempted us with several suspect opportunities in and around Eleuthera. My meetings with him were also useless, time consuming, frustrating and expensive, albeit more colorful and exciting than the Sarmiento meetings. Generally, negotiations with Wilson and his group involved a lot of feigned humility and obsequiousness, followed by prolonged posturing and protesting, and finally eroding into obscenity filled shouting matches. At one of the lowest points, I was pretty sure he would have swung at me if I'd been seated any closer to him. During another memorable meeting in a suite at the Atlantis, a young prostitute knocked on our door and claimed she was locked out of her room. She was

---

[19] Ledher's story was the subject of the 2004 movie *Blow* starring Johnny Depp.

gorgeous and wasted, and it was 9am in the morning. I got the feeling Wilson was playing games and trying to distract me. The Eleuthera deal never went anywhere, and more of Sidney's precious time was wasted.

One of the few redeeming experiences on Eleuthera was a dinner party Wilson hosted in the wine dungeon at the Greycliff Hotel in Nassau. The food and wine were exceptional, and the cave was cold, creepy, and kind of magical. It was filled with priceless vintages of French, Italian and California wines, and possibly the skeletal remains of former business partners. Wilson ordered off the menu and paired the delicious food with vintage Bordeaux and California Cabernet.

Wilson and his family were entwined in poisonwood. His gorgeous princesses both attended Ivy-league law schools, and his wife was a delightful and charming socialite. Dining with them was so pleasant and interesting that it was difficult to remember that I was dealing with potentially dangerous characters. It was like all rumors and innuendo disappeared, and there was no trace evidence of fangs or toxin. The Wilsons reminded me of some of the most prominent families in the United States and Canada (Kennedy, Bronfman, Annenberg, etc.) whose fortunes were derived from colossal criminal enterprises and prodigious corruption.[20] The immoral transgressions of the first generation, which result in massive wealth accumulation, are absolved with the succession of subsequent generations of artists, career socialites, and reluctant philanthropists, and all the prior crimes and nastiness are forgotten and forgiven. All the poisons disappear and the blood money is washed clean in the afterglow of good deeds and tax-deductible donations. High society has a short collective memory when substantial wealth is involved.

---

[20] To quote Balzac, *"Behind every great fortune lies a great crime"*.

Chapter 16
JägerBomb

I bolted up wide-awake in a hotel room in New Rochelle. I wasn't sure where I was at first, but I knew it was either late at night or early in the morning. It was that magical moment when the previous night slams into the next day like a freight train. It was still very dark, the room was spinning, I couldn't focus and my ears were ringing. It was the summer of 2005, and I'd been spending a lot of time traveling and promoting the brand. I was slightly ahead of the elephants, but the pack was closing and I had to pace myself to avoid exhaustion and cardiac arrest. I didn't want to die alone in a hotel room, naked and fetal, found by a hysterical Mexican maid screaming Santa Marias. I didn't want to expire on a hotel toilet like Elvis, surrounded by cloroxed towels, plastic soaps and toilet paper folded like a flower. But as I sat in bed hearing the piercing rings, I became very concerned about my brain. Could I have sprouted a major brain tumor overnight? Maybe the tequila shots were slowly creeping through my ear canals and launching a sneak attack on my neural circuits, and my brain was activating a mental panic room. As my head cleared and the room came into view, I traced the loud ringing to my cell phone. It was 4:30am, and it could only be one person.

"Good morning Sidney. It's early."

"Couldn't sleep." He coughed and wheezed. I could hear the television in the background. He had terrible insomnia, and Ambien was no longer effective for more than an hour or two. His legs throbbed, he couldn't breathe, and his lungs filled with fluid when he laid down, so now he mostly slept in a recliner. His tired, beat-up body was starting to fail, but his mind was still sharp as a tack and he knew he had limited time and an expired warranty.

"What's up?"

"Come see me. I have an idea."

I pulled myself out of bed, splashed water on my face, threw on some clothes and a ball cap, and arrived at his house around 5am. Sidney was in his recliner smoking and reading his book. He commissioned a professional writer named Martin Marxin to write his personal biography, and Sidney was proofing the manuscript. Marty was his fourth writer in as many years, and from the scowl on Sidney's face it was clear we'd soon be looking for number five. Sidney noticed me standing. "Come sit down," he pointed the claw at the chair next to him.

I sat. Nothing. Sidney was reading. I watched him read, shaking his head and occasionally grunting. This went on for almost two hours, and I was bored out of my skull. I studied the ceiling and the floors, and then I started conjuring designs out of the stains on the carpet. One looked like a brown bunny rabbit with yellowish teeth. Another one was a filthy snowman complete with crusty top hat and a concealed, orange colored weapon. I imagined the bunny and snowman might have known each other at some distant point in the past. Possibly participants in some sordid love triangle involving the dirty caterpillar that uncoiled luridly from my feet to the toilet. I was about to clear my throat to break the silence, when suddenly the intercom crackled to life. "Mr. Frank, Marty is here."

"Great. Send him in. Craig, up."

Craig appeared, as if out of thin air, and adjusted Sidney's recliner into a more upright position. "I'm sorry Seth, I need to meet quickly with Marty to talk about this…book."

"No problem, Mr. Frank, I'll just go wait outside…." I turned to walk out, but Sidney smiled and pointed the claw at my seat.

"No, stay here please. This will only take a minute." Even though he said please, it seemed much more command than request.

Marty breezed in casually and coolly. He was wearing a loud floral shirt and silky Bermuda shorts, and he was chewing on the stump of a fat Cohiba cigar.

Marty always looked like he'd just come from Atlantic City or the racetrack. He saw me sitting by the bed and he gave me a puzzled look, like I'd crashed his birthday party.

"Good morning Sidney, you're looking good." Marty flashed a big fake grin and went to sit down next to me.

"Don't sit down." Marty froze, half way seated, and looked curiously at Sidney and then at me. He smiled and continued moving his rear end towards the seat cushion, assuming Sidney was giving him a good-natured jab. "Did you hear me? Don't sit down." Sidney's bark snapped at my eardrum. Marty stood stiffly, now fully aware that Sidney wasn't kidding. Sidney held the manuscript aloft. "Marty, see this? You know what this is? This is a piece of shit." Sidney explained very calmly, as if solving a simple math equation, and then he casually tossed the script into the toilet next to his bed. The splash momentarily woke a dog that was curled up under the toilet. The fat Labrador lifted her massive head, blinked a few times, and then nestled back down and resumed hibernation.

"Craig, flush it." Craig lumbered over and attempted to flush the 200 plus page manuscript down the can, but it wouldn't go down without a fight. I heard some rumbling and gurgling, but it wasn't a fair fight and the commode quickly surrendered and fell silent.

"Marty, you are, unquestionably, the worst writer ever." Sidney reclined in his bed and raised the backs of his hands to his eyes. He was in a surly mood, which was good to see again after several weeks of malaise. Sidney was a voracious reader. Even when he wasn't feeling well, he read four to five newspapers, and several business and trade periodicals, cover to cover. He loved biographical novels, especially about Winston Churchill and other WWII war heroes. He'd read all of them, and several of them multiple times. He'd read biographies of almost every major historical figure, and he knew garbage when he read it. "You should put 'World's Worst Writer' on your resume." Sidney used the phrase 'World's Best' liberally in his marketing materials (i.e. World's Best Tasting Vodka), so he was thrilled to have the opportunity to use 'World's Worst' in casual conversation. I'd heard him tell Chad he was the world's worst putter several times. Chad spent most of the following year on the practice green. "How much am I paying you?" Sidney knew all of the staffer's salaries to the penny, but he wanted to see Marty squirm.

"Two hundred and seventy-five thousand...before bonus." Marty looked down at his highly polished loafers and twirled the wood buttons on his shirt. I looked around the room. Sidney's personal doctor was in one corner of the suite reviewing paperwork and pretending not to watch. Two of Sidney's chefs were loitering in the kitchenette area of the suite without any pretense of cooking. Craig was sitting at the nurse's station staring at his computer screen but not missing a word. He was a gentle giant with a dry wit and razor sharp intellect.

Sweat was starting to bead on Marty's forehead, and he rubbed his goatee as if pondering whether he should have mentioned his potential bonus compensation. His manuscript was garbage. It was a glorified term paper. I'd spent some time with Marty, and I enjoyed his company. He knew a lot about cigars and wine, and we did extensive research and testing on both. But business is business, and Marty clearly had no business attempting to foist his lousy book on Sidney.

Sidney gave Marty a huge break by hiring him, just like he'd done for all of all of his employees. There wasn't anyone on Sidney's staff or executive team that was hired purely on their merits, and most of his top talent were flawed individuals who would never be considered for equivalent jobs or salaries elsewhere. Sidney's hiring was almost philanthropic. He hired people he liked, and he liked people who were mildly fucked up and wanted more than they deserved.

He opened an extraordinary door for the unworthy, but they still had to pole vault through it. Marty needed to muster his abilities and produce a quality product that would almost substantiate the salary and validate Sidney's decision. This book wasn't going to do any of those things. It was full of facts and dates, but there was no passion or voice. It was empty and lifeless. I suspected that Marty was a more talented writer than suggested by the book, and I knew he'd been occupied with other projects and some personal issues. Marty had been working on Sidney's book for over a year, and he assumed Sidney would never actually take the time to read the full manuscript.

"Marty, I like you, but this book makes me ashamed that I hired you." Sidney could drop a bomb like a B-2. Marty's body was going limp and his face was pale. His goatee looked almost glazed. It was clear that his Sidney Frank gravy train was about to derail.

"Look at Seth over there. He can write, but he's my attorney, not my biographer." Suddenly I went from sideshow freak to center-stage attraction. "Maybe I should pay him double to do both." Sidney puffed his cigar and cackled.

At that very moment, I forgot Marty and felt overwhelmed with pride and consumed with love. I felt like the Grinch right after his heart grew three sizes. No matter how many times Sidney yelled at me, I knew right then and there that I loved that old bastard.

"Marty, you should consider a different career path. Maybe sales. Maybe something else. Now put that book back where it came from. Craig, TV." Craig magically appeared with a TiVo remote control and an empty plastic bag. He turned the TV on to a pre-recorded Yankee game, and Sidney was immediately absorbed into the action and puffing contentedly as if nothing happened. Marty looked dazed, and he scanned the room for a signal or cue from the assembled crowd. Craig was more than happy to oblige.

"Did I just get fired?"

"Yep." Craig smiled.

"What should I do now?"

Craig handed the plastic bag to Marty. "First, I'd fish that shit out of the toilet. Then I'd leave. Quickly."

Marty shuffled out of Sidney's room in a state of shock. He came in for chummy cocktails and chat, and he left with a soggy manuscript and a cold smack of reality. Even though he had it coming, I still felt sorry for him. We were all there for Sidney's personal amusement, and it was far from reality, but you still felt bad when a Sidney tsunami decimated someone's little slice of paradise.

I watched Sidney watching the game. He seemed indifferent to the trauma he'd just inflicted, but finding a good biographer was a high priority, and time was not his friend. I wondered if he had any remorse about the distress he'd just caused Marty. He could definitely be cold when he suspected someone was taking advantage of his generosity.

"You wanted to see me?"

Sidney looked at me with a slightly confused expression, as if he'd forgotten I was there. "Yes, I had something important to tell you, but I can't remember now. Want to play some cards? Craig, Cards."

Craig appeared with everything we needed. Table, cards, even custom poker chips with a tiny image of Sidney wearing a flashy fluorescent suit. We played a few hands of gin. Sidney was quiet, but I knew he was watching me and reading my hands. He knew all the cards I was holding. I didn't get close, didn't even sniff a win, but we played a dozen hands or so.

Sidney studied his hand, "Tough to be away all the time traveling around the world. Seems glamorous, but it's not. I remember how it used to be. I was away during the war. I met some women, but it was tough. I remember a woman I met while serving a tour in India. Her name was Enid Adams, and I will never forget her. Most beautiful girl I'd ever seen. A knockout, and smart. Brains and a body. She was the package. I think about her sometimes, and I hope she is well. I still have photos of her, unless the witch burned them. You ever been in a war?"

"Me? No sir, no wars, unless you count marriage."

Sidney smiled. "Of course. Shit, sometimes it's worse. You are too young to remember Vietnam. You probably don't even know about the Korean War. Doesn't get press these days. It was back in the early 50s. Just as the Korea conflict was brewing, Rosenstiel had a brilliant idea. Overproduce. Wars always caused shortages, especially in whisky. He decided to ramp-up Schenley's production and make millions of additional gallons, and parlay that product into hundreds of millions in quick profits. Lew had the equipment and manpower to do it. He could make more product than almost anyone, except maybe Bronfman. It was his chance to get ahead of Mr. Sam for the first time. He hated Seagram's with a passion you can't believe, and nothing would have given him more pleasure than beating Bronfman at his own game. And it would have worked, except for one small glitch."

Sidney looked at me as if I'd fill in the blank. I looked back at him blankly. "What was the glitch?"

"Do you know how long the Korean War lasted?"

"Nope."

"Well for fuck's sake! Me neither, but it was too damn fast, and that's the point. And then came the problem. Because of the tax structure in place, Lew was going to have to pay excise tax on Schenley's aged whisky. In those days, if you held whisky for more than 8 years, it was considered aged and you'd have to pay the government a $10 excise tax on every gallon every year. This would have cost Schenley over a billion dollars, and forced Lew into the shithouse. And worse, Bronfman would swallow him up for pennies on the dollar, and that was a fate worse than death.

"So Lew hired a guy named Lewis Nichols. Nichols was what you might call a lobbyist these days. Back then we called them bagmen. Nichols worked for the FBI for 30 years, and he had friends like Eisenhower, Johnson, Nixon and Hoover. Good friends to have. So Lew paid this guy 100 grand a year and bought him a beautiful place in Manhattan. 100 grand was a whole lot of simoleons in those days. It was a real sweet deal for Nichols. A lot of people thought Lew was crazy to pay him that much, but it was a good investment.

"Nichols greased just about every asshole in D.C., especially Lyndon Johnson. Lew had Johnson in his pocket. Paid him off for years, even before he became President. Johnson was crooked as a donkey's dick. I personally delivered a suitcase to him that Lew strictly forbade me to open. I opened it first chance I got. It was stuffed with stacks of twenties.

"So Nichols was persuasive, and he even wrangled some private meetings for Lew with President Eisenhower at the White House. Can you imagine? Lew and Ike drinking tea and discussing international trade policy in the oval office? I'll bet Mamie burned the china after Lew left.

"But Nichols did Lew a big favor by getting the Forand Bill passed in 1958, with Ike's blessing. The Forand Bill deferred the alcohol excise tax from 8 years to 20 years. It gave Lew 12 more years to unload the surplus whisky, and saved Lew billions of dollars and his ass." Sidney smiled and looked at me. "But he still had a lot of product to move. What's the best way to move product quickly?"

A tiny brain bulb flickered, "War?"

"Not just a war, but a long war. Juice consumption goes way up during wars, plus there's an ingenious bonus most people never considered. But Lew wasn't most people." Sidney looked around again and leaned in, as if he was about to disclose the location of Jimmy Hoffa's remains.

"Wars create alcoholics and drug addicts."

"Really?"

"No, not really. I make shit up to amuse you. Lew hired experts to run secret studies on troops returning home after seeing action on the battlefield. And you know what they learned?"

"Wars create alcoholics and drug addicts?"

"A big percentage of combat vets become alcoholics, and the demand for product skyrockets during and after wars. A war was a perfect marketing vehicle for Lew's products. He was making money going in, and more on the back end. And it was free, at least for Lew. He was bootstrapping his business to military spending. Greatest thing ever. But why stop there. There's more."

"More?"

"Much more. Vets were also becoming junkies. Asia was exposing young soldiers to opium and heroin, and they were getting hooked on smack. And guess who controlled the major heroin channels into the United States?"

"Lew?"

"And Lansky and an Italian fella named Lucky Lucianno. They had operations all over. They had compromised logistics officers flying it in on military transports. They also brought in lots of junk through Cuba and the Bahamas. Hey, that reminds me, I just remembered what I wanted to see you about. You need to go to the Bahamas, and you need to go today."

"The Bahamas?"

"Yes, the Bahamas."

"Today?"

"Jesus. Is there an echo? Today. Not tomorrow. Not next week. The Bahamas. Tooday.

"Why?"

"I had a dream about a cat."

"An imaginary cat told you that I should go to the Bahamas?

"Yes."

"Any particular Island?"

"Cat Island." Sidney flashed the toothy grin. "Get moving smart ass. I need some sleep.

Chapter 17
Bald Beaver

Cat Island was directly south of Eleuthera, and it was sparsely inhabited. I looked at the map, and it had some interesting elevations and topography. I made a call to Joe Morton, one of our Bahamas brokers, and by sheer coincidence his family happened to own a huge parcel of oceanfront land on Cat Island. Joe wasn't a golfer, but he told me the land was amenable to a golf course and boutique hotel. He'd considered telling me about it when we were looking at the Cotton Bay Club, but there was an issue. Even though the surrounding lands had some utilities, the Morton's parcel was pure jungle. It had absolutely no infrastructure. We would need to do everything. Roads, electricity, water, sewer, etc... Everything.

There was another little hitch he neglected to tell me during our first conversation. Cat Island had a reputation as a staging area for violent gangs of Colombian and Bahamian drug smugglers. The island itself was vast and largely uninhabited, and drug cartels used makeshift airstrips to load and unload small transport planes on their way between Florida and South America. It was also an easy place to hideout due to the dense jungles. Occasionally, people had been known to disappear on Cat Island if they asked too many questions.

In late August 2005, I flew from Nassau to Cat Island in a rental helicopter. My pilot was a former special forces operative, and he could have flown us through a Ferris wheel with his eyes closed, which was good since he smelled like he ate his raisin bran with dark rum instead of milk. Maybe there was some truth to Sidney's theory. Were all vets alcoholics at a minimum?

We spent a day flying over the property and working with satellite engineers to get a 3D topographical map. It was impossible to know exactly what was under the dense jungle canopy without a 3D rendering. The map was a fortune to produce, but from what I could see, it looked good. Really good. This piece of land had everything we were looking for. Elevation, contours, beautiful rocky stretches of coastline, and ivory white sandy beaches.

We quickly and quietly negotiated a deal to buy the property for $14 million. It was the most painless Bahamian negotiation to date. The vision was starting to take shape, but we had a long way to go. We would need government approval and a good golf course designer. Sidney wanted Rees Jones, the official "doctor" of designing U.S. Open courses, to create the course, and we retained a well-connected Bahamian law firm to represent us in the deal. We then submitted all of the initial plans and applications for Poisonwood to the Bahamian government for approval. The government's blessing was required for the sale, even though the transaction was between private parties. Their rationale was that they would not approve sales or transfers solely for speculative purposes. A buyer needed to show and commit to a cohesive and rational development plan. The government did not want wealthy people purchasing land and letting it mellow, like the Cotton Bay Club. They needed buyers who would build infrastructure, develop and populate the land, bringing commerce and cash flow to the poorer regions of paradise. With everything included in our master plans, our attorneys assured me that approval was a slam-dunk.

I'd met with almost every Bahamian official, and I was also actively scouting local New Blight talent. We would need a lot of help to get the project going, and I'd discovered a few local jewels, including a cook named Annie and Mickey the groundskeeper. I was also finding it difficult to keep the project under wraps. We were contacting landscape architects and clubhouse designers, and major golf development news traveled like wildfire. I started getting calls from heavy hitter developers. One day, I got a call on my cell from I number I did not recognize, but I answered anyway.

"Mr. Schechter? My name is Arnold, and I'd like to speak with you about the golf course you're building in the Bahamas. I heard about it from a friend, and I'd like to tell you a little about my development company and explore some partnership opportunities."

His voice sounded very familiar, but I just couldn't place it. "Thanks for the call, Arnold, but I don't think we are taking on partners at this point in time. I'm sure you understand."

"Well, of course I do. No skin off my back."

His voice was so familiar, I was sure I heard it somewhere. "I appreciate that Arnold. It was a real pleasure speaking with you. You know, Arnold, I didn't catch your last name."

"Palmer."

It took a moment or two to register.

I mentioned the call to Chad, but he didn't want to deal with or talk to anyone, even Arnold Palmer, who seemed much more pleasant than Rees Jones. Chad was a true cowboy, and we didn't need partners because we had an unlimited credit line and extremely generous terms at the Bank of Frank.

I planned to spend a solid week on Cat Island. I booked a room at the Greenwood and scheduled meetings with everyone we would need. Rees Jones was sending a crew out. I had landscape architects, hotel architects, spa designers, clubhouse designers, and hotel management companies on the way or on the phone. You name it, I had a meeting scheduled with it. I had meetings to schedule future meetings. My next week was completely booked.

I was also ready for my first ground assault of the property. I still hadn't actually set foot on the property because it was so remote and difficult to access by land. I rented a 4-wheel drive ground assault vehicle, and I had maps, machetes and Haitians. All systems were go, the green light was blinking and the countdown was on when my satellite phone rang.

"Hello Seth. How's everything?"

"Everything is perfect, Sidney. I am finally going in tomorrow to bushwhack."

"Sounds good. Chad has been showing me the photos. Looks beautiful.

You guys are doing good work." I'm sure Chad was taking all the credit, but I really didn't care. "Right now I need your help on something else. We are flying to London tomorrow. Probably for a month or so. I'm donating a million dollars to the Prince's Trust, and he's giving me an ugly bronze sculpture. I'm bringing some of the surviving Eagle Squadron members, and also setting up memorials for R.J. Mitchell and Alan Turing, something the Brits should have done years ago. Meet us there."

Chapter 18
Whiskey Dick

In early September of 2005, I put Cat Island on hold and flew from the Bahamas to London on British Airways in the economy-plus section because Polly wouldn't approve me for business class. Economy-plus was just slightly better than coach - you got a little more legroom and a few less screaming babies.

Sidney booked an entire wing at Claridge's, the posh and storied London hotel. It was his favorite. "See this room?" Sidney would direct the claw at some random suite, "I stayed here with Skippy in 1954. We hosted a big party for the Park and Tilford acquisition. Best party of my life." Sidney loved Claridge's. It was flooded with hazy, gin soaked memories of his glory days with Schenley. It was elegant and understated, and the service was impeccable. The doorman always knew your name and how to get anything you needed. In fact, he probably knew a little too much, and then some. Sidney reserved a corner suite for himself. They'd offered him a more grandiose penthouse, but he selected a room that had some kind of sentimental significance.

My first official assignment in London was escorting a group of bona fide war heroes and MOF to a cocktail party hosted by the Royal Air Force in honor of the 65th anniversary of the Battle of Britain. Sidney flew a group of surviving Eagle Squadron members to London, first class all expenses paid. And they were first class men - some of the greatest guys I'd ever met. The Eagle Squadron were American pilots who volunteered to fly Supermarine Spitfire and P51 Mustang fighter planes for the British Royal Air Force before the United States entered WWII, and they were still as spry and salty as ever. These guys weren't afraid of anything. Many had flown numerous combat missions and dogfights over enemy lines in flying machines that were little more than a metal coffin with a propeller, wings and guns. Our group of Eagles collectively had hundreds of confirmed kills and several were fighter ace status. They put their lives on the line to protect

England from the Nazis, and the British were extremely grateful for their sacrifices. They didn't make soldiers like these guys anymore.

The RAF threw a nice party, and MOF was mostly appropriate and well behaved, all things considered. I was having a good time talking to the Eagles and hearing their stories when I felt a light tap on my shoulder and heard a whimsical voice chirping near my ear.

"Beg your pardon sir, but are you Seth Schechter, counselor to a Mr. Sidney Frank?"

I turned and looked at the tapper. He was a quirky and amusing looking chap, with a little snicker on his pink cheeks, a receding hairline, a button nose and cheery disposition. He seemed the proper English gentlemen. I was wary.

"Why?"

"Allow me to introduce myself. Randolph Churchill IV."

Holy shit. I was talking to Randolph Churchill.

"My father is Winston S. Churchill III."

"Pleasure." It's a Churchill. I resumed my conversation comparing the virtues of the Spitfire to the P51 Mustang. The P51 was faster, had bigger guns, more artillery storage and a range four times farther than the Spitfire. All concurred that the Spitfire saved Britain, and the P51 ended WWII.

"I understand that your benefactor is an admirer of my great grandfather, Sir Winston Churchill."

"Yes. One of his heroes," I smiled.

Randolph passed me his business card. He was an associate with Rathbones, a London based financial services company. "I'd love to take you and Sidney to see Sir Winston's war room. Are you available sometime this week?" Randolph had done his homework. You can't donate a million dollars to the Prince's Trust or set up memorials for British war heroes and hope to fly under the Churchill's radar. Randolph was good. He was polished. Sidney loved Churchill, and was going to love Randolph.

"Well, let me think. Our schedule is tight. Tomorrow we are going to the Royal Science Museum to dedicate the R.J. Mitchell exhibit. The next day we are off to Bletchley Park to dedicate the new Alan Turing wing. Friday we meet Prince Charles and Lady Camilla. But, I'm sure we can squeeze you in somewhere."

"Splendid."

....

We had a busy schedule. One of Sidney's main reasons for coming to London was next on the hit parade. We were all going to the London's Science Museum for the unveiling of a sculpture of R.J. Mitchell that Sidney commissioned. Mitchell was the inventor of the Supermarine Spitfire, and Sidney believed that Mitchell was a true unsung war hero. According to Sidney, the Spitfire was one of the reasons the allied forces won WWII, and Mitchell never received the recognition he rightly deserved. So he was doing something about it.

Sidney commissioned a sculpture of Mitchell that was made from 400,000 small pieces of grey slate, and had it installed in the Science Museum while they were having a major exhibition dedicated to R.J. Mitchell and his Spitfire (which Sidney also commissioned and funded). They sculpture was very unusual, and strangely lifelike. It bore an uncanny resemblance to Mitchell, although he was now monochromatic and coated with very tiny rocks. He looked very much like some kind of new Marvel Comics superhero named "Spitfire Man". Sidney loved it. Like an Agam work, the Mitchell sculpture seemed to move and morph as you walked around it and shadows and light changed. Words just can't do it justice.

Spitfire Man (aka R.J. Mitchell)

The museum dedicated the Mitchell statue with grand gestures and a big fanfare, and they invited local press, WWII veterans and celebrities, including Mitchell's son Gordon who was 85 at the time. Sidney gave a brief speech and unveiled the statue and everyone gasped in awe. Some of the assembled guests gasped for more oxygen from their respirator tanks.

....

The day following the R.J. Mitchell event was another important dedication at Bletchley Park. Bletchley was the nerve center of England's

212

decryption unit, and the superstar of the decryption unit was a man named Alan Turing. Many people consider Turning to be the father of computer science and artificial intelligence. His code-breaking contributions were integral in decoding the German Enigma cipher, giving the Allied forces a huge advantage over Germany and leading to their defeat in 1945. Turing was a genius cryptanalyst and war hero who never received the gratitude of his nation or the world. In point of fact, quite the opposite.

There is no question that Turing was one of England's national treasures. There is also no question that Turing was gay, and in the 1950s homosexuality was still illegal in England. In 1952, after helping rid the world of the scourge of Hitler and Nazism, Turing was prosecuted by the British government for engaging in consensual sex with another adult male. He was chemically castrated, but worst of all his security clearances were denied and he was no longer allowed to do the work he loved. His beloved country's intolerance and inhumanity overwhelmed him, and he killed himself in 1954 by eating an apple filled with cyanide, reminiscent of a true life sleeping beauty except he never woke up again. Some believe he was poisoned because he knew too much.

The British government issued a formal apology to Turing in 2009, but until then he had received almost no national recognition for his extraordinary contributions to humanity. Sidney wanted to do more, so he commissioned another morphing slate sculpture of Turing to be installed in the bunker at Bletchley where he did the majority of his work.

Alan Turing and his Enigma Machine

Sidney also made a large donation to Bletchley to incentivize them to install the slate sculpture. Bletchley threw a nice dedication ceremony and reception to celebrate the gift, but Sidney was preoccupied and we didn't stay long. We had to squeeze another major event into the itinerary, and Sidney was really excited about this one.

Chapter 19

Johnnie Highballs

Sidney on Churchill's Chair. Winston III in the background.

Never was so much owed by so many to Sidney Frank.

Sidney sat proudly on the British throne of power, one of his most sacred and revered seats in history, puffing a big cigar and wearing an ear-to-ear grin. It was not some jewel-encrusted throne in Buckingham Palace. This was Sir Winston Churchill's seat in his underground war room. This was the historic hot seat where Churchill strategized and commanded British forces while Nazi bombs rained on London. The Churchills opened up the War Museum underneath the Treasury building for Sidney's personal amusement, and he loved it. This was better than Disneyland for a Churchill fanatic like Sidney. And he had a backstage, all-access pass. He was allowed to play on the rides, to sit on the plastic treasure trove and share a mug of grog with the Pirates of the Caribbean.

Winston Churchill III, grandson of the legendary Sir Winston, was leading this parade. He was a playboy with slick grey hair and a tan that George Hamilton would have envied. Winston III had served seven years in the House of Commons, but after mounting bills and public service pay, he decided to see what his country could do for him. He auctioned off many of his grandfather's priceless papers and artifacts, including the original Finest Hour speech, for $20 million dollars. Winnie was also connected to a number of socialites and high maintenance women, including Soraya Khashoggi, the ex-wife of Saudi arms dealer Adnan Khashoggi.

Randolph was playing the dutiful son, following his father and chuckling at his fond recollections of crusty old gramps with his omnipresent cigar and diluted whiskey snifter. Winnie and Randy were a dangerous duo. I wondered how many wealthy admirers opened their vaults after a privately curated showing of the Churchill collection. Judging from their donor wall of fame, more than a few.

"No one is allowed back here, except for you my good friend." Winston smiled. His deeply tan skin creased and crinkled around his twinkly blue eyes. "My grandfather would have been honored. And we've arranged for a private tour of Chartwell, my grandfather's ancestral country estate, and lunch at one of our favorite greasy spoons. Please, the cars are waiting." Danny and the guards lifted Sidney from his perch and rolled him out the door to a waiting armored limo.

I felt that familiar tapping on my shoulder. "Mr. Schechter, you will ride with me." Randolph caught me a little off guard, but I rolled with it.

I was surprised, and a little disappointed, by the modest BMW wagon that he was driving. I was expecting an Aston Martin or Jaguar. Something more Bond-like and less Mr. Bean-like. But in a way, I was relieved. How bad could he be driving a BMW wagon? I relaxed as we made our way out of London, fully prepared to enjoy a pleasant drive into the country.

"So, it seemed like Sidney is enjoying himself."

"Yep."

"And you are his counselor, and you advise him and his foundation?"

I started to feel a pinch of tension in the pit of up my stomach.

"You must realize we don't do this type of thing for everyone. This is Top shelf, I assume Sidney will show his appreciation?"

"He will." I looked out the window and watched the tightly packed London flats flying through my periphery. I knew the proposition was coming at some point, but I didn't expect Randolph to be so direct. I was expecting a nice note on fine parchment, sealed with a wax and stamped with the Churchill crest. Not the classic old hard sell in a soccer mom-mobile.

"Possibly through a donation to the Churchill Museum? We have many American patrons. The Annenbergs are major supporters of the Churchill Museum. Are you familiar with them?"

"Very. Lee Annenberg was Sidney's former mother-in-law, years before she became a diplomat. He knew her back when she was a mobster moll shagging her way up the food chain."

We spent the remainder of the journey enjoying the lovely British country in silence.

....

Last but very far from least, Sidney had a private meet and greet with Prince Charles at Buckingham Palace. His Royal Highness wanted to thank Sidney personally for the million-dollar donation the Prince's Trust, and Sidney was happy to show up and accept a bronze replica of the 65th Battle of Brittan memorial. It was not a handsome piece of art, but it was an offer he couldn't refuse.

Sidney was probably the only person in history to arrive for a meet and greet with the Windsors wearing a fluorescent green blazer.

Sidney and Prince Charles at Buckingham Palace

In the image above, Sidney could be a the poster boy for the fringe theorists who believe the British throne uses wealthy Jews, like the Rothschild family, to control international crime syndicates, including opium, blood diamond, and liquor distribution chains. Why the hell would Sidney give such a huge amount of money to the Royals? It just didn't make sense to me initially. They didn't need it. They weren't unrecognized heroes...at least not in my mind.

But then again, it wasn't my mind I was dealing with. Sidney participated in the war effort and lived through the roughest times, and his perspective was flavored by his experiences. In Sidney's reality, his support of Prince Charles and the Churchill family represented tribute to partners that helped defeat the Nazis and liberate victims of unspeakable atrocities, some of whom were his relatives. Winston Churchill was a true hero in every sense of the word. He was one of the greatest wartime leaders in history as well as a Nobel Prize winner in literature. Prince Charles would soon rule a country that, besides being America's closest ally, helped establish Israel as a Jewish State and safe haven for holocaust survivors and war victims. The United Kingdom and the United States were united in a global humanitarian cause that was greater than the sum, and both Britain's future King and most legendary leader should be shown proper respect and gratitude, even if their financial houses were already in good working order.

The Queen is Dead. Long Live the Martini King.

....

There were a few other memorable evenings in London, including the night Sidney and entourage were invited to game at a private casino. The casino owner hosted a lavish and lengthy Indian dinner served by a crew of Ukrainian contortionists. After an incredibly spicy meal, casks of vintage wine and barrels of blended whiskey, a stuffed and shitfaced Sidney moseyed on down to the gaming tables.

The casino owner was trying to contain his merriment. He had a tipsy, mildly demented American whale rolling up to play blackjack. The Yankee piñata was primed, and bendy sirens were luring him to double down and go full monty.

Sidney slapped $50,000 on the opening hand. The casino jockey grinned and the spectators gasped. Sidney had some Bob's your uncle balls and he was throwing down big. Eyes were wide and the room was electric. The cards were dealt. Sidney had two face cards, the dealer a 12. The dealer's hit was a face card, and Sidney won. The crowd cheered and tightened their seat belts.

Sidney stood up abruptly and flashed a toothy grin at the adoring ladies. I immediately had a sinking feeling. Sidney leaned over, grunted and discharged curried gumbo into his diaper. The diaper contained most of it.

"Danny?"

"Yes champ?"

"Let's skedaddle." Sidney grabbed his chips and slogged merrily out followed closely by security and medical crew. The rest of us followed closely behind, but not too close.

The casino owner looked very pale and I think he may have experienced his own muted expulsion as he watched our grand exit.

....

Our crew assembled in the Claridge's bar almost every night. It was one of the hot spots in London, and it was right outside our rooms. Tabloid stars were regularly photographed sneaking in and stumbling out. The tables were small and cozy, and the lounge area was ample and bustling. It was staffed by stunning Baltic women who looked like lingerie models. Chic London hotels imported crews of young Eastern European women because they were incredibly beautiful and willing to work for nothing. They were just happy to get away from long lines for bread and borsht.

Sidney's squadron always had 15 to 20 people drinking cocktails, and we reconfigured tables so we dominated the lounge. We had all the golfers, security, nurses, cooks, and lawyers assembled, and we raised a little ruckus. We engaged in obscene amounts of promotion for many different brands, none of which were Sidney's. We ordered rounds and rounds of drinks, drinks for the house, drinks for the bartenders, doubles for the waitresses. Perturbed bystanders would inquire about our particulars. They could never unravel the mystery, and none of us offered a rational explanation. Even the truth sounded implausible.

"So, how's Enid?" Mr. Brown was knocking back a tall glass of single malt and taking it all in. He leaned back in his chair and savored my confusion.

"Who?"

"Enid" He winked as if he knew something, and he obviously did. Brown was our Claridge's anchor. He was there every night, devising an engagement strategy while defending our position from hostile Russian incursions. I had no idea what he was talking about, and I was trying to relax after three stressful events. I didn't have much on my calendar, and was looking forward to some R&R. Maybe go see Big Ben, Buckingham and all the touristy shit, or buy some hideously expensive Burberry bauble for Laurel. Looked like leisure time was not in my cards.

The name Enid sounded very familiar. Sydney said something about Enid once, but I couldn't place her. "Oh yeah, how could I forget Enid. She's napping in my room. She's a tiger, and double jointed too."

"She's 78." Mr. Brown smiled and sipped his drink.

"Gross."

"You see Sidney today?"

"Nope. I've been a little busy." I'd been on the phone for several hours with attorneys and most of the Cat Island team, reconfiguring my land assault. I couldn't wait to get in there with machetes. London was amusing and I enjoyed spending time with the Eagle Squad guys, but I was getting itchy to return to island business.

"Well, you should go see him. He's got a little project for you." Mr. Brown gave me a wink and kept nursing his cocktail.

....

Sadly, I knew what "little project" really meant. Sidney had a cockamamie errand, and no one else wanted to do it, so I'd been involuntarily volunteered. I'd already delivered ancient newspaper articles to John Malarkey, and old friend of Sidney's who was recovering from hip replacement surgery in a grim and remote London hospital. I handed him the newspapers and snapped a quick photo. The poor old guy had no clue what was happening, and I was quickly invited to leave by hospital security.

John Malarkey displaying the delivered newspaper

I excused myself from the party and took the elevator to Sidney's floor. A guard open the door and escorted me in to his suite. It looked just like home. They'd decorated his room with imported blackout curtains, and the air conditioner was on hyperdrive. Sidney was in his usual repose, semi-naked on his back in bed. His head was propped up with pillows so he could watch TV, although he generally dozed more than he watched. He had his smoking shirt on with all of the assorted holes burned into it, and his huge Jägermeister ashtray was sitting on the asbestos mat covering his chest. There were random playing cards scattered all over the mat. I was in luck. He appeared to be sleeping. I turned around to leave.

"Seth?" Damn, how could he see me with his eyes closed?

"Yes Sidney?"

"I want you to go see Enid."

"Enid?"

"Enid Adams. She's outside of London. Go see if she's comfortable. And give her this note."

I now realize that Project Enid was probably Sidney's primary motivation for returning to England.

Chapter 20
Red Headed Slut

"What do you want?"

"Nothing ma'am. Sorry to intrude. Sidney Frank sent me."

"Yes, I know. I got your message. What does he want?"

Enid Adams lived in a very modest cottage in the country. She lived there alone and took care of all of the chores herself. Her daughter visited from London every couple of weeks to help out. It took me almost three hours to drive there, and she wasn't exactly thrilled to see me.

I thought I'd gone to the wrong house. Time had not been kind to Enid. She had become quite round and wrinkly, and her red ruddy skin was spotted and sun damaged. Her teeth were heavily stained and almost wooden looking, but bad teeth didn't seem uncommon for most Brits. Enid moved around the little cottage very slowly and deliberately, and I could see a walker in the corner that she was too proud to use in my company.

"Sidney sent me to make sure you are comfortable."

"Comfortable?"

"Yes, comfortable."

"Do I appear comfortable to you?"

"Not really, but I'm not sure we're talking about the same kind of comfort."

"So, what you're really asking is, do I need his charity?" This old bird caught on quickly.

"Yes, Mrs. Adams, that's exactly what he wanted to know. Do you need any money." I looked around her little cottage. It had been quaint and maybe charming in its day, but now was shabby and in serious disrepair. Enid was getting far too elderly to keep up with the chores and required maintenance, and it appeared to me that she could use some assistance.

"Well, he has some nerve sending his henchman out here to insult me. I don't need his charity. You can tell that to your master. I don't care if he is the Sultan of Brunei, I won't take a pound. Not a shilling. I have a few aches and pains, and I don't get around so well anymore, but I'm doing just fine." She snorted at me, hobbled into the kitchen and started banging pots and pans around.

I wasn't sure what to do, so I started walking around the living room, waiting for some indication from her as to whether I should stay or go. The walls were covered with photographs of her children and grandchildren. Normal looking British people, nothing exceptional. Then something on the wall caught my eye.

Enid Adams

There was an old dusty photograph of a very beautiful woman. No make-up, no fancy lights, just pure and natural beauty. Her big grey eyes were mesmerizing. Her skin looked like alabaster. The photo reminded me of an old

Hollywood glamour shot, only without the heavy touch ups. I was awestruck. Who was this vintage vision? As I studied the ancient photo, it slowly dawned on me that this exquisite creature was Enid many years ago. She was smiling in the photo, but there was something hidden and mysterious in her eyes, like she had a forbidden secret.

Enid was probably Sidney's true love. I know he had strong feelings for Skippy, including the strong feeling he was going to get very rich, but it wasn't the same thing he felt for Enid. She wasn't wealthy or politically connected, and falling for her provided Sidney no immediate material benefit. His love for Enid was pure, and she broke his heart and left it to rot under the sweltering Karachi sun. She was the one that got away, and he sent me to figure out what he missed.

Sidney fell madly in love with Enid while they were both in India. Sidney was stationed there during his WWII service, and Enid was there as a nurse for the RAF. She had been informed that her husband, Lt. Colonel Thomas Adams, had been captured by the Japanese in Burma and was presumed dead, and Sidney was there to console her and pick up the pieces. He did a good job. They were inseparable for two years.

And then, as if by some kind of Burmese black magic, Colonel Adams reappeared. Burma was liberated, and Adams was released from the prison. He returned to Enid. She was now deeply in love with Sidney, but she felt it was her duty to be with Adams, so Enid let Sidney go. She broke him into a million little pieces, and all the King's horses and men trampled over him again.

"I suppose I'll be going then..." I started feeling guilty about loitering, and Enid was still in the kitchen banging the pots.

"What? Going? Absolutely not. I won't hear of it. I'm making tea."

I took my camera out and snapped a few pictures of her living room and photographs, including a close-up of her old picture.

"What in world do you think you are doing?" She walked out of the kitchen holding two cups of tea on a silver tray.

Before she could turn away, I snapped a photo of her, as I knew that's what Sidney really wanted. That's what I would have wanted. The money shot. I almost didn't want to show him.

"Taking pictures for Sidney."

"Really? Well, it's quite rude to snap a photo without asking first. You didn't even allow me proper time to spruce up."

I didn't have the kind of time that would take. "Sorry. Do you mind if I take a few pictures of your house?" Before she could answer, I aimed and start shooting everything. The dirty walls. The decrepit furniture. Enid was living from Colonel Adams' pension benefits, and those were modest at best.

Enid placed the tray on her coffee table and gingerly sat down on the couch. I could see that she was clearly in pain. Her pain was probably constant and debilitating. I'm sure that taking care of all the household responsibilities was not an easy task, especially out in the country. She still drew water from a well, and heated the house with peat and firewood. She obviously cherished her independence. That was abundantly clear. I'm sure her fierce independence and confidence also beguiled Sidney, on top of her formerly bewitching looks.

I put the camera down. We stared at each other and the walls for about five minutes without saying anything. We both drank our tea politely. I finally broke the tension.

"So, what was Sidney like back when you met?"

She sat silent for what seemed like many minutes, carefully considering her response.

"He was brilliant. He made me laugh and want to live at a time when I wanted to curl up and die. He was one of the kindest and most caring people I ever knew. I loved him more than I thought I was capable, and I'll never forgive myself for leaving him, but I had no choice." She smiled and fell silent. There was a distant, melancholy look in her pale grey eyes. A happy lingering memory. A fading ray of sunshine. I suddenly felt sorry for her. She seemed so frail and lonely.

I walked over and handed her the envelope. She peered at it, and then gave me a quizzical look. She opened the envelope and pulled the note out. She read it. I could see tears welling up in her eyes.

I snapped a few shots of a happier Enid before I left.

Enid Adams

I returned to Claridge's and went directly to Sidney's room. Sidney was in bed smoking and reading a book. I sat down on a chair next to the bed. He didn't look at me.

"How was she?"

"She was ok."

"Yeah? Just ok? Did you give her the note?"

229

"Yes."

"Was she a pain in the ass?

"Yep."

"She hasn't changed."

"She's changed a little."

"You take photos?"

"You want to see them?

"No." Sidney was quiet and pretending to read.

"I saw an old photo of her on the wall."

"Not bad right?" Sidney smiled.

"Yeah. Not bad."

....

I flew directly from London to Cat Island and checked into the Greenwood Hotel. Lucy would be in the kitchen all week, and I resolved to do some serious bushwhacking this time around. I had all the supplies I needed, and the Haitians were on standby. The countdown was on again. I would not be denied.

My cell phone rang. It was Craig back in New York.

"I got some interesting information...." Craig was always coy and mysterious when he had something good.

"Spill it."

"I thought you might want to know that Winston is flying in from London to meet with Sidney and the executive team tomorrow."

"I'm interested. Any idea why?"

"I have an idea."

"Mind telling me?"

"Not at all."

"Is it going to cost me?"

"The usual." I considered it $500 well spent.

"Done."

"Because Winston wants to create Churchill cigars, and he wants Sidney to be his partner."

The Haitians would have to wait, again. I was on the next flight to Nassau, and then on to New York. Winston wanted to pimp out his grandfather's image and family name by developing Winston Churchill brand cigars. He was seeking Sidney's sage wisdom and marketing advice, and a little venture capital between new chums never hurt. After all, Sidney's Midas touch could turn shit into gold, and he had the sterling to float a risky venture with a fancy British socialite. Winston was nobody's fool, and he knew the most important business lesson. Never use your own money if you don't have to.

I walked into SFIC boardroom and scanned the occupants. Sidney had assembled his executive dream team, primed and ready to heap praise and adoration on whatever plan he concocted. They looked unanimously agitated when I walked into the meeting and sat down at the table. I was intruding on their sacred sales domain. I was feeding from their trough and diluting their pie. They had no clue that I was responsible for getting Winston and Sidney in bed in the first place, but I wasn't about to give them the satisfaction.

The executives enlisted the expertise of an eager Davidoff sales representative who was ready to pounce on what must have sounded like a dream come true. The Churchill name was almost synonymous with the image of a cigar, and the Churchill family had never considered licensing their name or Sir Winston's distinctive image to something as vulgar and mundane as a tobacco venture.

Winston waltzed in looking the dapper English gent, draped in a bespoke suite and handmade loafers. He worked the room, pressing the flesh and sharing a chuckle with most of the executives. Sidney was wheeled in last and rolled to the head of the table, cigar in his mouth and his eyes barely open. The London trip had taken a toll on him, and he was still recovering his energy. He was sitting fairly still, and I was not entirely sure he was awake.

We sat through Mr. Davidoff's tediously well-heeled pitch. We feigned interest in his colorful charts and graphs, market research, metrics and forecasts. They would source tobacco from the finest plantations in Nicaragua, and the marketing campaign would be exponential. Churchill cigars would be the biggest thing to come out of England in years. Bigger than the Beatles. Davidoff had gone all out on this sucker. They even prepared branded cigar boxes and mock-up labels with tiny pictures of Sir Winston on the cigar rings. First class. Top shelf. The Davidoff show finally ended, and it was the rep's finest hour. He was prepared to accept Winston's and Sidney's undying gratitude and signatures on the exclusive licensing agreement conveniently stashed in his expensive leather attaché. He primed his Monte Blanc fountain pen out and prepared to bask in mega deal afterglow.

All of the executives at the table looked at Sidney. He was fast asleep, head slumped to the side and cigar dangling dangerously from the corner of his mouth. Sidney's office was filled with hundreds of bottles full of alcohol, and his Cuban combustible could have ignited the world's biggest Molotov cocktail. No one made an overt move to wake Sidney or extinguish the detonator, but several executives eyeballed it cautiously. Some of the executives threw caution to the wind and looked over at Winston. Winston had a perplexed expression, and he was silent for a few minutes while the executives stared.

"Did you say, Nicaragua?"

"Yes. Niiicarrrragua." The *Davidoff* representative looked slightly indignant as he drew out each syllable and rolled his r's.

"Does it have to be Niiicarrrragua?" Winston drew out his syllables also. He wasn't about to suffer condescension from a cheeky tobacco peddler.

"No, of course not. Nicaragua grows the best tobacco, but we could do Honduras, maybe Dominican Republic if you prefer. But I would recommend

Nicaragua for this blend. It's the best option."

"What about Cuba?"

"Cuba?" The word seemed to burn the *Davidoff* rep's lips on the way out, like he'd inhaled from the wrong end.

"Yes, Cuba."

"Simply not. Out of the question."

"Why not?"

"For any number of reasons."

"Well, you may have your reasons and I'm sure they're entirely reasonable, but my grandfather smoked good Cuban cigars exclusively, and any cigar bearing his name and likeness needs to be authentic." Good lord, old Winston III actually had a set and a sack to hold them up. Pappy would have been proud. "I will only make cigars that my grandfather would have smoked. No exceptions."

"That's impossible." The Davidoff rep was irked. This was not going to be the slam-dunk he expected. His thin mustache sagged, and his once shiny suit seemed to have dulled.

"Why not."

"Because, Davidoff doesn't produce in Cuba."

"I see, well, other companies do."

"Yes, but then you could never sell them in the United States."

"No?"

"No. There's a small issue called an embargo."

"Yes, I've heard about that. Well, it's bollocks but I could live with it." All the SFIC executives collectively sighed and pouted.

"Then I suppose we are done here." The rep made no effort to hide his disdain. He'd spent a lot of time polishing his pitch and printing tiny Winston stickers, and it was all for naught. Cuban production would never happen. Churchill cigars would never happen. Cheerio and bugger off.

"What about a dual production?" All executives were now looking at me.

"What's that? Dual production. Please explain." Winston leaned in and turned up the volume in his almost invisible hearing aids.

"Most of the cigar companies that produce in Cuba also produce in other, non-embargoed countries. Cohiba. Montecristo. Romeo & Julietta. We could make both Cuban and non-Cubans under the same Churchill label. Problem solved."

"Wait, wait, hold on. Problem not solved. The Cuban and non-Cuban brands aren't the same companies, even if it would appear so on their labels." The Davidoff aficionado was reengaging. "The non-Cuban brands are produced by companies that stole the Cuban labels and intellectual property rights years ago. Essentially, they are counterfeit brands. Davidoff takes pride in the fact that we never produced cigars in Cuba, and never will." He smiled and looked at the assembled guests triumphantly, as if he'd just cured cancer. I looked over at Sidney and Winston. Winston looked annoyed. Sidney, who had recently awakened, looked confused. He saw me and smiled a little, but I could tell he had no idea where he was or what was happening.

"I like the dual production idea." Winston was ready to start today. I could see the pound signs rolling through his retinas.

"You just can't do it. You can't produce in Cuba, and also sell in the United States. It will never happen."

"We don't have to. We'll sell the non-Cuban cigars domestically, and we'll sell the Cuban cigars everywhere else. We just need to negotiate deals with the original Cuban company and the phony foreign fabricators. Maybe we'll do Nicaraguans for the United States market."

"The Cubans won't go for it."

"Really? Have you ever asked them?"

"No. Why don't you call Fidel and ask him."

Winston and Sidney looked at each other and smiled.

I was on the next plane back to Nassau, but I was not going to Cat Island.

Chapter 21
Cuba Libre

In October of 2005 I found myself standing in line for the CubaJet flight from Nassau to Havana. I noticed some other American travelers standing in line and peering around nervously. It was like we all expected to be busted and searched at any moment, like something out of *Midnight Express*. I pictured several years of marching in tiny circles around a palm tree with other Bahamian prisoners, eating rotten shrimp and coconuts and smoking crappy cigars. I noticed people in line behind me who looked conspicuously inconspicuous, but I tried not to think about them. I was about to embark on a crazy adventure per official orders, and I didn't care whom the company hired to keep tabs on me.

The plane ride was just the appetizer. Everything in the plane's cabin seemed loose or broken, and my seatbelt didn't work. The overhead luggage compartment kept opening and expelling its contents onto passengers below. I didn't want to think about the plane's engine if the cabin was an indicator of maintenance standards. It was like walking into a putrid restroom at a restaurant and wondering if the same squad cleaned the kitchen.

Jose Marti International Airport was antiquated, although it was more modernized than many of the decrepit and deteriorating buildings of Havana. The airport was allegedly going through some kind of major renovations, but the Cuban workers seemed as driven as many of the Central American road-crews I saw during the ill-advised road trips of my youth. They huddled around in large groups, and while a few half-heartedly worked, the others took siestas. Progress moves slowly when you're paid in *cacahuetes*.

I didn't check any bags due to my unfounded fear they would disappear in some Cuban lost baggage vortex, so I humped my luggage through the terminal and was greeted by four National police officers who asked for my passport and then interrogated me for 10 minutes regarding my reasons for being in Cuba. When I told them I was a guest of Partagas, the Red Sea of police parted and I was flushed through like a tiny kernel of corn down Che Guevara's lower intestine. Partagas was the most famous tobacco house in Cuba and a huge source of national pride, and an invitation from them was almost better than an invitation from Fidel.

They were having a lavish party to celebrate a special occasion, and I was staying at the Hotel Nacional. The Nacional was another fading Havana relic that had been a very special place in the distant past. It was the best hotel in Cuba when it opened in 1930, and it catered to guests like John Wayne and Hemingway. But the mob infiltrated it slowly and systemically, and by 1950 Meyer Lansky was heavily invested in the Nacional and its operations. He built a separate wing and opened the Casino Internacional, and it quickly became Havana's high-rolling hot spot. Things kept right on rolling until Castro shut the hotel and casino down in 1960. Since that time, the hotel slowly wilted and decomposed like the rest of Havana around it, although it still retained some traces of its former glory. My room was pleasant despite the fact that my television and toilet were broken. I showered and went downstairs to check out the action.

The hotel bar had some activity. It was a popular spot for Americans, Canadians and Europeans. I bellied up and ordered my first Cuba Libre in Cuba. I glanced around and noticed some suspicious looking characters who seemed out of place in a Havana bar. They looked too clean. As I sat and drank, I again experienced the uneasy feeling that I was being monitored. I was certain that most Americans in Cuba were under observation in some form or another, although it wasn't intrusive and there was no way to avoid it.

I noticed a very attractive girl sitting at the bar a few feet away. She smiled and winked at me. The universal signal. I knew she was a pro, as are many of the Cuban ladies who prowl hotel bars. Prostitution at $100 a pop is a lucrative career in a country where most of population is subsisting on $12 a week and upward mobility is nonexistent.

A car service picked me up at the hotel around 7pm and delivered me to the Partagas factory building. There was a tent set up in the back, and the building was already swarming with Europeans and South Americans when I arrived. There were rumors Fidel might show up, and everything was alive and buzzing.

I made my way to a very special smoking room in the Partagas factory with buttery soft leather recliners. There was a photo on the wall of Arnold Schwarzenegger sitting in the same chairs smoking a fat Partagas cigar. So much for the embargo. The room had tables with numerous humidors containing the rarest vintage cigars in Cuba. Many of these cigars were made with Robaina tobacco, the most revered tobacco house in all of Cuba. Alejandro Robaina was in attendance, and he was holding court on one side of the room. He was so dark and leathery that his head resembled an enormous raisin. He looked like the evolutionary reptilian to human missing link.

Alejandro Robaina

Robaina was the undisputed emperor of Cuban cigars. He started smoking at the tender age of seven, and began working his family's tobacco fields in western Cuba when he was 10. He went on to achieve cult status for the luscious tobacco leaves he grew on his 40-acre plantation, Finca la Piña. I was never a cigar fan before I was sent to Cuba. I recalled the few times I smoked at weddings, probably after a couple of shots of Jägermeister. I always woke up with an excruciating hangover and the suspicion that I'd been tonguing an ashtray. But there was something about smoking a Robaina at the Partagas factory in the heart of Havana that just felt right. I found a chair and reclined with my Robaina in one hand and a snifter of Havana Club rum in the other. The rum and smoke were soothing, and I felt like I could smoke an entire box while melting into that chair.

There were Latin drums and Cuban beats coming from somewhere in the building, and the warm rhythms mixed with sweet smoke and strong drinks were getting me buzzed. I was starting to feel adrenaline and electricity coming up my spine, so I closed my eyes and sank further into the leather chair. I wanted to capture and hold the magic in my mind for as long as possible, but it was hard to focus with all of the commotion around me. I opened my eyes and, like a magic trick, a girl appeared out of the smoke.

She was standing on the opposite side of the room, through the thick cloud of haze, talking to some European guy with blonde spiky hair. I could tell she wasn't listening to a word he said. She was wearing a short, skin-tight dress that displayed her tan, sculpted legs and perfect bubble butt. She noticed me staring and gave me a very slight smile. Just the tiniest little crack of recognition. She had big hazel eyes, dark silky hair, and a flawless athletic body. I had a momentary lapse of reason and too much rum. My brain melted as I walked over to her.

"Hi."

She looked at me and didn't say a word. My rival rolled his eyes and strolled away.

"Do you speak English?"

She nodded. "Very leetle." She told me her name was Daniela and that she worked as a flight attendant for CubaJet. I know she didn't work my flight. I would have remembered her. Her accent seemed Cuban, but I thought I detected a slight South American flavor as well, maybe Brazilian or Colombian. We drank a few more rounds, and between the rum, cigars and drums, I was getting hammered. She invited me to a club with her friends, and I was powerless to resist. We left Partagas and wandered through Havana's crumbling streets and decaying facades, passing vintage American cars, old women with moustaches, old men smoking old cigar butts, starving dogs sleeping on street corners, and dirty children laughing and playing with brightly colored garbage. The Cuban scenery was fascinating, but I was having difficulty appreciating it. Daniela's honeydew skin and sweet rum sweat were intoxicating. We hit about three different clubs, and then returned to the bar at the Nacional. I ordered a round of drinks and went to use the bathroom.

When I returned to the bar, I could have sworn my drink tasted slightly different, but I didn't give it much thought. I was preoccupied.

"Let's go to your room." Daniela grabbed my leg and squeezed hard. She started to walk towards the elevator before I could protest. I wasn't sure what to do, so I followed her.

We got in the elevator together, and I was definitely feeling a little loopy. I'd had a few too many Robainas and way too much rum. I was also feeling a little guilty, although I couldn't think clearly. We were just going to my room, I told myself. Nothing had happened, and nothing was going to happen.

We got to my room and I had trouble opening the door. Daniela was more than happy to assist. She didn't seem all that drunk even though she matched me drink for drink.

She walked in and sat down on the bed. She patted the seat next to her. I sat

239

down and tried to look at her, but I was having trouble focusing. I was also starting to think about my wife, and I was feeling guilty about what I thought might possibly be about to happen.

"I think there might be rum in the mini-bar." I needed more rum like a hole in the head.

"I check." Daniela got up and walked over. She did a straight leg bend over at the mini-bar, and I caught a full shot of her perfect toned and tapered legs coming from what appeared to be a perfect ass and it was all perfectly spectacular. As I stared, I noticed that Daniela's two perfect legs became four perfect legs. I remember laughing and rubbing my eyes, and then I was out.

....

When I regained consciousness the next morning, Daniela was long gone. I was disoriented and woozy with the second worst headache of my life, almost but not quite as bad as the hangover following my welcome night with Sidney's crew. My room had been ransacked. All my clothes, personal items and papers we strewn about the floor. I stood up a little too quickly, and sat right back down before I passed out again. The room was still spinning, but I could think semi-lucidly. I needed water badly. I hobbled to the bathroom and drank directly from the faucet. I probably would have slurped from the toilet if the faucet were broken.

I walked around the room taking inventory. My computer and cell phone were missing, but my Rolex was still on my wrist and my wallet was in my back pocket. I opened my wallet and there was still a wad of bills and all of my credit cards. I picked up the phone and thought about calling security, but what was I going to tell them. I put the phone down and tried to collect my thoughts. Had I been targeted, or was this just a crime of opportunity? Why did she go through my papers and what did she want with my computer? She was going to have a hard time accessing any useful information on it due to the fingerprint reader and airtight security system. She may not have noticed that before she left, but it was just going to be a useless metal box.

I was actually somewhat relieved that my computer was the only missing item, and that I still had my organs in tact. I wondered momentarily what a stolen kidney or heart would be worth on the Cuban black market, but I didn't care to dwell on it. I strongly suspected that Daniela was not Cuban and that someone had hired her to steal my computer, but the question was who? It seemed unlikely that SFIC would take measures this extreme, but then again they were capable of anything. One overriding thought took precedence. I needed to get the fuck out of Cuba.

Chapter 22
Irish Car Bomb

I never said a thing to anyone. The next morning I packed up and got the hell out of Havana as fast as I could. I flew to Nassau for more useless meetings that I couldn't focus on, and then back to New York.

I walked in to Sidney's room. It was a full house again. Along with the usual nurses and golfers, I noticed some doctors and therapists that I'd never seen before. Chad was sitting by the bed reading a magazine.

"How are you Sidney?"

"Great." He smiled and coughed and I heard him gasp for breaths. He wasn't well. He desperately needed a new heart valve, but he couldn't get one because the procedure was too risky for someone in his poor state of health and American doctors would not take the risk. He needed to get better before they would operate on him. Irony can strike in many terrible ways when you are terminal. He made a few extended trips to the hospital in White Plains, but he was now at home resting and trying to improve. "How was Cuba?"

"Interesting. Incredible country, but I think we are going to have some trouble with cigar production. It might be tricky."

"Yeah? That's what I was thinking too. You know what? Fuck it. I already got enough tricky projects, don't need any more bullshit. Let Winston deal with Fidel." Sidney gave me a knowing glance and a nod. "I always enjoyed my trips to Cuba. Went there a few times with Lew and his crew. Lansky ran that place like the emperor of Rome, and he always took good care of us." Sidney smiled and was reflective for a few moments, probably remembering some Cuban concubine. "How's Poisonwood coming along?"

"Everything's on schedule. I still need to have it surveyed, but we should be getting government approval shortly. Our attorneys have assured me that everything checks out, title is clear and good to go." We had recently decided to name the golf course and development Poisonwood. It was the perfect name. Beautiful and dangerous. A championship golf course with an edge. Most people hated the name. Sidney loved it.

"Good." Sidney coughed a little more. He looked around at all of the assembled staff members in the room, most of them loitering and casually burglarizing our conversation. "Let's go for a ride."

The disappointed staffers looked at Sidney and then at me. Chad glanced up from the magazine with a frown.

"A ride?"

"Yes. A ride."

"Ok."

Sidney was rolled to the Maybach and helped into the back seat. Chad followed us out and he started to climb in.

"No. Just Seth."

"What?" Chad managed his best sad puppy dog look. Even I felt a little sorry for him.

"Get back in the house." Chad stared at me and shook his head in disbelief. His world was coming to an end.

Gary started to climb into the drivers seat.

"Seth will drive me."

"Seth?" I was as surprised as Gary. We looked at each other. I had never chauffeured Sidney anywhere, and I had never driven the Maybach.

"Yes.

I got in and started it up. The 550 hp bi-turbos came roaring to life, and the car purred like a Grizzly Bear. I shifted into drive and started rolling out of the driveway.

"Where are we going?"

Silence.

"Mr. Frank?"

Silence.

"Are you alright back there?"

"Just drive."

I drove a few miles into the Westchester countryside, and things were quiet. I was busy trying to keep the car on the narrow roads, which were difficult enough to navigate in a midsize automobile. Westchester was an awful place for driving. The Hutch was designed for horse buggies, not cars, and definitely not German luxury missiles.

"Seth?"

"Yes?"

"Are you listening to me?"

"Yes, Sidney. Always."

"I need to tell you something."

"Okay."

"I got some regrets. Big ones. Most involve women and money. Skippy was both. She was a mess. Some people blame me for her problems and addictions, and a few even thought that I had something to do with her death, that I poisoned her for her money or some crazy shit like that. She didn't have any money after Lew kicked her out of his will. If you ask me, that old piece of shit broke her heart when he picked pussy over his own children, and she never recovered. She lost everything, and she spiraled down. Cancer just fueled her decision to end her life. But I don't want to dwell on her pain. She's at peace and life goes on. And don't get me started on Marian's problems.

"As far as money, I made fortunes and lost fortunes, but money comes and money goes. Money is magnificent, but it's not everything. Sooner or later, you realize that some things are much more important. And you think about all the time you wasted chasing bullshit and illusions, and you get regrets. I realized it too late, but you got your whole life. You're a smart kid, and I like you, so I'm going to give you a piece of advice that I wish someone had given me." Sidney now had my full attention, although I almost drove the car into a ravine. Fortunately he didn't notice. "Get out of this business and do something you care about. Something that makes a difference. Give people opportunities to help themselves. Find unknown heroes and get them known. You like to surf, right? So teach kids to surf. Even better, teach retarded kids to surf. Help abused animals. Do something to help, something you care about. You won't regret it. Trust me on that. You will still be happy and satisfied, even if you don't make any money. You can hold your head up and know that you made the world better. And if you make a little money along the way, and there's no harm in that, then enjoy the shit out of it. But don't let it control you. It will ruin you if you are weak. It will make you doubt everything and mistrust everyone. Even the people you love most of all."

"Ok."

"There's only one thing that's permanent. The most valuable gift you can give, and the one treasure worth guarding with your life."

Sidney sat silently. I waited a few minutes. I thought he might have fallen asleep. I glanced in the rear-view mirror. He was wide-awake.

"Love."

"Sidney?"

"I know, I'm an old fart singing a sad sack song, but it's true. When you get to my age and you've done everything, you will understand. I've had a lot of women in my life, but not much love, at least not real love. And my children are a fucking mess, but I still love them. Someday when you have kids you will understand. Nobody is perfect, and you will screw up and make mistakes, and so will they, trust me on that. But you need to forgive them and love them, or you will regret it.

"I did my best with my kids. I know I wasn't the world's greatest father, but I didn't want them to make the same mistakes I made. I wanted them to be better than me, and I thought that would happen if I gave them everything and saved them from the struggles and suffering I experienced. I didn't want them to know that pain.

"But that was a mistake. I now know that a little suffering is good for kids. It builds their character and makes them appreciate things and understand people better. Suffering makes them better people. So does teaching them to help and to give, and you can't start them too early. Take them to animal shelters, soup kitchens, homeless shelters, wherever. Show them real life. Don't sugar coat it. Show them the shit all around us. They need to see what others lack to appreciate what they got, and they will be happier because there is so much more joy in giving. Encourage them to give whenever they can and any way they can. Let them give their allowance away, or their toys to children that don't have anything. Giving is the best feeling there is. My kids never learned that, and that is my fault. Turns out that wasn't the biggest mistake I made."

"What was your…"

"Don't interrupt, I'm getting to it. Like I said, I made lots of mistakes with my kids, even though I always loved them, but my biggest was not showing them enough affection, or as much as they needed. I thought throwing money counted as love, but it doesn't. I didn't spend enough time with them or really take the time to show them how much I loved them. I was too busy with other bullshit, trying to make money and chasing pussy. I didn't notice that the family poison was making them toxic. By the time I noticed what was happening to them it was too late. They were deep in the disease and there was nothing I could do to get them back.

"The reason I'm telling you all this is that I don't want to see you make the same mistakes I made. You remind me a little of myself, just not as handsome or smart." I glanced in the rear-view mirror and saw the toothy grin.

"I can see my flaws in you. Trust me, you got them. You don't realize it, but you wouldn't be sitting there if you didn't. So do yourself a favor. Go home and love your wife, even if she drives you crazy. And when you have kids, make sure to love them as much as you can. Love them more than that. More than they deserve."

"Ok."

"Good. And promise that you will help my family after I'm gone. They need someone to take care of them, because they damn well can't take care of themselves. It will be difficult, but promise me you will help them, until the time comes. "

"How will I know when the time comes?"

"You will know."

He was quiet and I was hoping tonight's lesson was over.

"Also, you need to complete my legacy. Poisonwood is my greatest dream. It's my vision and gift to the world. Ever since I can remember, I wanted to build a golf course. And you are going to make that happen for me because I can't do it myself. I will be a part of that course forever. Dewar's, Jägermeister, Grey Goose, they are all good, but they are just brands and brands are business. They aren't really mine. They aren't part of me. My children are probably going to take my money and do crazy shit with it, and that's life. But that golf course is mine. I want to be buried there if possible, or moved there after I crap out. You are doing my most important work. Do you understand?"

"Yes."

"Good. I have something else to tell you that I've never told anyone else."

"Why are you telling me?"

"Because you are sitting there, and I trust you, and because you need to know the real reason I couldn't stand the Rosenstiel family. Lew was a son-of-a-bitch, a womanizer and terrible father, but those are things I can't fault too much," Sidney smiled, but he slowed down and chose his words deliberately. "The real reason I hated Lew was something very different, and tragic. One of the worst things that ever happened in my life. Most of the time I try not to think about it. I try to forget, but it's been buried deep inside me for a long time, gnawing away at me. I need to tell you, and I need to tell you now. Before it's too late."

I wasn't sure I wanted to know. "Sidney, you don't need to..."

"Shut up and listen. I told you that Lew needed Vietnam to move his juice and junk. It was the best thing that could have happened for Lew and his buddy Lansky. Whisky started moving again, Schenley was making a dent in their stockpile, the heroin market was booming, Lansky and Luciano were happy as pigs in shit and business had never been better for the mob. Just when they thought it was a fairytale ending and they would all ride off into the sunset and live happily ever after, things changed.

"In 1960, Lansky took some big hits. John F. Kennedy, the prodigal son of his archrival Joe Kennedy, was elected President of the United States. John installed Bobby as Attorney General, and Bobby started a crusade against organized crime, including many of his father's former buddies. John and Bobby were making life difficult for Lansky, Lew and their associates, and business started slipping.

"And then came the grand finale in Lansky's landslide. Castro seized all of Lansky's hotel, casino and real estate holdings in Cuba. He lost everything. That idiot had most of his nut tied up in Havana with the Riviera and the Nacional. Lansky was more than a little upset, but he really blew a gasket when Kennedy botched the Bay of Pigs and failed to reunite him with his beloved assets. Deep down, Lansky didn't think Kennedy really gave a shit about Cuba. Lansky hated the Kennedy family anyway, and now he blamed them for ruining him. The Kennedy boys were running the government, and the government was fucking Lansky six ways to Sunday. He was losing his fortune and his mind.

"Then in early 1963, Robert McNamara, the Secretary of Defense, announces that Kennedy is pulling out of Vietnam. That scared the shit out of Lew. He began to think that Vietnam might be Korea all over again. A quick war would be disaster for Schenley, and it would close off their smack supply channels and end free military cargo transport. Withdrawal from Vietnam would ruin Lew. He couldn't let that happen.

"I remember a very strange meeting in the summer of 1963. I stopped by

Lew's office to check in about something, and I bumped into a crazy group of people. Sam Bronfman, Bronfman's attorney Louis Bloomfield, Lansky, and a couple guys I didn't recognize were coming out of Lew's office. I swore one of them was Richard Nixon, but I wasn't sure and he scurried away before I got a good look. Whoever he was, he looked nervous as hell.

"I'd seen Lansky lurking around Lew's office a few times, but never Sam Bronfman. Lew hated Sam. It was like seeing Hitler come skipping out of a temple after High Holy Days services. Never thought I'd see the day. I asked Lew about it, and he blew some happy horse shit about a political cause they had an interest in. And I tried to let it go, but I just couldn't get over the fact that Lew allowed Sam Bronfman inside his office. I mean he had a goddamn war room in there dedicated to destroying Sam. And he just opens the door, rolls out the red carpet and lets Bronfman come waltzing in. It didn't add up. I smelled a rat.

"Then a few months later, something happened that changed the world forever. One of the worst days I can remember. John Kennedy got his brains blown out in Dallas. I knew that Lew hated him and his family, but I actually liked him. I think I liked him more because Lew hated him, and I believed John was trying to change things for the better. Get rid of the established government assholes, and make the world a better place. John was handsome, charming and charismatic, and a great speaker. He tore Nixon up on the televised debates. It was night and day. Nixon had a good face for radio. When John spoke, he was sincere and inspiring. He spoke from the heart, and he could tell a story. He was a decent poker player, and he had a wandering eye and weakness for blondes with big tits. I'll tell you something, he would have made a hell of a liquor salesman.

"So when he was killed, I was upset. It seemed like Oswald was stealing the future from us, and I wanted to kill him for it. And then, lo and behold, Jack Ruby plugs him in the guts on live TV. And that's when I knew something wasn't right. I knew Jack pretty well. We'd crossed paths a number of times. He was a Jew, and Jews didn't pull that kind of shit in public. Jack also owned a bar and had business dealings with Schenley. I knew that he'd also done some work for Lansky in Cuba before Castro. And Ruby was claiming he killed Oswald because he loved Kennedy. I knew that was bullshit. He was a rat, and he was covering something up.

"So I called Lew, and Lew didn't want to talk about it, but he sounded nervous as hell. Lew never sounded calm, but I could tell that something was different this time. So I went over to see him, and I got a funny feeling. Something wasn't right. I could see in Lew's face that he knew something, something big, and he wasn't telling me, but I could tell that motherfucker wanted to spill it. I pressed him a little, and it didn't take much. Lew opened up like a stuck pig. He closed the door, turned off the taps and recorders, and he told me a story that still gives me nightmares."

I started to get chills down my neck. I wasn't sure if I really wanted to hear any more, but I couldn't stop him now.

"It turns out that after Joe Kennedy's crew gunned down Lansky's guys in 1927, many children were left without fathers. In those days, it was next to impossible for a woman to support a big family on her own. Lansky paid for several widows and their families to relocate to the Holy Land. One of these families was a young mother and her three infant children. She was also pregnant with her fourth child, a boy named David.

"David grew up in Israel and joined the Israeli army when he was 16 years old. He was a quiet boy, but this kid was a stone cold killer. His marksmanship skills were like nothing the Israelis had ever seen. He had balls the size of grapefruits and ice water running through his veins, and he could put a bullet through a pinhead. David racked up more sniper kills than any other soldier, several well beyond 2000 meters. That was something special in the days before lasers and computers and all the high-tech shit they got now. David had a gift. They called him the Scorpion because he could live in the desert, alone, no spotter, virtually undetected for weeks at a time while stalking his prey. David

251

became one of the most highly decorated members of the Israeli army. By 1960, he was considered the most lethal assassin in the world.

"Lansky kept in touch with David's family, making sure they had everything they needed. Lansky also made sure the David never forgot his father, or the powerful American dynasty that caused his father's death. David killed many people for his country, but deep down he wanted vengeance for his family.

"In 1963, Lansky and Lew gave him that opportunity. They arranged for David to return to the United States for a very special mission. David was provided with everything he needed. After all the shit he'd been through, blowing Kennedy's head off would be like a day at the zoo. Besides, Lansky knew that it would give David immense personal pleasure to pull the trigger. It would finally bring him closure, and he would have done it for free. The $100,000 they paid him was icing. Lew and Lansky masterminded the greatest hit in history with two simple yet powerful motives, revenge and greed. Lew had the connections, and Lansky had the firepower.

"Lew and Bronfman owned Lyndon Johnson and Nixon. Lew told me Johnson was his puppet, and that Johnson promised to escalate Vietnam and keep the gravy train rolling if Lew took Kennedy out of the way. Johnson also cleared the way for Bronfman to buy Texas Pacific Coal and Oil Company.[21] Nixon knew he'd never get the Presidency while Kennedy was alive, and history has shown that his judgment was suspect.

"Lansky knew David had the tools to complete the job. They considered using CIA operatives, but they couldn't be sure the cowboys wouldn't flip on them. They also couldn't rely on a Chicago hired gun to sack up and pull the trigger with the President in the sights. Lansky needed someone with a deep personal vendetta and a passion for the kill. David had both. The Chicago

---

[21] Sam Bronfman bought Texas Pacific in 1963 for $50 million. In 1980, the Bronfman heirs sold the Texas Pacific Oil holdings to Sun Oil Co. for $2.3 billion.

syndicate provided Oswald as the ideal patsy, and Lew assumed that Oswald would get nervous and either not shoot or miss the target completely, which went exactly according to plan. Oswald must have been surprised, to say the least, when Kennedy's skull exploded while he was trying to reload his Carcano carbine. Ruby was persuaded to remove Oswald, and Lew knew they could control Ruby until he was gone. The clock was ticking on that schmuck. Terminal brain cancer, plus they gave him a suitcase full of cash and threatened to kill his family if he snitched.

"The Feds sniffed around a little, but Lew got to Hoover and made the entire investigation disappear. Turns out that Hoover hated the Kennedys almost as much as Lansky. Lew also did some entertaining at his Connecticut estate and had glossy, graphic close-ups of Hoover buggering blonde boys. Hoover was just as sick as Lew.

"So Hoover did Lew a big favor and shit canned the investigation. Lew and Lansky pulled off the perfect hit on the most powerful man in the world, and Hoover just rolled over, crumpled it up and threw it away. But Lew was the kingpin. That old bastard bragged that he was the merchant of death, like he was some kind of national hero. And for his grand finale, Lew donates a million dollars to create the J. Edgar Hoover Foundation. Can you believe it? A decorated member of the Jewish mob donates a million dollars to fund a foundation for the head of the FBI, and nobody lifts a goddamn eyebrow? Doesn't that seem odd to you? I'll tell you what, it's fucking crazy.

"I'm sitting there listening to Lew, and I can't believe what I was hearing. I looked at his fat smug face, and his thick smudged glasses, and the burning cigar clenched between his brown teeth, and the room started spinning. He was laughing, and grinding the cigar with his teeth, and his teeth turned into fangs, and his eyes turned bright red, and I saw blood oozing from his scalp and pieces of brain falling on his desk. I got sick. Literally. I lost my shit all over Lew's marble flooring and his fucking Italian loafers.

"I knew that Joe Kennedy was a scumbag, and that Lansky hated anything named Kennedy. I knew John and Bobby weren't playing nice with the mobsters that helped John get elected. I knew about Cuba, and Vietnam, I knew they had Johnson in their pockets, and I knew some other shit also. But they didn't have to blow John's brains out in front of his wife and children, for Christ's sake. No one deserves that."

Sidney was quiet.

"So, I left. I got the fuck away from Lew as fast as I could. I couldn't look at him without getting sick to my stomach. I had to work with him for a couple more years, and those were the worst years of my life. Even now, there is not a day that goes by that I don't think about it. There is not a day that I don't wonder if there was something I could have done to stop it. It kills me to think about it. It will haunt me the rest of my life, and there is nothing I can do. I have dedicated myself to making the world a better place, but that's not going to change what happened, and it doesn't make up for anything. But it's all I can do now. It's my way of trying to make peace. Do you understand me?"

"Yes."

"Good. I have another favor to ask."

My mind was spinning. I felt unsteady and squeamish. I wasn't sure if I wanted to hear anymore.

"I want you to write my book."

"Me?"

"You have to tell my story. It's the world's greatest story about the most interesting person you will ever know, and the world needs to hear it. They need to know the truth after I'm gone. They need to know everything. These other writers I've hired can't write a comic book. They couldn't write a baby book. You need to promise me that you'll write it."

"Ok."

"Say it."

"What?"

"Give me your word that you will write it." Sidney locked his eyes on mine.

"I promise to write your book."

"Good enough. One last thing. The staff, you, the golfers and nurses and cooks, all of you, you are my family. You have taken care of me. You have been there for me, and you helped me take care of lots of unfinished business. You helped me close deals that I thought would never be closed. You helped me make some things right in my life. You helped me find some peace. I'm ready to go now, and I'm not worried because I know you will all continue my legacy, and because you will tell my story. I never want any of you to have to work for assholes again. I never want any of you to have to suffer. I want you to be comfortable, but not too comfortable. I don't want to make you all useless. You will all be taken care of. I have made arrangements." Sidney coughed a little, and winced. He was in pain, and he was starting to struggle just to catch his breath. It was hard to watch.

"Sidney, that is very thoughtful, but you're not going anywhere. Besides, just being with you is a reward in itself."

"Cut the bullshit."

"Ok."

"I'm a billionaire, and I can afford it. I've made arrangements." He coughed.

"With an attorney?"

"No, with my daughter."

"Your daughter?"

"Yes, my daughter the painter."

His daughter the painter? That didn't sound too good.

"Mr. Frank, did you want any assistance with this?"

"No. It's all taken care of. You will all be taken care of. I've made sure of it."

"Ok." I had a bad feeling. Sidney started coughing again, and I noticed he spit a little blood into a tissue.

"Let's go home."

....

I limped into my bed at the Residence Inn. I felt like I'd been smacked around with a sock full of nickels. How the hell was I going to write a book about Sidney? And even more to the point, should I write this book? I knew some of his stories were true, but this last one was a doozy. It seemed plausible, but then again many of Sidney's wacked stories seemed plausible. And supposing, hypothetically, that I did write his book. What were the consequences? Would the mob make me disappear? Would the feds protecting Sidney's company and family shut me down? And, would I be a traitor to my people?

There is an expression unique to the Jewish people. Whenever anything significant happens around the world, we ask whether "it's good for the Jews?" For example, when a cruel Middle Eastern dictator is overthrown, a tribal elder will ask, "So, Mordi, did you hear that bastard Saddam was killed and his government overthrown? Good riddance, yes of course, but still I wonder, is it good for the Jews?" So, we must ask, was the assassination of Kennedy good for the Jews? Seems likely, especially for a certain subset of Jews.

If what Sidney was telling me was true, the Jewish mafia appeared to be primarily responsible for overthrowing the United States government, and for better or worse, I was a Jew. Jews have a long and colorful history, with some very high points (Natalie Portman, Albert Einstein, Jonas Salk), and some very low points (David Berkowitz, Bernie Madoff, Phil Spector). I'd read some of the conspiracy theories about the powerful Jewish families who served as bankers and financiers for European aristocracy who did not want to taint their delicate sensibilities with debt collection, tax assessment and compounding interest. These Court Jews, or "*Hofjuden*," were portrayed as bankers, loan makers and financial advisors who stashed the royal bouillon and hatched their own tribal dynasties. Names like Montefiore, Goldsmid, Oppenheimer, de Hirsch, and Sassoon were purportedly at the top of *Hofjuden* food chain. The most revered and storied family was the Rothschilds. According to Illuminati lore, the Rothschilds controlled vast legitimate and criminal enterprises under the auspices of the British throne, including most of the world's drug trade, organized crime, the U.S. government, Wall Street and Hollywood. And while I found those theories to be provocative and disturbing, I mainly attributed them to anti-Semitic propaganda and conspiracy theory paranoia. But after hearing Sidney's story, I could not help wondering whether the Illuminati might be on to something.

Conventional stereotypes peg Jews as greedy, cheap, and moderately unattractive people with whiney voices and abrasive personalities. It would seem that we are all aggressive, arrogant and obsessed with money, power and status. Jews essentially resemble every witch, warlock or otherwise wicked character in every Disney movie ever made. And to be brutally honest, I can understand some of this generalized intolerance. I'd grown up amidst clans of haughty and pretentious South African and Mexican Jews, and I attended college with a plethora of New York's finest. I'd met more than my share of Jews who made me feel guilty and ashamed of my own religious identity. Fortunately, guilt and shame are at the core of Jewish identity. We embrace self-loathing. We celebrate grief and rejoice in regret. We were raised by competitive, overbearing parents who equipped us with precious few practical skills and lifelong neuroses that will never be cured despite years of therapy. We are encouraged to marry within the faith to perpetuate our "chosen" status, but we also perpetuate undesirable physical phenotypes and genetic disorders. And the icing on the Judaic cake is that many of us live with the irrational fear that our gentile friends assume we secretly wear robes, chant in dead languages, drink gentile baby blood and are destined to suffer eternal combustion in Hell.

On the bright side, if Jews do control the western world (including the United States, UK, Europe and Canada), then we are doing a far better job of it than our Muslim managed neighbors. Jews have no problem enforcing swift justice and defending ourselves against violence and oppression, and we are unified in promoting and embracing peace, love and tolerance for all people regardless of race, color or creed. The western world is certainly not without its issues, but things generally work here, and when they don't we have the freedom to rise up and question, debate and disagree with our governments without too much fear of imprisonment, torture, and/or execution. This was the vision of the founding fathers of the United States, and it is the same vision cherished and perpetuated by Jews worldwide. This still doesn't absolve the Jews of guilt for [hypothetically] taking over the western world. But it could be worse. Much worse. Last time I checked my neighbors were not getting necklaced with burning tires or beheaded in town squares, and women are not publically whipped or stoned to death for having the audacity to show their ankles or walk down the street without a male overlord.

I was not an observant Jew, and I couldn't sit through a service without feeling like a phony when I bowed my head or lip-synced prayers and songs. But I was extremely proud of the Jewish culture of tenacity and toughness. Jews had been persecuted and tortured for thousands of years, and many attempts had been made to eradicate us, but we were still digging in and hanging on to our traditions, ideology and freedom. Nonetheless, I was now connected, albeit remotely, to what was possibly the greatest crime of the 20th century. Sidney's confession was really not going to help anyone at the end of the day, and certainly would not be good for the Jews.

But I made a promise to Sidney to tell his story, and a promise is a promise. My word was good.

Chapter 23

Screaming Orgasm

My phone rang. It was my wife. I hadn't seen her for almost two months.

"I'm pregnant."

"Say what?"

"I'm pregnant."

"Holy shit. How did that happen?"

"How do you think?"

"Holy shit."

"That's nice."

"Sorry. Damn, that's great news honey. Wow. Holy shit."

"Yeah. I didn't want to have to tell you over the phone, but I wasn't sure when you were coming home and I thought you might want to know."

"Are you sure?"

"Yes."

"Well, that's amazing. Holy shit. So great."

I felt woozy and on the verge of puking.

"Amazing?"

"Sorry, I don't know what to say right now. I'm in shock. I wasn't expecting this at all."

"Okay."

"How are you feeling?"

"Sick."

"Sorry. Anything I can do?"

"Come home."

I was going to be a daddy. Holy shit.

Chapter 24
Cock Sucking Cowboy

Sidney decided to return to San Diego in late November 2005, which was perfect timing for me. Chad settled the illegal contribution pickle by paying a $40,000 fine with Sidney's money. Laurel was starting to show, and I was getting the Fear again. I was taking responsibility for another life, a little person growing inside my wife's stomach, and Sidney's poor health was weighing heavily on my mind. Laurel wanted to buy a house in a nicer part of San Diego that had good schools, dog parks and wide sidewalks. Nice houses in San Diego did not come cheap. Shitty houses in San Diego didn't come cheap either.

We were not back in the heartland for very long before Sidney was back in the hospital. His failing heart valve was causing his lungs to fill with fluid, and in order to breath he needed to have his lungs drained, which meant extended stays in the ER. The staffers kept themselves occupied with the usual business (mainly drinking and gambling), but the house had a much different feel. The king was not holding court and the jesters were without mirth and folly. There was no golf, no bridge, no Clint Eastwood movies playing on the big screen. The faint aroma of burning cigar drifting through the hallways and air ducts every few hours was conspicuously absent. I know it's cliché, but sometimes the things you find most annoying are the things you miss when they're gone.

The staff visited Sidney in the hospital daily. At times there were more than 20 people in Sidney's private room in the ICU. The other ICU inmates, at least those who were conscious, seemed confused. The nurses seemed irritated and they rolled their eyes every time they walked by, but they wouldn't dare do anything to upset a terminal billionaire and his buddies.

"I'm bored. Get me some movies." We remodeled his hospital room. A huge portable LCD TV Screen with Bose surround sound system and subwoofers was delivered. We brought in about 500 of his favorite movies, including the porn, and we played them so loudly that other inmates complained about their vibrating beds.

"The food here is awful. Bring me good food." The chefs hauled in huge coolers of gourmet delicacies. There was something wonderfully ironic about watching an ICU patient with terminal cardiovascular disease devouring Kobe beef sliders topped with cheese and foie gras.

But Sidney was deteriorating, and I knew things were getting grim when his offspring started appearing. I was surprised to see the Tainted Painter finally make a showing, and alarmed when the Moet Poet popped up.

The Artists

Behold, les Artistes. I had never actually met the Poet during my entire tenure with Sidney, but I'd heard that Sidney couldn't stand him. And I'd only seen the Painter a handful of times at most. She started appearing more frequently as Sidney's condition worsened. After making her grand entrance, she would spend several minutes getting briefed by the medical team, then off to comfort her poor rich papa.

My first close encounter with the Painter occurred randomly. She was standing outside Sidney's room, whispering on a cell phone to her handlers. The phone was literally buried in her massive kinky hair nest. It looked like most of her forearm was in the process of being consumed by some kind of swarming grey fungus. Her head was cocked and her eyes pointed straight down at the ground.

"Can you fax me a copy of the agreement? And forward a copy of the notarized papers to our attorney in Hawaii, and he'll courier them to our attorneys in Seattle, who will UPS them on to our attorneys in New York, who will FedEx them back to Hawaii. Goose, you're it! Then we should schedule a conference call to discuss the merits of sending them back to Seattle and starting over." The Painter took a breath, "Yes, I spoke to the doctors, and they are not optimistic. I keep asking if everything is in order, because the last thing I need is what happened when my grandfather..." She picked up her head and saw me watching her. She flashed a crooked smirk with crinkled eyes and a frizzy head bob or two, and then immediately retreated to a more private lair.

The Painter was in her fifties, but you wouldn't have guessed it. From her appearance you would almost expect her to continually shed dust and stray fuzz balls, and you would not be surprised to find small tangles of hairy lint beneath her if she was stationary for any significant period of time. She was an artist, and her monstrous artworks adorned the walls of her Hawaiian and Colorado compounds. She somehow managed to mask her talent and avoid critical acclaim. Fortunately for her, the potbellied Poet was comfortable wallowing in grandeur.

"Ladies and gentlemen of the jury, my mind is blurry, so sit back and rewind while I spin you some yarn from my ample behind. Roses are red, and blood is red too, red fingerprints in the snow, you know, are the trappings of a fool. Dorian Hasselhoff, the Swiss mist lily gilding maniac pianist mountaineer,

263

contrived this epic opera, though rarely did he rest, while subliminally summiting Mt. Everest. He looked into the teeth of the offing and saw what he could see, under mucky blue infinity, my thigh crust glued and glittery. Dodo consummated the summit, just before his plummet, when the dude like collapsed into a big ass crevasse. Exhibit A, if I may. A memorandum in tandem with Dodo's surprise demise. And I quote, 'Lost in the frost, I am broken and bleeding in that cold dark space, my brain absorbed in a mindless race, preparing for a foul descent to the bottom of my bottomless tent. When I close my eyes I can still see my blank reflection on black windowless night skies, my mind's eye darker than opaque window blinds...'"

The Poet's morose prose and gloomy hyperbole could inspire Sylvia Plath to ratchet up to high broil. He resembled an obese garden gnome, just a hair over five feet tall in his signature Gore-Tex trekking boots, although his natural stride was closer to a waddle. He had Fabio flowing ashy locks and a crusty amber beard framing his cherubic face. His smudged spectacles rested on the tip of his pink button nose, and he was partial to bucket hats (generally covered with odd ink scrawl) and chunky wool sweaters. I don't think the Poet expected anyone to believe he was a hardcore mountaineer, but that didn't deter him from dressing the part. His stature and gait were better suited to prospecting or spelunking in wide caves.

The squatty squire was the absolute worst-case scenario cocktail party companion. You would chew your arm off trying to get away from him. You might consider setting yourself ablaze to keep him at a safe distance. He would prattle on and on in syncopated rhythms, rambling rhymes and tangential rants, pontificating on all sorts of tedious topics, his favorites being the arts and politics. The Poet could recite entire chapters of Nabokov from memory. The first [and only] evening my wife and I joined the Artists for quiet dinner, the Poet regurgitated lengthy sections from *Lolita* with such fervor and lunacy that almost everyone in the restaurant, besides the Artists, was spooked.

In addition to his mad lyrical skills, the Poet was also a self-proclaimed musical prodigy. He pounded out Rachmaninoff and beef stroganoff with similar gusto, usually while dressed up as a centaur, minotaur or other obscure mythical beast. The Poet kept three priceless Steinways stashed in different secure locations around the country. These beauties required hermetically sealed environments with precise humidity and temperature to keep their tune, and the carbon conscious conservationist spent a fortune on heating and air conditioning to keep his babies cozy and comfy during the cold winter months. On one memorable occasion, the Poet was in Hawaii when an ice storm hit the Northwest, and he "invited" me to fly from San Diego to Seattle to stoke the furnaces and wrap a baby grand with fuzzy blankets.

....

In April of 2011, the Poet fulfilled a lifelong dream of *performing the piano upon a remote wilderness peak.* He chartered a helicopter to drop him and a Steinway on an isolated section of the Chugach mountain range in Alaska. Just a puny Poet and his priceless piano braving the frozen tundra. Naturally, the Poet wore a full Yeti costume. On a 6,000 foot glacier in the middle of nowhere, the Abominable Poet pounded out frigid show tunes while dressed like a pygmy Sasquatch.

The Abominable Poet

266

"Seth, would you care to join us for a brief meeting?" Both Artists looked concerned.

"Sure." I had never had much more than a few words with either of them. The Artists were sitting in one of Rancho Limon's spare rooms, drinking Sidney's wine and sampling liberally from a platter of pungent cheeses. We sat in silence and stared at each other.

Finally, the Painter broke the silence. "We realize you work for my father, and we'd never betray his confidence or compromise ourselves, but we heard you are more or less trustworthy. You're one of the few staff members who doesn't have a free car or house, or any other valuable company property that we could verify, and you never took advantage of Sidney, as far as we can tell at this point of our ongoing internal investigations, although counsel has advised us to reserve the right to defer final binding determinations with regard to the validity of that claim to an undetermined date, to be determined and disclosed at a subsequent indeterminate and undisclosed time. The accountants claim that your project budgets are accurate, even when audited, again qualified with a similar disclaimer as above with the addition of a full forensic audit and optional colonoscopy. Further, your base compensation is surprisingly reasonable, all things considered. Henceforth, we might, should our attorneys deem you fit and reasonably sane or at least manageably insane, have a place for you, you know, afterwards...."

"Afterwards what?"

"Afterwards...after the transition."

And there it was. A position with the Artists. My golden ticket was now a gilded toilet. I supposed a place was preferable to absence of place.

"Please don't discuss this with anyone. We'd like to keep it quiet. Obviously, we can't keep everyone." Keep a lid on it kid, and say goodbye to your former friends forever. I hadn't given it much thought, but the transition was inevitable, and obviously there would be minimal need for the golfers, nurses, jugglers, jesters and contortionists under the new regime.

I looked at the Artists. They looked at me. We stared at each other in silence and it started getting awkward again.

. . . .

The Painter was also an accomplished Actress. She nailed dutiful daughter, making impromptu appearances at the hospital and catching up on all the years and financials. I assumed Sidney would see through her faux finish, but he bought it. He named the Painter as his official successor, and she promised to run the business and manage his foundation as if he were still alive and kicking ass. She assured Sidney that his legacy was secure, his company protected, and his staffers would be comfortable. Sidney seemed at peace with this decision. In all truth, the Painter was the lesser of the evils. The Scientist is not worth mentioning.

The transition was in motion, the heir was apparent, and the drama and nastiness that accompanied Lew Rosenstiel's death would be averted.

. . . .

"Did I ever tell you about the Roy Cohn clusterfuck?" Sidney leaned back and put his hands behind his head.

He didn't have to. That story was well documented. Sidney and Jerry Finkelstein, the Painter's ex-father-in-law and a notorious New York power broker, conspired to hire the most corrupt lawyer money could buy to infiltrate and sabotage Lew Rosenstiel's estate while he lay vegetative on death's doormat. Dollars to donuts, they couldn't have done better than Roy Cohn. Not only was he repugnant and morally bankrupt, but as luck would have it, Cohn was already connected to Rosenstiel through their mutual association with J. Edgar Hoover. Cohn's father was also a New York state judge and close personal friend of the Finkelsteins. Cohn was their ace in the hole.

At the time of Rosenstiel's prolonged death march in the mid 1970s, he still had considerable wealth and an estate estimated at $75 million dollars, although he'd diluted most of the original family shareholders through multiple marriages. He was on his fifth wife, and he had one living daughter named Libby. His other daughter Skippy (Sidney's wife and the Painter's mother) had predeceased him, and neither the Painter nor Sidney figured to be high on the receiving end of Rosenstiel's largesse due to the fact that he'd essentially disowned and disinherited them. This problem was further exacerbated by the $5 million dollars in unsettled claims Sidney and his issue had pending against Rosenstiel and his estate.

By December 1975, Rosenstiel was sequestered in a Florida hospital room suffering from a laundry list of terminal ailments, the most bothersome being paralysis from a massive stroke and advanced dementia. He was severely incapacitated and he spent most of his time catatonic and drooling. Time was not on his side, and quick action was needed if Sidney and his brood hoped to scavenge anything from the Rosenstiel carcass. A foolproof plan was hatched.

Cohn made an unannounced, late-night visit to Rosenstiel's hospital deathbed armed with a slick codicil that added Cohn, the Painter and the Painter's then husband, Jimmy Finkelstein[22], as executors and trustees of his estate. This minor addition would have given Cohn and the Painter a majority vote and control over the disposition of Rosenstiel's estate, including all outstanding unsettled claims against the estate, which coincidentally included their own $5 million in unsettled claims.

Rosenstiel passed away six weeks later, and Cohn attempted to introduce the signed codicil into Rosenstiel's estate. The codicil was contested, and litigation ensued. According to his own sworn testimony, Cohn was able, by some

---

[22] You might recall Jimmy Finkelstein's charming brother, Andrew Stein, from Chapter 10. Stein dropped the "Finkel" from his last name.

superhuman stroke of good fortune, to revive the comatose Rosenstiel just long enough for him to be fully aware and cognizant of the profound legal changes he was authorizing, sign the codicil, and shoot the bull for a few minutes before he peacefully slipped back into sweet oblivion. Jerry Finkelstein's sworn testimony backed up Cohn's story, although some questioned his veracity, particularly in light of the fact that numerous witnesses placed him in New York on the day of Cohn's surprise Florida visit. Several hospital staffers, who became key witnesses in subsequent hearings, testified that only Cohn was present in Rosenstiel's hospital room, and that Rosenstiel was especially unconscious that entire day.

During a formal inquest conducted by the New York State Bar, Cohn claimed that Rosenstiel wanted to add him and the Painter as executors to 'protect his daughter Libby's interests and ward off attacks from malicious persons trying to raid his estate.' The codicil was eventually revoked, and Cohn was ultimately disbarred for this and a laundry list of other egregious offenses.

The kicker of this story is that the entire Rosenstiel caper was absolutely pointless. Rosenstiel had transferred the bulk of his assets to a special *inter-vivos* trust for Libby several months before Cohn visited him. This special trust was irrevocable and beyond the reach of Rosenstiel's estate's executors who would only control a pittance of his wealth after his death. So even if the phony codicil had been legitimate, Cohn and the Painter would have been helpless to protect Rosenstiel's estate or enforce their own claims against it. It was a circus of errors, and the Painter and Cohn were the clowns.

....

I stopped by the hospital to see Sidney before I flew back to the Bahamas. He did not look well. I was used to seeing him tired and uncomfortable, but he was deteriorating quickly. His speech was so slow and labored, that it was difficult to understand him. He was sedated to keep him as comfortable as possible. His heart valve was shot, and things were getting grim.

But there was also some good news for a change. A surgeon in Canada was willing to perform a high-risk heart valve replacement, and Sidney was getting ready to fly to Vancouver in a matter of days. His San Diego doctors wanted to make sure he was as healthy and stable as possible before they cleared him to travel. I had flown to Vancouver to scout the hospital a few weeks earlier, and all systems were go. He had hope, and hope was the best medicine available.

I sat down next to his bed. There were no nurses or staff around, and it was very quiet. Sidney was asleep, and he looked peaceful for a change. His left hand was on top of his stomach. I reached out and put my hand on top of his. His eyes fluttered open, and he gave me a confused look. Then he noticed my hand on top of his. He grasped my hand and squeezed it firmly for several minutes.

"I'm flying back to Cat Island tomorrow. I wanted to say goodbye and I'll see you in Canada."

"Good. Before you go. I want you to hold something for me, for safekeeping. It's the most valuable thing I have. The most important thing in my life. Just promise me one thing. Promise you won't open it."

"Ok. I promise."

The claw emerged from under the sheets, and it was gripping a small box. Sidney held it out to me, and I removed it from his clench and looked at it. It was a pack of playing cards. I shrugged and put it in my pocket. "I will guard them with my life."

"You should, smart ass. Let's play some cards, but with a different pack."

And we played gin for an hour and enjoyed the quiet. He even let me win a few hands.

Chapter 25
Blue Balls

In early January 2006, I returned to Cat Island for my final attempt to hike the Union Estate tract before the sale closed. I had been foiled in all my previous attempts, but I was determined to get in deep. Sidney would buy it regardless, but I needed to know exactly what was under the hood, and I needed to see a poisonwood tree.

Chad decided to tag along on this trip to get away from all the stress for a few days, although he stayed in his luxury suite in Nassau. My tiny island commuter airplane landed on Cat Island on January 8th, and I realized that I'd come at a bad time. It was incredibly hot, and it was January. I started second guessing the decision to build in the Bahamas. Hawaii was also very nice, and it was in the United States. We'd heard rumors that Rupert Murdoch was considering selling Lanai. The weather in Hawaii was better, but you just couldn't beat the Bahamian water. It was so clear and blue that it almost looked green, and there were times when it was almost too warm.

I spent two days recollecting supplies, rearranging off-road transportation, and reassembling my Haitian troupe for the third time. I think they were even beginning to doubt the ground assault would ever happen. It was hotter than Hades, and I tried to spend as much time as possible indoors. In the evenings I gorged on Annie's cooking and rum. On the second night I managed to get some sleep, but the rum wore off around 4 am and I watched mosquito aerobatics above my bed for a couple of hours.

I picked up the Haitians around 8am on January 10th, and about two hours later I was knee deep in poisonous sap and spider shit when I confirmed that we'd made the right choice. We found the most perfect piece of land for Sidney's sublime golf course. Poisonwood was going to be his pot of gold.

....

"Stewardess, a shot of tequila for me, and a double for the pilot," would be his last call. At approximately 10am on January 10, 2006, Sidney Frank dropped dead on top of the king-sized bed in the master cabin of his BBJ. Reports that Sidney crapped out on top of the stacked flight attendant remain unconfirmed. I like to imagine that he took his final trip over the rainbow clutching a Davidoff in one hand and a size D silicon implant in the other.

....

After a minor panic attack and an entire bottle of rum, I revived on the beach in front of the Greenwood Hotel. Accompanying the empty bottle and me were a pack of sandy playing cards and a massive hangover. I took a quick shower and booked the next flight to Nassau, and then on to New York for Sidney's memorial.

Chapter 26
Angel's Tit

Sidney's staffers were flown from San Diego to New York on a chartered JetBlue red-eye, and we were all to be lodged in a mid-tier mid-town hotel, but none of the rooms were ready when the group arrived at 5am. Everyone camped out in the lobby drinking and playing cards for almost five hours. The Artists reserved a palatial suite for themselves at the Four Seasons, to be ready upon arrival of their private jet. I got a note to meet them following the funeral services.

The service itself was fairly low-key considering the high life of the man being memorialized. Some notable tribal elders, retired mobsters and rubberneckers turned out, but it was not the absurd theater I expected. No brawls. No mistresses. No love children. Frankly, most of us were a little disappointed. The lowlight of the funeral was a touching eulogy from Lenny "Penishead" Sidewinder that sounded very little like a tribute and much more like a sales pitch for SFIC's newest product, Tommy Bahama Rum.[23] I half expected him to open the casket and pose for a photo with Sidney and a bottle of Tommy.

As I walked through the lobby at the Four Seasons, I felt the box of playing cards in my pocket. I promised Sidney that I'd take care of the Artists, and my word was good. I quickly spotted them at a table in the lounge. I walked up slowly and studied them from a distance. The Poet was reenacting a scene from one of his epic works, and the Painter was cackling loudly. I noticed they were mourning Sidney with a bottle of vintage Champagne, and the Poet was wearing a lobster bib. I didn't see any lobster. The festivities quickly subdued when they noticed me watching them.

The Artists stood up and we exchanged awkward hugs. They smelled fishy

---

[23] The collaboration of loud leisurewear and overpriced rum was one of the most ill conceived products since New Coke. SFIC dumped it in 2010.

and sour, and my eyes started to burn. I sat down and the Poet became very solemn and sanctimonious.

"Thank you so much for coming. We are so incredibly sad and like heartbroken, you know? It's all like so sadly unspoken. As you know, things have changed, and we've rearranged. Just so you know, we are letting Chad go, tomorrow, just so you know the ebb and the flow." These Artists sure didn't waste any time chopping heads. "We are going to need your help to sort out Sidney's affairs. We need your skills and *Savior-faire*. Will you be our Sherpa, our Tenzing Norgay from here to payday and throughout all time and the days of our lives to the ends of this endless eternity?"

The power had shifted and Chad was no longer in control. My hand was being called, and I had to play it or dump. I looked at the two loathsome creatures celebrating Sidney's demise, and I didn't have a shred of sympathy for either of them. I couldn't stand the thought of working for them. I couldn't stand the thought sitting at that table much longer, waiting for the Poet to get tipsy and the inescapable Nabakovian barking. But I made a promise to Sidney, and, in truth, I was weak. I couldn't afford to be unemployed, and now we had a child on the way. I thought about the house we purchased near good schools and wide sidewalks, and the jumbo mortgage payments due every month. I thought about looking my wife in her furrowed, frowning face, staring into her bottomless blue eyes and telling her that I tucked my tail and dumped. I asked myself what Sidney would do.

I sold my soul quickly. I felt violated and unclean, and I couldn't wait to take a shower and fly home.

Chapter 27
Adios Mother Fucker

In late January of 2006, I received the letter. *Dear Mr. Schechter, you are in Group #2. Please report to Rancho Valencia, and bring all company property with you, including phones, computers, automobiles, surveillance devices, firearms, treasure maps, envelopes full of cash, compromising photos, etc.*

It happened relatively quickly. A week after the funeral, all staffers were summoned to Rancho Valencia, a luxurious and exclusive hotel and spa in Rancho Santa Fe favored by the Artists when visiting Sidney. It was one of the most beautiful resorts in California, and relatively unknown and off the grid. It was an ironic setting for a firing squad.

Group #1 went first. They comprised the majority of the staff, including golfers, cooks, nurses, etc. These were the people who took care of Sidney six and sometimes seven days a week. These people lived with him in New York for six months every year, and out of suitcases the rest of the year. This group flew around the world with him at a moment's notice. These were the staffers with whom Sidney golfed, played cards, watched movies and ballgames, lectured, advised, mentored, bullshitted, laughed, teased, taunted and abused. These caregivers prepared his food, bathed him, dressed him, kept him from torching himself with cigars, drove him to meet prostitutes, administered injections directly into his penis, changed his diapers, wiped him clean, drove him home, tucked him in and kissed him goodnight. These were the employees who got the most out of him, yet stole from him the least. These were the people he trusted most of all. This group was more family than his family.

The Artists read a contrived statement to Group #1 about how hard it was to make this decision, and they really wanted everyone to know just how much they genuinely appreciated everything they did, and that even though things would change they really wanted to stay in touch and play a big part in everyone's lives, and they really wanted to know how everyone was doing for years and years to come, and so on and so forth. In the meantime, thank you for your services, and please turn over your car keys and any other valuable company property immediately. Good luck with your future endeavors and good day.

Many of the Group #1 members had no alternate means of transportation. They were forced to surrender the cars they drove to the meeting, and catch rides with friends or take taxis. As far as I am aware, the Artists never contacted any of them again, except through their attorneys.

Group #2 was spared termination, momentarily. We were of some limited use. Several of us knew where skeletons were buried. A few of us knew where nuclear warheads were deployed.

Group #1 was stunned. They'd expected much more than an Artist's boot in their asses. For most of the staff, the opportunity to work for Sidney was a gift in itself, but it wasn't a day at the beach. Working for Sidney came at a steep price. Some key members of the staff were corrupted beyond repair. They probably weren't saints to begin with, but Sidney's wealth and indulgences contributed to their moral demise. Most of the rest of us suffered collateral damage. We lost some of the most productive years of our professional lives. We lost time with families and loved ones. We lived out of suitcases. We lived between coasts and continents. We worked in substandard conditions, and we were housed in substandard accommodations. We braved MOF's psychotic rage on a daily basis. We faced hostility and resentment from company executives and employees. We were on-call all-day, every-day, all year long.

Most of the former staff never really went anywhere after getting let go. Sidney's tough love mentorship wasn't effective, and the skills we learned on the job were not highly transferrable, unless you could find another eccentric billionaire who was putting together a traveling freak show for his personal amusement. The prospect of entering the real world was far too grim for many to handle. At least three former staffers, inspired by Sidney's entrepreneurial spirit, started businesses that failed. Most of the golfers retired from competition, and none of them ever won a significant professional tournament (one golfer qualified for the U.S. Open, and another for the British Open). Several former staffers sued the family and SFIC for specious reasons. Several marriages and lives were irreparably destroyed. Staffers (and their spouses) became accustomed to a lifestyle that was unsustainable and unrealistic. Money can't buy happiness, but lack of money can destroy it quickly.

The great irony of that mass dismissal, and the subsequent dilution of gifts Sidney promised to leave for his staff, was that I spent years finding Sidney's long lost friends and making sure they were comfortable, usually by treating them kindly and giving them huge sums of money. Sidney never would have treated his enemies as poorly as his personal staffers were treated following his death.

....

I was sitting in my kitchen trying to relax and enjoy a pleasant Sunday afternoon when my cell phone rang. I saw it was the bitty bard calling, and was very tempted to let it roll to voicemail. I just didn't have the stamina to tolerate his rambling bullshit on a Sunday. I looked at the phone again, flinched, and answered.

"Mahalo Prince Seth, it's King Pelu. Mahalo means hello, or goodbye, or something sly, although there are like a myriad of tangential derivatives and intangible dirigibles floating through the offing of the smudged windows of my mind, and the sloe eyed dusky mongrels in the Swiss mist mad mud pie sky," fast-forward through another 15 or 20 minutes of gibberish. "Listen, we need to speak to you about the Poisonwood project because something is rotten in the dirty Bahamas. Hang on, I think I just soiled my pajamas."

I heard the Painter pick up another extension and scream out "Helloooooo!" so loudly that I pulled the handset away from my ear to protect my remaining hearing. Now I had both of them on the call - a live streaming dunce duet in dynamic stereo.

"Poisonwood?" I'd suspected this call was coming. Not a matter of if but more a matter of when, and now was apparently when.

The Poet came back on, now breathing a little more heavily than usual. "We've been ruminating, perseverating, obsessing and compulsing, and we decided that Poisonwood is nondoable."

Nondoable? Was that really a word? I suppose you can't argue semantics with a puffy Poet. "It will be a challenge, but it's doable. Poisonwood was Sidney's dream."

"That might be true, and not to poo poo, but it clearly seems to be the impossiblist of all the impossible dreams to me."

I considered trying to defend Sidney's dream, but I was in no position to argue. Poisonwood was going to be a challenge. It would require grit, determination and strength of character that the Artists couldn't fake. I could have pushed harder. I could have dug in and defended the fort. At the very least, I should have politely excused myself from the table and shuffled. But I wasn't ready to say goodbye. My word was good, and I was still holding on to the increasingly unrealistic notion of helping Sidney's foundation realize his legacy. I also still quietly yearned for the elusive everything lurking just beyond my grasp, although I was beginning to see that money rarely brought the happiness or fulfillment I was chasing. I had two prime miserable misers on the other end of the line.

I wasn't learning, growing or doing anything particularly interesting or useful. I was definitely not getting any dynamic opportunities to build companies or develop new products. My professional development was stunted, and now I had turned the corner and was heading towards regression. I had succumbed to helping the Artists dismantle and destroy Sidney's projects, the very same projects I had been charging at only weeks earlier. I thought of my promise to Sidney. It was not my primary motivation, but it was still in the back of my mind and clinging to a few low hanging neurons. I had to take care of the Artists. I had to counsel them to the best of my ability. It wasn't time to walk. I had to put my personal feelings aside, lean forward and brace myself for impact. I took a deep breath.

"Ok. We can try to cancel the deal, but there's a $1.4 million deposit on the property."

"Is it refundable?"

"No."

"No?"

"No."

"Oh." Things got very quiet. It required strenuous concentration and mathematic gymnastics to weigh the loss of the deposit against other tangible assets and accounts receivable.

"Listen, I know you guys are going through a rough time now, but I would suggest that you take a little vacation to the islands. Fly down to the Bahamas and speak to the owner, Mr. Morton. He is a nice older gentleman. Patriarch of the family. Solid old school values, integrity, etc. He might be sensitive to your...situation." I secretly hoped old man Morton would keep all of the money and tell them to go fuck themselves. Morton wasn't getting any younger himself. I wondered if he suspected that his family might stick the same blade between his buttocks.

The prospect of a prostrated plea did not please the pudgy Poet. "Perhaps we could write a letter?"

Brilliant. *Dear Sir, I have a small favor to ask. Hope it's not a bother really, but I wonder if you wouldn't mind refunding the $1.4 million nonrefundable deposit my dear old dead dad paid to buy your lovely seaside lot. You see, funny story really, we've decided to destroy his dreams. Be a sport and send us a big fat check. Thanks a million, or 1.4 million to be precise. Fondly, the*

Artists.

"I wouldn't recommend a letter. I think a personal visit is always better. Face to face. Old school."

They sent a letter. Morton turned out to be amazingly honorable and he actually refunded some of the deposit. He then turned around and sold the same parcel for $30 million to another group of investors.

And that was the end of Poisonwood. More than any of Sidney's crazy projects, I am still haunted by Poisonwood. I have nightmares about Father Jerome resurrecting and flogging me with huge black and yellow spiders. I also have nightmares of the bodies of Haitians scattered all over the beaches after a storm, some on golf holes and greens. But worst of all, I have visions of Myles Ingraham, the toddler with muscular dystrophy, sitting in a little wooden chair in Mickey's perfect little garden, rubbing his painful legs and waiting for doctors and a hospital that will never come.

....

A few weeks later I got a gloomy call from Karl. The company had officially shit canned the wine project. They gave Karl a month to bulk out the remaining inventory and return his computer. He sounded like he'd been crying. It was a bad time to try to find a wine making job, and Karl had been very fond of Sidney. He'd flown out to New York for the memorial service on his own dime because Polly refused to reimburse his travel costs.

I hung up the phone and stared at the wall. Was this the time? The cards were falling, and I could see the end coming into view. I opened my wallet and took out the photo from Sidney's pack of cards. I looked at some other photos of my pregnant wife. I needed to hang in there. Maybe things would change after they reshuffled some projects and assets. Maybe they would decide to start building and growing. The Poet had asked me to buy domain names for hypothetical wineries, and only later did I realize he never intended to do anything with them other than give me false hope and keep me hoping.

It was difficult to see the wine project come to abrupt end. Sidney would have loved to see it grow and flourish, but it was not going to happen under the Artists' reign. It was just another baby flushed with the bathwater. I had a horrible vision of Karl sitting on his deck, head in his hands, surrounded by broken rosé bottles and thousands of sharp swarming beaks.

....

The cigar concept seemed to fizzle out for SFIC as well, but in 2007 Davidoff and Winston III announced an unusual collaborative deal where Davidoff would produce Winston Churchill brand cigars in the Dominican Republic using tobacco produced from Cuban seeds. I suppose this seed concession appeased Winston's Cuban requirements. Officially, I don't think SFIC had any part of this deal, but it's impossible to know for certain.

Davidoff's Winston Churchill brand garnered some media coverage when they were initially released, but they never lived up to the hype. They received consistently low ratings and minimal praise, and as of the writing of this sentence they were available in bulk, deeply discounted, from several shady online outlets. Winston III passed away in 2010 from prostate cancer.

....

I was at the beach with Cooper. It was one of the few places where I could find momentary peace. I loved watching him swim out through the waves to retrieve his squeaky ball. He dug cavernous holes to nowhere. He stalked seagulls and sandpipers incessantly, true to his birddog roots. He hunted slowly and precisely, crouching and moving slowly on his tippy toes, taking small deliberate steps, finally coming to a point like a petrified bronze statue. He never actually caught a bird, but that didn't bother him in the least.

I took deep breaths and tried to relax. I didn't want to think about the Artists, because I knew the stress might set me off and I'd either have a seizure or rip my clothes off and join Cooper in the bird hunt. There was a large swell building, and I watched some big set waves rolling in and a few brave surfers paddling out. I'd surfed big waves in my youth, and it was always an intense and terrifying experience. You had to clear your mind of doubt and stay in the moment. You had to fully commit to the wave, or doubt and hesitation could get you pummeled and possibly killed.

I saw a large channel forming, allowing the surfers quick access to the outside waves. I watched as they paddled hard for the channel, hoping not to get sucked into the churning shore break. Some made it safely, others took a long, cold tumble through the rinse cycle. To the untrained eye, it looked like a game of chance. But there was more to it. Experienced surfers knew how to read the sets and rhythms, and when to wait or charge. They also knew when they were in trouble, and that it was sometimes better to relax, hold your breath and ride it out. Almost everyone pops to the surface eventually.

As I watched, I felt my phone buzzing in my pocket. It was the Artists. It seemed like they had the ability to detect and destroy any fleeting moment of tranquility.

It was the summer of 2006, and the Artists rented a house in La Jolla to serve as home base while they sold off most of Sidney's property and estate. I served as their driver/houseboy for much of that glorious summer. I was soon off to the airport to shuttle them back to La Jolla.

"Helloooo." The Painter looked as if she'd flown across the country with the windows open. I sometimes wondered whether small birds would alight from the bushy thatch on her head and chirp merry little melodies.

"*Buenos dias, amigo*." Being a savvy world traveler, the Poet affected the native tongue and customs of his surroundings to blend in, although he was still dressed like a midget Sir Edmund Hillary. In addition to his heavy wool sweater and surplus army britches, he was wearing a bucket hat with some kind of secret code or treasure map scribbled on it with a Sharpie.

"So, how was your flight?" They had just purchased a fractional share in a private jet service company.

"Super duper Captain Pooper. We asked our pilot to fly slower to like save fuel, you know? We need to stay green, even aboard that jet engine flying thing. Maybe we should create an electric airline and call it Jet Green? By the way, can you look into how many credits we need to book to offset our flight's carbon footprint, maybe just a hint?"

"I'll get right on that."

"Fabulous. And we conjured some new voodoo for you to do while we flew."

They wanted me to fly to Sacramento to personally file the formation articles for Skippy LLC, a holding company for their new Hawaiian properties, and I would have to do this shameful act in front of live recording clerks. The pinnacle of humiliation would be when a recording clerk at the California Secretary of State office announced that the paperwork for Skippy was ready to be picked up, over the main intercom, in front of all the other attorneys waiting for their corporate papers, and I would have to skip to the counter, retrieve it, and skip out before the ridicule started.

After that, they wanted me to go to San Francisco to meet with the mayor, Gavin Newsome.

"In order to avoid energy disaster, we've decided to fund the Gavster. We are giving him $200,000 from Sidney's foundation to fund tidal energy in the Frisco nation." The Artists met Gavin at the Clinton Global Initiative Conference, and old Gavalicious charmed the wallet right out of the Poet's tight little lederhosen.

I flew to Sacramento and filed the Skippy LLC paperwork. I then packed my remaining dignity into a half empty box of tic tacs and flew to San Francisco to meet the Mayor.

Gavin Newsome and the Sidney Frank Foundation team

I drove from the San Francisco airport to a scenic area near the historic Fort with a beautiful view of the Golden Gate Bridge. There were press people and politicos already converging for a buzz worthy press conference. Gavin was orchestrating a convergence of city bureaucrats, executives from PG&E and private energy companies.

"Hi there you handsome devil, Seth Frank, right? Welcome. Welcome. I met your folks in D.C. Awesome people. Super cool. Please thank them again for funding me, I mean, funding my project, of course. It's phenomenal. Just phenomenal. We're having a little clambake to kick off this fucking kick ass phenomenal project." Gavin flashed his $200,000 smile and shook my hand firmly. I could see why the Poet was attracted to him. He was charming in a huckstery way with his slick hair and shiny sharkskin suit.

Gavin sauntered away and was quickly engulfed by several agents who worked for a prestigious philanthropic advisory firm hired by the Artists to help guide them through the vexing world of giving Sidney's money away. One of Sidney's grandsons was also attending the event, although he looked like he had just rolled out of bed after a heavy night of huffing and masturbation. Gavin sauntered away for more handshakes and photo ops, but I saw him lean in and whisper "foundation piñatas" to one of his aides.

"He kissed me," Gabby giggled in my ear. Gabby was wearing a pair of sunglasses with rose tinted lenses that were subtly heart shaped. She was blushing and flustered – her cheeks were almost the same color as her glasses. Gabby worked for the philanthropic advisory group, but her true passion was attending Burning Man every year.

Scorching Women

"Who?"

"Gavin."

"Seriously?"

"Yes. Why?" She glared at me.

"No reason." Gavin was a pro. This guy would kiss a porcupine if he thought he could squeeze a buck out of it. I could definitely learn something from him.

"We have a meeting with the San Francisco Department of Energy after the press conference."

"Swell."

....

The San Francisco Department of the Environment representatives were a nice group of kids who were genuinely concerned about climate change and protecting the environment, but they presented a flimsy report detailing their lackluster achievements and findings. The only thing I could glean was that they distributed all of Sidney's $200,000 to 'stakeholders' and at some point, some flunky ran a few tests and determined that tidal energy from the San Francisco bay was unfeasible. It was apparently too expensive and time-consuming for such a small return. And then, when Sidney's seed money was gone, they made the executive decision to change directions and pursue wave energy. After all, wave energy came from waves and was way cooler than tidal energy.

I called the Poet immediately following the meeting.

"*Bonjour Monsieur*. We're in Paris, you know? It's delicious, all the lovely soft cheese, *si vous* please. *Fromage* in my garage. *Quel dommage*. So delightful and spiteful to my bulging waist."

"Happy for you, but can you believe it? $200,000 and nada to show for it, and now they want more." Sidney would never have made this grant in the first place, and it was even more difficult to watch all that money get sucked out with the Golden Gate tide. I was fairly sure we could find more impactful ways to invest in alternative energy development.

"And the Burgundian wines are juicy and fine, right off the vine, and sublimely divine in my asinine mind." I wasn't sure how much more I could take. I tried to focus on my paycheck and my child's eventual need for braces and tuition.

"Did you hear anything I just said?"

"*Mais oui. Monsieur Guapo* needs $250,000 for wave energy."

"Yes."

"That's it?"

"What?"

"He only wants $250,000?"

"Well, at this point, but..."

"Yes, of course, that's fine. Give him the bread, and leave me to my wine."

"Are you serious?" I wondered if the *pequeño* piñata Poet realized that pesos were pouring out of his ass like horchata.

"So serious, I'm delirious."

Somewhere a village was not missing the Poet. It was no use reasoning with him. I was sickened by the thought of Sidney's money being flushed down the toilet by an over indulged dwarf. I was embarrassed to be associated with the Artists, and I was thoroughly disgusted with myself. I was ashamed of my weakness. My vulnerabilities. The Fear. I was unable to leave them. I was paralyzed. They were kryptonite. I would just put blinders on, turn my brain off, and hang on.

I looked at the little photo from the cards. It was almost time. I should have cashed out right then and there. But I held on, knowing I'd regret it.

....

I spent most of the remainder of 2006 trying to represent Sidney's interests within the foundation, but it was almost impossible. The Artists were going to do what they wanted to do with his money, and there was little I could do to sway them. And the things they wanted to do were not horrible things. Alternative energy development, conserving land and translating foreign plays were worthy investments, but they really weren't what Sidney was interested in, and to me his intent was sacred. Sidney trusted the Artists to keep his interests alive through his foundation, not to preserve land in Hawaii (that coincidentally bordered their compounds), build an artist colony in Montana or fund multiple Moliere adaptations, regardless of the potential upside to the obscure French playwright fan base.

But what really drove me to the brink were the multitude of meaningless tasks and ridiculous errands I was expected to perform daily. I limbo danced to depths of shame and degradation I barely thought possible. I kept detailed records of the absurdity, but I'm too proud to disclose them. I will admit that I was once requested to inflate pool toys, with a pump. I actually drove to their rental house with the sole purpose of inflating pink rubber rafts and purple latex balls. I would have found the experience even more humiliating if the Artists actually had the skills to inflate pool toys by themselves. Even so, I felt obliged to pee in the pool before I departed.

....

"Thanks for coming. Sorry that we pulled you away from your daughter's delightful soirée, but this is an emergencée. Deranged minds call for spastic measures. There has been a grand theft. Malfeasance on a senseless scale with preposterous proportions. There has been a criminal caper, or a craper. A King

Kong kerfuffle with a side of seared truffles. We have proof, and it's in the pudding. Or maybe it's in the tarts. And by the way, I heart tarts. Would you happen to know where I might go for tasty tarts around these parts?"

I received a frantic call from the Artists, and they instructed me to meet them immediately. It was a Saturday, and we were celebrating my daughter's second birthday party with all of our friends and family at our house. My wife just shook her head when I told her I had to attend another meeting with the Artists.

The Artists were sitting at an outdoor table at the Lodge at Torrey Pines, overlooking the blue Pacific and the breathtaking cliffs of La Jolla. They were playing cards and drinking wine, and the Poet was ranting about a multitude of unethical schemes foisted upon Sidney. He'd apparently concluded that several of Sidney's key staffers and close friends were criminals. The Painter was holding her wine glass and a handful of cards, but she appeared to be glazed over and lost in rapture.

The Artists hired additional lawyers to confirm their suspicions, and the lawyers were eating it up. They were slurping the nectar of Sidney's estate. These were high-octane Manhattan partners billing over $1,000 per hour, pulling in associates, forensic accountants and expert consultants to maximize dysfunction and optimize obsessions. And the legal teams scheduled meetings, meetings to schedule more meetings, conference calls to schedule meetings, meetings to schedule calls to schedule more meetings, and they produced volumes and volumes of useless memos and random research reports. They brought in more experts, who scheduled more meetings and calls, and wrote more thoroughly meaningless reports. They killed small rain forests and raised the earth's median core temperature. But the meetings kept coming, the lawyers kept billing, and Sidney's estate kept shrinking. The Artists were chasing their tales and spilling out cash and prizes as their handlers and enablers whipped them into a frenzy.

Attorneys generally feed on human misery, and they love it when everything turns to shit. For many law firms, bad estate planning is actually preferable, as long as the level of competence exceeds malpractice. Clean estate plans with smooth transitions yield very low returns for law firms. The worst mistake a law firm can make is to draft a well thought-out, well-reasoned and rational estate plan that anticipates potential sources of tension and successfully avoids turmoil and conflict. That won't get any junior associate on the partnership track. The big legal fees are in conflict. The even bigger legal fees come after conflict deteriorates into guerrilla warfare. Their L word is not Love. It's Litigation, and lawyers love them some good old litigation. They adore batshit crazy clients with big ugly estates and bitter beneficiaries. They are partial to paranoid executors. They yearn for the train wreck. They crave the nuclear meltdown. Throw in a bitter step-mom and or two, a few disgruntled half-siblings, and a multi-racial love child if you're really lucky, and watch the sparks fly and bills balloon. A good extended will contest involving multiple heirs with old grudges will eat up astounding chunks of an estate. The jackals, hyenas, vultures, rats, worms, maggots, attorneys, parasites, bacteria and various other scavengers will feast on the putrefied carcass of that estate for years and years.

"These gypsy Judases, they played Sidney like a clown. They schemed and they scammed and they blew his houses down. They robbed him blind, and now my mind is as blank as a black window blind... wait a second.... didn't I already say that? Hey dummy, I've got gin rummy! Slap Jack!" The Poet slapped his hand down and the wine bottle jumped but remained upright. The Painter didn't even flinch. I noticed they were drowning their outrage with a bottle of vintage Bordeaux.

The Poet composed several lengthy narratives and algorithms detailing the enormous web of schemes and conspiracies surrounding Sidney and the staff, and he also had hired a private investigation firm to work with the attorneys to prepare a comprehensive report with lots of colorful charts and diagrams. It had taken the Poet months to put all the pieces together, but he finally had it all figured out.

"The smoking gun," the Poet smugly produced a large binder and passed it to me with such care and reverence that you would think it was the Magna Carta. It was enormous. I tried to read the first few pages, and then resorted to scanning it. I saw the names of people I knew very well, several of Sidney's employees and associates, followed by extremely detailed information about their personal lives and financial holdings. It was clear that certain members of the inner-circle benefitted greatly from their employment. But Sidney was an extremely generous billionaire and the amounts didn't seem unreasonable, certainly not what I was expecting after the dramatic build-up.

This binder was the Poet's crowning achievement and the product of hundreds of thousands of dollars in legal costs. He was quite pleased with himself. I looked down at the huge report, and then I took a hard look at the Artists. They had already reaped substantial rewards from Sidney's estate, and yet they were obsessed with getting more. They were completely incapable of enjoying their good fortune because they were consumed with keeping everyone else from sharing scraps from their hog trough.

"You know they are guilty, right?" the Painter had emerged from her trance and was joining the fray. The unbearable in pursuit of the unemployed. The waitress came to the table, and I ordered coffee. Black.

"And look. We found these agreements. They're between Sidney, Chad and one of Sidney's contractors. And look here, Sidney even signed them."

The documents were obvious forgeries. Sidney's signatures were perfect calligraphy, which was impossible since his hand was so gnarled and shaky that he could barely hold a pen. Besides the perfect penmanship, Sidney rarely signed anything. He did business the old school way, on his word and his handshake. No paper trail. No documentation. Just a man and his word, stemming from the days a contract for bootleg whisky wasn't enforceable in court. Sidney's word was good, and it said more than reams of agreements. His handshake was more permanent than a signature etched with a thick black sharpie.

"I'm not so sure..."

"Wait, before you respond, there's a bond. We appreciate your invaluable assistance, and we have a retainer to detain you." The Poet produced another voluminous document from somewhere near his groin region.

I glanced at the agreement and payment terms they were offering. It was considerable. It meant partial security and comfort for my family. It meant not having to worry too much about the mortgage, college tuition or retirement. I looked out over the Pacific Ocean and a huge line of pelicans was flying in a fluid V-shaped formation. I could hear the waves pounding against the cliffs below. I took a deep breath and looked at the Artists. I studied them closely for several minutes in complete silence, and then I shut my eyes. I heard the waves crashing and the pelicans calling each other as they drafted the bird on the point. I could see the Artists in my mind, but they were enveloped in a brown festering cloud. I took some deep breaths. I saw the pelicans circling the Artists, faster and faster, creating a vortex of living energy. A gargantuan black wave was rising on the horizon like a watery dragon, just at the edge of my periphery, gaining strength and speed as the birds circled. The monster peaked and came crashing down on the Artists, completely obscuring them from view. The pelican formation rose from the receding water and shot straight up at the sun like a bullet. The water finally dissipated and the Artists were huddled naked, cold and shivering on the empty beach. The shroud was gone and everything was crystal clear.

I opened my eyes and stared at the Artists, but they didn't look human. They had become enormous wet rats with their legs stuck in the wet sand. I saw their mouths jabbering and their beady, vacant eyes staring at me, waiting for me to validate their wretched crusade. I saw the venomous web that surrounded and constricted them. They were drowning in their own poison.

I wasn't angry anymore, and I didn't hate them. I thought about the little photo from the card box. And then it hit me like a second massive wave. I knew it was time. I experienced a moment of clarity and complete lapse of reason and accountability. I was a burning ash that becomes a firefly, following the light and looking down on the rats gnawing their tails. The black waves would wash them away. I would follow the pelicans.

"Fold."

"What?"

"You should fold."

"Come again? Fold? What does that mean exactly?" It was the first time I'd heard the Poet not rhyme, and I was certain it wasn't a very good sign.

"Yes, yes, what does that mean?" The Painter portrayed a pained expression, and she set her glass down and stared at me. "Explain that please."

I cleared my throat and took a deep breath. "It isn't worth it. Be happy with what you have, and leave the table while you're way ahead. This report and those agreements are just going to cause you hours of aggravation, grief, and millions more in legal costs, and the end will be the same. Go try to enjoy your lives and leave Sidney's friends alone. Time to cash in your chips, let go and walk away."

Sidney loved the people in the report, and he wanted them to be taken care of and comfortable. He was aware that some of his favorites were taking liberties, and he didn't care. He was probably also aware that the Artists' were going to screw the staff after he died. There was absolutely no way to prove Sidney's knowledge or ignorance of anything in that report. His word was good, his paper trail was not so good.

I could see from the blank expressions on the Artists' faces that my advice wasn't getting any traction. "Look, you aren't really artists. You're phonies, lazy and essentially useless. You like to play philanthropists, but it's a charade. You're a house of cards. Everyone knows it, except you, although deep down I suspect you do too. And the truth is that nobody gives a shit, nobody will remember you, and no one is going to miss you. You've already destroyed most of Sidney's dreams, don't you think you've done enough?"

You could have heard a firefly fart. I grabbed the wine bottle, took a big long slug, and slammed it back down on the table. "I'm going back to my daughter's birthday party. Have a nice day."

....

My phone rang a few days later on a Sunday, in the early spring of 2007. Caller ID displayed a number in Seattle that I didn't recognize. I was enjoying some time with my daughter, Sydney. She was starting to talk, and we were making each other laugh. She was hilarious. Sydney did not have a shy bone in her body. She would talk to anyone, at length, on virtually any subject. She said hello to everyone she passed. When we took her to restaurants, she would grab a crayon and a children's menu and walk around taking orders from other tables. She would make me call my friends so she could talk to them. She loved everyone and was curious about everything.

My phone was still ringing. Reluctantly, I answered.

"Mr. Schechter, I represent the Artists and I'm calling on their behalf. After careful consideration and numerous lengthy meetings with other high priced employment attorneys and highly compensated human relations consultants, they decided to go in a different direction with the foundation. Thus, they are letting you go. Best of luck in your future endeavors, and good day to you."

Good day? I knew it was coming, and I figured it would be quick, but I had to smile about their rationale. They had never gone in a consistent direction with Sidney's foundation (nor anything else), so how could any direction be different? Neither Artist was capable of making a rational decision or articulating a reasonable plan without consulting their cabal of advisors, and every decision was second and third guessed, poorly executed, and frequently modified or aborted altogether. I rarely completed any of the absurd tasks I was instructed to do without waiting a day or two for the predictable decision to pursue a different, and generally more irrational course of action.

"Great." And that was that. I was fully expecting it, and they weren't going to get any argument out of me. I was relieved and I was free, but I was disappointed. After all I'd been through with this family, these chicken shits didn't even have the spine to fire me in person. All my time with Sidney, and the years following his death, ended with a lawyer's phone call. Not surprising, but still disappointing. The dream was dead.

....

I recalled the last couple of years with the Artists, and they were a definite lowlight. Not quite as bad as my years with Butterbean, but not much better. On the bright side, I wouldn't have to answer the idiotic phone calls, blow up pool toys or respond to the byproducts of their madness. I wouldn't have to feign ignorance of their hypocrisy, pretend that I respected their self-serving agenda, or perpetuate their delusions of artistic talent and philanthropic commitment.

But even the bullshit Artists couldn't ruin my memories of Sidney Frank. I will always think of him dressed up in his fluorescent suits, flanked by Jagerette skanks, making a spectacle of himself in a five star restaurant or dumpy dive bar. I thought about the way things could have been if he'd lived another five years, and I wondered if I'd be playing Poisonwood with him. I pictured him perched in a golf cart on a tee box overlooking the Atlantic, sucking on a big stogie and beaming at his golfing Xanadu.

No one can replace Sidney. They can't dream his dreams or run his empire. He is an unsung hero deserving of recognition he will hopefully receive someday. His legacy will endure, not through his family or foundation, but through the memories he created and the lives he touched. Sidney was also living proof that anything is possible, including the grim possibility of having everything and nothing at the same time.

Sidney wasn't a saint and he was far from perfect. Exceedingly far. He had profound faults and extensive weaknesses. He wasn't a model father, yet despite his volatile relationship with his children, he still loved them more than anything. Maybe giving control of his business, estate and foundation to the Painter was his ultimate act of contrition and redemption. He was giving her the opportunity to do something *after* giving her a life of doing nothing, and it was an opportunity she clearly didn't deserve. Maybe he felt responsible for his brood's limited slop from the Rosenstiel hog trough. Maybe he understood and accepted his children's faults because he was partially culpable. Perhaps he hoped that his love would conquer their anger, greed and pettiness, and that his huge flawed heart would cure their poisoned blood. Maybe it was his final attempt to restore a small piece of his own lost soul.

Sidney was one of the least boring people I have ever known, and he was very good to me and to the countless recipients of his generosity. He was always happy to see and spend time with me. He knew what I was supposed to be doing, and also what I was really doing. He remembered names, places and seemingly insignificant details with the precision of a hard drive. With all of the people competing for his time and attention, all of the financiers, bankers, lawyers, doctors, developers, dealers, brokers, investors, salesmen, schemers, scammers, gangsters, killers, politicians, family members and the entire cast of characters in his martini wonderland, he always had time to sit down, talk, share a drink and watch a movie. Sidney plucked me away from a mundane existence and tedious career path, and he gave me the gift of priceless opportunities and extraordinary experiences that I wouldn't trade for the world. He was a hero, a mentor, and most importantly, a friend.

Sidney completely changed the way I measured success. He made me understand that success isn't measured by net worth, ranking on the Forbes list, or material possessions. Success is finding your own brand of happiness. Success is enjoying your brief time on earth, helping others enjoy their time, spending as much time as you possibly can with people that make you happy, and realizing that everything is replaceable except love and time. Success is living an interesting life, never becoming boring, overcoming hardship and adversity, and becoming stronger and smarter from each failure. Success is loving your children more than they deserve, giving people a chance they don't deserve, and giving them a second chance after they fuck up the first chance. Success is making your children better than you, giving away more than you make, and telling the world's greatest stories.

....

I hung up the phone and walked back towards the family room. I experienced waves of relief, disappointment and sadness, but not the Fear. The Artists had lost their power over me, and their money wasn't important. In fact, it was unnecessary. I knew I could lose it all and still have everything.

Sydney was sleeping on the couch. The television was blaring cartoons and she had her arms wrapped around a bag of cheese puffs and a white and orange-tinted fuzzy bunny. I watched her sleep for close to an hour. She was dreaming about a fairytale land with cheesy puff clouds, mountains of ice cream and Kool-Aid lakes. She had no cares. She had no fear. She loved everything. Sydney's heart was open and pure. I was going to make sure she turned out better than me. I would make sure she followed her heart.

Our backyard was not very large. It had a small patch of grass, a patio area with a table and grill, and a few fruit trees near the perimeter wall. But if you looked closely, you could see a very small, very special tree growing in a sunny spot near the fruit trees. I'm fairly sure none of our neighbors had a similar tree, and I'm almost positive none of our neighbors had a tree named Sidney.

I planted Mr. Sidney Poisonwood not long after our Sydney was born. I was not sure if a poisonwood would grow in the San Diego climate. He was not only growing, he was thriving. I walked outside and gave him some water. I could see some new leaves starting to bud, and the faintest traces of sap starting to ooze from his bark. I warned Sydney that she was never to touch Mr. Poisonwood, and she thought I was funny, but she was complying so far. I figured curiosity would get the better of her someday and she'd learn a hard lesson, but it would make her stronger. For now all was good.

I walked back in the house and into the bathroom. I pulled out my wallet and removed the little photo from the deck of cards. It was Sidney Frank with his two children and two large dogs. The children looked to be around five or six years old. Back in those days Sidney was partial to obese golden retrievers. They were on the beach somewhere, and Sidney was holding the kids and smiling. The dogs were licking the kids, and the kids were laughing.

"Thank you Sidney," I kissed the photo, dropped it in the toilet and flushed.

Printed in Great Britain
by Amazon

12903679R00180